# HIGH-POWERED INVESTING

## A Financial Planner's Guide to Making Money in Today's Uncertain Markets

Gary M. Goldberg
Donald Jay Korn

WILEY

John Wiley & Sons, Inc.
New York • Chichester • Brisbane • Toronto • Singapore

Publisher: Stephen Kippur
Editor: Katherine Schowalter
Managing Editor: Corinne McCormick
Editing, Design, and Production: Publications Development Company of
Crockett, Texas

**Library of Congress Cataloging-in-Publication Data**

Goldberg, Gary (Gary M.)
   High-powered investing : a financial planner's guide to making money in
today's uncertain markets / Gary Goldberg & Donald Korn.
      p.    cm.
   Bibliography: p.
   ISBN 0-471-61127-1
   1. Finance, Personal.   2. Investments.   I. Korn, Donald.
II. Title.
HG179.G65   1988
332.6'78—dc19                          88-19094
                                                  CIP

Printed in the United States of America

88 89 10 9 8 7 6 5 4 3 2 1

# Preface

Whenever we told people that we were writing a book on investing, we heard comments like, "So you're going to tell me how to make a lot of money?"

Not really. We hope to show you how to make a little money— how to make real money from your investments, *after* taxes and *above inflation.* If you earn a little real money each year, and reinvest it so that your real money compounds, you will be way ahead over the long term. Certainly, you will be better off than the vast majority of speculators, bottom fishers, market timers, and in-and-out day traders.

Our book is based on *cash-flow investing*—taking cash distributions and reinvesting for shorter term, more frequent gains. We describe 22 ways to earn regular cash distributions. In some cases, the cash flow is tax-sheltered; in others, you have to pay taxes, but at today's relatively low tax rates. Then the after-tax cash flow is reinvested and compounded.

Cash-flow investing is not new; investors always have had bonds and dividend-paying stocks to choose among. However, today cash-flow investing is more attractive than ever.

First, yields are higher. After the inflation of the 1970s, investors in bonds and bond equivalents have learned their lesson. Yields are higher in relation to inflation than they have been historically. Every upward blip in the inflation rate sends yields higher still, as markets react quickly.

Second, taxes are lower. It's better to pay 28 or 33 percent on investment income (or perhaps 38 percent, if we get a future tax hike) than to pay 50 or 70 percent, as was the case under prior tax laws.

iii

Third, new cash-flow vehicles can give you protection. Runaway inflation, if it reappears, would be disastrous for investors who hold only bonds and bond proxies. Now, there is a new category of nonbonds. These are investments that give you bondlike cash flow, yet they're designed to gain value in inflationary times.

Nobody knows what the future will bring: inflation, disinflation, or muddling through. However, you now can build a balanced portfolio of cash-flow vehicles that will hold up in any foreseeable economic environment.

Cash-flow investing is more predictable than simply "buy-stocks-and-hope-for-the-best." Because it's more predictable, it's less risky; for example, cash-flow portfolios held up in the October 19, 1987, stock market crash.

Our strategy is "take-your-money-upfront." Take it often. Pay taxes, if necessary. Reinvest and compound. Long-term, you can build wealth with cash-flow investing.

# Contents

v

• Get Cash, Owe No Taxes • Single
Premium Comes in Two Varieties • A Lifetime
Commitment • Only Buy Insurance If You Need It

Three Kinds of REITs • REITs Look Sweeter
after Tax Reform • Market Discount Plagues
REIT Investors • Making the Payout More
Certain • No Need to Buy Blind

A One-Decision Investment • Certain Return at a
Low Cost • No Flexibility • Why Put Stocks into
Unit Trusts?

More Red Flags on Mutual Funds • Putting Part
of Your Portfolio in Partnerships • One Tax
Instead of Two • Pay Taxes Later, Rather Than
Sooner • Partnership Investments Are Smaller,
More Targeted Than Mutual Funds • Two Faces
of Limited Partnerships • A Look at the Dark
Side • How Have Limited Partnerships
Performed? • Not All Gloom and Doom • Keeping
Your Balance

The Three Categories of Real Estate
Partnerships • Mortgage Partnerships May
Offer Participation • How Mortgage Partnerships
Differ • Why Loan-to-Value Ratios Are
Crucial • Now for the Fancy Stuff • Low Risks,
Low Returns

Checking the Math • Going for Growth
• Owning Real Estate for Inflation

# Introduction

# When Cash Was a Four-Letter Word

Investing is a paradox. People earn money. They spend it on what they need and what they want. Anything left over, they invest. Therefore, the only people who invest are those with more money than they need.

Yet why do they invest? To acquire more money. Presumably, this will provide them with an even greater excess of funds. And more to invest. And so on.

Obviously, there's often a method behind this seeming madness. People forgo current consumption—they refrain from spending all of their money—in order to prepare for an uncertain future. They invest to have money during retirement . . . to create an emergency fund . . . to pay for a child's college tuition or a parent's nursing home stay . . . to provide for their family, once their final accounts are paid.

## BUILDING WEALTH WITH CASH-FLOW INVESTING

A few years ago, this illusory paradox of investing grew so robust that it toppled traditional thinking. Investors literally didn't want to receive money, at least not in the form of spendable cash. Sophisticated investors, the heavy hitters so beloved by financial advisers, turned to these advisers for the advice that makes investors sophisticated. Their advice? Keep away from cash.

Why were investment advisers advising against cash? It's a tale that's worth a few pages to tell. You need to recall the economic

1

and tax climate of the late 1970s and early 1980s to understand why cash investments were unwelcome.

Things are different now. Today, cash-flow investing makes sense. You want vehicles where you receive an immediate return, "cash-on-cash," as insiders put it. Get your cash upfront and reinvest it. You will avoid roller coasters like the 1987 stock market. If you have a substantial portfolio—say $50,000 or more—or if you expect to accumulate such a portfolio, cash-flow investing is the safest and most predictable way to build up that portfolio over the long term.

We have written this book for those investors. We want you to know how various investments work—where the cash comes from. That doesn't change, no matter what happens to the economy. Once you're familiar with the investment vehicles available, you can decide which ones are most appropriate to help reach your goals. You may want to work with advisers, but the more you know about investments, the better you will be able to use their advice. It's your money—you worked for it—so it's worth taking the time and effort to learn how that money can work for you.

## THE FLIGHT FROM CASH

Let's take a look at the days when investing for cash was a bad idea—in the late 1970s and 1980s. Money market funds were paying 10, 12, even 15 percent—Astronomical numbers, by today's standards. All manner of bank accounts and bonds were comfortably in double figures. Great news for the little old ladies in tennis sneakers. But the heavy hitters, with their heavy advisers urging them on, were running away from bonds and banks as fast as they could.

Why were they running? Because they were pursued by two relentless adversaries, taxes and inflation. In this race, cash was a burden rather than a blessing.

The graduated income tax system was burden number one. Suppose a member of the investing class earned $100 a year and spent $90. He had $10 left to invest. At 15 percent interest, that's a quick $1.50.

However, federal tax law dictates that his first $1.50 of investment income be stacked on top of his $100 in earned income. Now, he had $101.50 in taxable income. The $1.50 in investment income was his most heavily taxed income. It fell in his highest tax bracket. If he was in a 50 percent tax bracket, 75 cents from the $1.50 was diverted to the Internal Revenue Service. He was left with 75 cents: just 7.5 percent of his $10 investment. After a year, that $10 investment portfolio had grown to $10.75, after taxes.

Back in the days of 15 percent money market rates, though, inflation was likely to be 10 percent. So he would need $11 in Year Two, just to buy the things he could have bought for $10 in Year One. Instead, he had only $10.75. Clearly, he was losing the race.

This sort of calculation was performed over and over, by countless investors, in the late 1970s and early 1980s. For some, the answer was to avoid the tax bite and buy tax-exempt bonds. The municipal bond market (munis), once the province of banks and insurance companies, became dominated by individual investors during this period.

But munis weren't always the answer. An 8 percent tax-exempt yield looked great until interest rates rose to 10 percent. Or 12 percent. Each time rates went up, the value of existing bonds went down. Often, even a tax-free yield wasn't enough to keep up with the inflation rate. The obvious conclusion was to stay away from cash or from any investment where the payoff was to be a stream of dollars.

## GOING FOR GROWTH INSTEAD OF CASH FLOW

If you want to invest for an uncertain future, but you don't want cash, what do you want? You want growth. You want tax benefits. You may even want a combination of both.

Investing for growth is easy to understand. Instead of putting your surplus $10 into a money market fund, you buy a rare stamp. Other collectors, also fleeing from cash, bid up the price of rare stamps. You hold onto yours, but you know you could sell it for $20, or $30. As long as you're in the investing class, making more money than you need to spend, you can hold on to your stamp. No matter how much the stamp appreciates, you pay no taxes as long as you don't sell it.

Finally, the day comes when you need more money than you're earning. You turn to your stamp, your investment. If you sell it for

$30, you've tripled your investment over the years. The $20 profit is a taxable gain.

In the old days, before the 1986 tax act, that sale would be favorably taxed as a long-term capital gain. Your tax on that gain would be less than half the taxes you would have paid if you had invested for cash, year after year.

You might not even have to sell your stamp when you wanted to cash in on it. You might borrow the money you needed using the stamp as collateral. With a stamp worth $30 as security, a lender would gladly lend you $20. That $20 would go right into your pocket, tax-free, because money that you get from a loan is not taxed as income.

You would have to pay interest on the loan, but the interest payment would be tax deductible, and your cost of borrowing would be lower. In addition, you would still own the stamp, benefiting as it rose in value to $40 or $50.

That's growth. Buy something that will become more valuable over the years. Pay no taxes while it grows in value. Sell it when you want to and pay taxes at less than half the going rate, or borrow against it and pay no taxes at all. Most stock market investments fall into this category, because most stocks offer low current cash (dividends) and the promise of high appreciation.

## ADDING TAX BENEFITS TO GROWTH

Tax benefits are a little harder to understand. Suppose you invest your $10 in a $100 apartment building, borrowing the other $90. You might owe $12 a year in interest on your loan, but you have money from rents to cover most or all of the $12. In the meantime, you're taking depreciation on a $100 building.

When it comes time to prepare your tax return, you find that you have a $20 loss on your apartment building, including depreciation. That $20 loss is matched against your $100 in income, giving you only $80 to pay taxes on. By cutting your income by $20, you reduce your tax bill by $10—if you're in a 50 percent tax bracket. You can claim a refund or reduce your estimated tax payments to reflect the difference. Thus, you wind up with an extra $10 in your pocket from your tax savings. And you still own an apartment building that may appreciate.

## THE RETURN OF CASH-FLOW INVESTING

No wonder growth and tax benefits looked more appealing than cash, a few years ago. Now, things have changed. First came disinflation and then came tax reform.

Disinflation makes it less attractive to invest purely for long-term growth. That stamp you bought for $10 no longer is rolling along to $20, $30, $40, $50. Instead, with inflation of 3 and 4 percent a year, as in the 1980s, your stamp grows in value to $10.30, $10.70, $11, etc—if it grows in value at all. Some classic inflation hedges actually lose value. Gold, which sold at $850 per ounce in 1980, slumped to less than $300 per ounce, three years later, and remains far below its peak price.

The 1986 tax law was the final blow, knocking out growth investments as well as those designed for tax benefits. If you invested for growth, you expected to take your profits eventually at long-term capital gain rates, less than half of your ordinary tax rate. The top rate on long-term gains was 20 percent, and many people paid 15 or 16 percent.

Under the 1986 tax law, there is no advantage to long-term capital gains. They're taxed at the same rate as any other income. So there's no advantage to holding on for the long-term. Indeed, investors who previously bought long-term assets will have to pay taxes on their gains at a 28 percent or a 33 percent rate, much higher than they expected when they first invested.

It's true that you still can borrow against long-term assets and take the loan proceeds, tax-free. But now the interest you'll pay on those loans may no longer be tax-deductible. The 1986 tax law gives a yellow light to growth investments.

At the same time, it gives a red light to investing for tax benefits. Virtually all types of tax-oriented investments—real estate, computer leasing, movies, cattle breeding—are now classified as *passive*. If you have passive losses, you can't deduct them unless you have passive income.

Let's look at the same example of the investor with $100 in income from his job and a $20 loss from an apartment investment. Previously, he'd net them and pay taxes on $80 in income.

He can no longer do that. Now he has to pay taxes on his full $100 in income and eat the $20 real estate loss. That loss is only deductible if he can use it to offset some income from a passive investment, such as another real estate deal. If not, he has to carry it forward, until he has some passive income to offset, or until he gets out of his apartment investment.

There are some limited exceptions to this rule. For example, if you were in a passive investment before the 1986 tax law was passed, you'll get partial deductions for the next few years. If your income is under $150,000, some real estate losses may be deductible. Even in these circumstances, though, the 1986 tax law is discouraging.

That's because tax rates are now lower. If you're paying taxes at a 50 percent rate, a $1 tax deduction saves you 50 cents. But, at a 28 percent rate, the $1 deduction saves you only 28 cents.

Back to our $100 earner with the $20 apartment loss. Let's assume he invested before the 1986 tax law took effect. In 1988, for example, he's entitled to deduct 40 percent of his passive losses or $8. This brings his income down to $92 while the other $12 worth of losses will be "banked" until they can be used.

In 1988, he's in a 28 percent bracket, and his $8 in tax deductions saves him only $2.24. That's a far cry from the $10 in tax savings he enjoyed in 1986, with the same numbers, under prior tax law.

As before, he still owns an apartment building. But that building isn't appreciating as fast as it did a few years earlier, now that inflation is down. And his ultimate long-term profit will be taxed at 28 or 33 percent, not 15 or 20 percent.

|  | *Old Tax Law* | *Current Tax Law* |
|---|---|---|
| 1988 Real estate loss | $20.00 | $20.00 |
| Amount deductible | $20.00 | $ 8.00 |
| Tax bracket | 50% | 28% |
| Tax saving | $10.00 | $ 2.24 |
| 1989 Real estate loss | $20.00 | $20.00 |
| Amount deductible | $20.00 | $ 4.00 |
| Tax bracket | 50% | 28% |
| Tax saving | $10.00 | $ 1.12 |

*Instead of the $10 annual tax saving that the investor expected, when he originally went into the deal, the 1986 tax law permits only $2.24 in tax saving in 1988, $1.12 in 1989, 56 cents in 1990, and zero thereafter.*

It no longer makes sense to invest for growth or for tax benefits. What's left? We're back to cash. Cash is still a four-letter word, but now that word is G-O-O-D.

## CASH-FLOW INVESTING BECOMES MORE COMPLEX

Let's take another look at our cash example using the new rules. Suppose a money market fund yields 6 percent in this age of disinflation. With a 28 percent tax bracket, you keep 72 percent of your investment income. If you invest $10 and earn 60 cents in interest, you can keep about 43 cents for a 4.3 percent after-tax yield.

Suppose inflation this year is 4 percent, about the average for the 1980s. At this rate, it will take $10.40 to maintain the purchasing power of your original $10, yet you now have $10.43. You're ahead of the game. Even if inflation moves up to 5 or 6 percent, you are a lot better off than you were when you had $10.75 to buy $11 worth of goods and services. As long as inflation and tax rates remain at their current levels, it pays to invest for current cash flow. Take your earnings right now, up front, while the taking is good.

If that's all there is to it, this would be a short book. Invest in money market funds, CDs, or Treasury bills, pay the taxes, and come out ahead . . . or almost ahead. However, if you want to build up your portfolio, through cash-flow compounding, you must invest in higher-yielding vehicles. That means taking some risks. The purpose of this book is to acquaint you with the most popular cash-flow vehicles and explain the risks and probable rewards.

## CASH-FLOW INVESTING UNDER THE 1986 TAX LAW

After tax reform, cash has two new wrinkles. First, suppose you are one of the thousands of investors who played the tax benefit game during the past several years. Especially if you invested in real estate, you probably can expect several years of losses from those old deals, and these losses, as mentioned above, won't be fully deductible.

If that's the case, you want taxable cash from a passive investment—nothing to do with stocks, bonds, or interest-paying accounts will quality. The passive investment taxable income will enable you to use your losses from previous deals. In effect, you'll convert taxable cash to tax-free cash.

The second new wrinkle in cash will appeal to many investors, not just those with old tax shelter losses. It's tax-free cash, plus growth potential.

This is a new breed of investment that competes with and complements tax-exempt municipal bonds. The tax-exempt yields on munis are extremely high these days, compared to other investments, and they have a great appeal to individuals. But munis are still bonds, with all the negatives. The interest rate is fixed over the life of the bond, and there's no chance for growth. Buy a $1,000 muni with an 8 percent coupon and you will receive $80 in interest—until the bond matures and you get your $1,000 back.

At the same time, inflation is eating away at your bonds. Even at a 4 percent inflation rate, the money you invest in a 20-year bond will lose more than half of its purchasing power by maturity. And there's no guarantee that inflation will stay at 4 percent over the next 20 years.

"Non-bonds" address this problem. They're designed to pay cash to investors right from the start. They involve businesses (usually related to real estate or equipment leasing), and the tax benefits from that business offset the income, resulting in little or no tax obligation. In varying amounts, your cash is nontaxable.

At the same time, cash payments may grow if the business prospers. The value of the underlying assets may grow to keep pace with inflation. These new tax-sheltered cash vehicles can give you current yields, growth protection, and inflation protection. No bond can do all that. If you hold municipal bonds in your portfolio, which makes you vulnerable to inflation, these nonbonds can be used as a hedge. They may go up if your munis go down.

## MAKING THE RIGHT DECISIONS

Investors face a new world when they want to cash in today. There are traditional interest-bearing vehicles, new "passive income" investments to soak up shelter losses, as well as the category of nonbonds.

You have to make the decisions, whether you're a "do-it-yourself" investor or if you work with financial advisers. Before you can decide, you have to know what your options are. That's the purpose of this book.

## OUR BUILDING-BLOCK APPROACH

You can easily be overwhelmed by today's investment choices. When a broker recommends an enhanced government open-ended mutual fund or a public equipment leasing limited partnership or a multi-sectored closed-end fund, you can be excused if your eye-blink rate picks up. There really are only a few ways to invest money. Once you know the basics, the variations will be easier to understand.

That's our approach in this book. In the first section, "Cash-It-Yourself," we'll cover the basic investment vehicles: banks, stocks, bonds, real estate. We'll explain how they work. You'll see where the cash really comes from. After you understand these basics, you're ready to make investment decisions—if you do your home-work.

Most investors can handle their own portfolios if they're willing to devote the necessary time and effort. Or, you may want to leave your money management to a professional. In Sections II and III, "Managed Cash" and "Partners-in-Cash," we cover the major types of investments that are directed by others. Even here, though, it's up to you to choose the right professionals—the money managers or the general partners.

When you read those later sections, remember to build on what you've read in the first section. If you understand the economics of buying real estate on your own, for example, you'll have no trouble figuring out the workings of a real estate investment trust or a real estate limited partnership.

Why do we cover so many different types of investments? If there's one thing that any investment adviser should have learned during the last 10 years, it's humility. No one—not the smartest Ph.D. in economics—can accurately predict what will happen in the financial markets. In 1987 alone, one of the century's worst bear markets in bonds was punctuated by the October 19 stock market crash. Few advisers predicted those events, no matter what they said after the fact. After the crash, one investor quipped, "If all the economists in the United States were laid end to end, that would be a good thing!"

Anyone who tells you that a specific investment is a sure thing is a sure loser. That's why diversification is the most important aspect of any investment portfolio. Rather than just buy stocks, buy stocks and bonds and real estate. The more diverse your portfolio, the better you're protected against disaster's striking one specific investment. And, the more types of investments familiar to you, the better you will be able to diversify.

There is a saying: *If it's to be, it's up to me.* No adviser, no matter how conscientious, will pay as much attention to your investments as you can yourself.

## A LAST NOTE

In some examples in this book we assume that investors have a 30 percent tax bracket. There really is no 30 percent bracket. Officially, the top federal income tax bracket is 28 percent, but a 5 percent surcharge puts some investors into the 33 percent tax bracket. So 30 percent is a compromise, easy to use for calculations.

Finally, there's a story attributed to Ann Landers we would like to relate. She received a letter from a man who devoted himself solely to his work and to his investments. "Ann," he wrote, "I have a generous expense account, my own Ferrari, my own Cessna. But I also have my doubts. Am I doing right? Am I doing wrong?"

Ann wrote back, "You ain't doing bad!"

# SECTION I

## Cash-It-Yourself

When you invest for cash, there are two directions to take. You can invest on your own, or you can hire a professional to assist you.

Sometimes, it's obvious that you're hiring a professional. When you work with an accountant, an attorney, a financial planner, or an insurance agent, you generally meet with that adviser or speak with him or her on the phone. You explain what you want or need; the professional advises you. The professional is compensated directly by fee or by a sales commission.

In other cases, the presence of an investment adviser is not so clear. When you invest in a no-load mutual fund, for example, you simply send a check to a specified fund. There's no upfront sales charge, so all of your money is invested in securities.

However, that mutual fund is managed by professionals, and those professionals are paid. They're paid by you, the mutual fund investor, through ongoing fees. The same is true when you invest in a limited partnership and pay the general partner for running the business.

You pay more for professional investment management. If investor A buys a bond portfolio directly while investor B buys shares in a mutual fund that holds the same bonds, A is likely to wind up with a higher yield, because he hasn't paid the fund manager.

11

There are many who prefer making investments themselves. They want more control of their personal finances. Not only do they save money on advisers' fees, they often use discount brokers to save commissions when they buy and sell securities.

If you choose your own investments, you can save a great deal of money by using a discounter. However, some investors try to have it both ways: a professional's advice and discount rates.

They ask their broker for a stock recommendation, for example, and buy 100 shares on a full-commission basis. Then they buy another 2,000 shares of the same stock through a discounter. We don't recommend such tactics—they verge on dishonesty. Most financial advisers will refuse to give further advice to such clients when they find evidence of heavy buying through a discounter.

But not all investors need recommendations from someone else. If you're really determined to do your own homework, to make your own investment decisions instead of using professional advisers, you may wind up with more cash for yourself. In the next seven chapters, you will learn what you need to know if you're going to act as your own investment adviser.

## Summary

*Pros:*

- Avoiding advisers' fees can lead to higher returns.
- You have more control over your portfolio.

*Cons:*

- You need to spend time and effort to keep up with the changing investment environment.

# 1

# Banking on Cash

John S. had a simple approach to investing. Every day, around lunchtime, he would listen to his favorite radio phone-in host. Whatever this guru told him to do, he did.

In the early 1980s, interest rates reached their highest levels in recent memory. Twelve percent, 15 percent—you name it, you could get it. All the while, John's radio know-it-all had the same advice: "Stay short-term."

Following this advice John kept nearly all of his $500,000 capital in one local bank, in a day-to-day account. From 1982 to 1987, as interest rates dropped, John listened to his adviser and stayed short. All the while, his investment returns were dropping, too. At the same time, John missed out on one of the greatest bull markets ever in the stock and bond markets.

John actually did better than his radio expert, who wound up losing his show, but John's experience illustrates a point many investors don't appreciate about banks: Banks have many advantages, but you can have too much of a good thing.

## WHY GO TO THE BANK FOR CASH?

What's good about counting on banks for cash? Let's look at some of the positives:

1. *Banks are convenient.* This may not be readily apparent to anyone who has stood in line in a bank, but getting your cash into and out of a bank is relatively easy. Banks can be especially convenient if you are willing to leave more than a minimal amount on deposit. For $20,000, some banks will give you access to an express

line, which may please you as much as it aggravates your not-so-fortunate fellow depositors.

2. *Banks are safe.* Each account is guaranteed up to $100,000 by the Federal Deposit Insurance Corp. (FDIC) or the Federal Savings & Loan Insurance Corp. (FSLIC). Some critics have expressed doubts about FDIC and FSLIC insurance coverage, because neither has sufficient funds to cover severe runs. According to one cynic, if you're concerned about FDIC coverage, put your money in the worst bank in town. That likely will be the first bank to go broke, so you will collect your insurance money while there's still enough left to pay off. However, there's really little chance that the federal government will allow small (under $100,000) investors to be victimized in case a bank or thrift fails.

3. *Bank products have become flexible.* Not many years ago, bank accounts were of two kinds: passbook savings account or a checking account. In recent years, banks have added more variety. Depositors became dissatisfied with the low-yield passbook rate and downright mutinous about the no-yield checking account rate. Today, yields on bank accounts go up and down with the money markets.

Banks now devote most of their ad money to promoting certificates of deposit (CDs). Here, you agree to leave your money in a bank for a set time period, anywhere from three months to 10 years. There are some tax advantages to CDs. If you invest in a one-year CD in January 1989, for example, it won't mature until January 1990. All of the interest is considered 1990 income, with taxes payable by April 15, 1991, even though most of the interest is earned in 1989.

You can go the other way and choose ready cash over deferral. Some banks offer you the option of taking out CD interest monthly or quarterly, while you leave the principal intact. A newspaper ad for one bank, for example, tells of a businesswoman who used $63,000 worth of CDs to fund a trust. Every month, $400 worth of interest is paid out to cover her mother's housing costs in Florida.

## BANK DEPOSITORS ARE REALLY LENDERS

What are the drawbacks of relying on a bank for cash? To understand the negatives, you need to recognize where your bank cash comes from.

Whenever you make a bank deposit, you're going into the loan business. Your bank takes your money and lends it to selected borrowers, generally local businesses. Or, the bank may buy Treasury securities thereby lending money to the federal government.

Therefore, bank depositors have all the negatives faced by lenders except the risk of default, which you can avoid by staying within the $100,000 limit for federal insurance. If you lend short-term, your yield is likely to be low. If you lend long-term, to get a higher yield, you risk a rise in interest rates. An 8 percent yield on a five-year CD would not be a great investment if inflation and interest rates are back up in double digits, two years later.

Bank depositors are indirect lenders. The bank lends the money and gets the going loan rate; the bank's expenses, including salaries, come out before the loan interest can be passed through to you. So bank depositors are getting no-growth investments with relatively low yields. The interest is fully taxable, unless held in a tax-exempt retirement account, such as an IRA or Keogh.

There have been some attempts to combine the safety of bank accounts with growth investments, such as stocks or real estate. One hybrid is a *participating CD*. Investors buy CDs that are earmarked for a specific real estate project. They get a stated yield, usually a bit lower than the standard CD rate, but they also get a chance to share in the profits of the real estate venture.

For example, E.F. Hutton (since acquired by Shearson Lehman) has sold deals involving participating CDs. In one, Far West Savings and Loan Association, a thrift headquartered in Newport Beach, California, issued $62 million worth of 10-year CDs. Minimum investment was $5,000, or $2,000 for IRAs. The money was used for mortgage loans, including the financing of new apartments in California and Florida. The loans called for developers to pay a stated loan interest, about 25 percent of operating income, plus another 25 percent of any profit on sale.

Investors are guaranteed an 8 percent return. The next 1.3 percent of earnings from the venture were to go to the Savings and Loan. After that, the CD investors get all the earnings, until they realize a 13 percent return; they get 85 percent of the profits thereafter. Thus, investors who were willing to accept 8 percent on a 10-year CD—below the going rate—received some growth potential through participation in real estate.

You don't have to wait for a Wall Street firm to come along with a packaged deal if this idea appeals to you. You can invest, say, $5,000 in a long-term CD, to get safe cash, and invest another $5,000 in a real estate partnership or real estate trust with a reputable sponsor. This will give you a similar combination of safety and opportunity.

## STOCK-MARKET SPECULATING WITH CDS

A later wrinkle in CDs, pioneered by Chase Manhattan, combines a bank deposit with equity in the stock market. Investors are offered a base return that generally runs from 0 percent (this is actually a guarantee against a loss of principal) to 4 percent. The return may be somewhat higher if the stock market moves up. That's because the yield on these CDs is tied to the performance of a stock market index. A depositor willing to accept a 0 percent guarantee will get more stock market growth potential than a depositor who wants to hedge his bets with a 4 percent guarantee.

For example, you invest in a market-linked CD for a year, getting a 4 percent minimum and 20 percent stock market participation. In that year, the Standard & Poor's (S&P) 500 index goes up 20 percent. Your total return is your base 4 percent plus 4 percent stock market participation (20 percent of 20 percent). That is an 8 percent yield, perhaps a bit better than you would have earned on a straight one-year CD. If the market shoots up by 40 percent in that year, your CD return will be 12 percent. If the market goes down, you will still get your base 4 percent.

On the other hand, consider the situation where you choose a CD with no minimum return but a 70 percent participation. You will earn 14 percent if the market goes up 20 percent, and 28 percent if the market goes up 40 percent. If the market goes down, you will get your principal back.

Some banks offer bear market CDs, where you can earn more money if the stock market goes down. Or CDs with the up side pegged to the price of gold.

These "gimmick" CDs aren't pure cash investments. They're speculations because of the wide range of possible returns. Most people are better off making a well-thought-out investment directly in real estate or stocks or gold, while also keeping an appropriate amount of safe cash in the bank.

Recently, banks have been offering various forms of inflation-proof CDs. You agree to lock your money up for a given time period, at a certain interest rate. If inflation increases and interest rates move up, you have an escape clause. You can get a higher rate for the second half of your deposit time, or you can borrow against your first CD, to invest in a higher-yield new CD. Alternatively, your interest rate will float to keep ahead of inflation.

In every case, the gimmicks are there because the banks want to lock in your money. You're probably better off by staying away from these exotic CDs and staying short-term, rolling over into new CDs if rates rise. Or, just keep your money in a bank's money market account where you get day-to-day yield adjustment and no withdrawal penalties.

## MAKING ROOM FOR BANK CASH
## IN YOUR PORTFOLIO

Bank cash generally should be part of your portfolio, enough to cover three to six months' worth of expenses. In case of unforeseen circumstances, you'll have ready cash to tap. The more predictable your income, the less of a reserve you'll need. A 20-year executive with a Fortune 500 company may need three months' worth of income in the bank while a freelance writer may need six months' worth—at least!

If you look upon the bank as a place to keep emergency money, it's natural you should lean toward an interest-bearing checking account with day-to-day access. With a CD, you're locked in, exposed to rising interest rates.

It's true that CDs may have higher yields than other bank accounts, but the carrot may not be worth the stick. Suppose you decide you need $20,000 in the bank: $4,000 per month for five months. Every extra 1 percent you earn will provide you with an added $200 per year, about $140 a year after taxes. For $140 a year, is it worth locking up your money in a CD?

Many investors do extensive bank comparison shopping. They'll take their money out of First National, where it's earning 6.82 percent, and shoot it over to Second Federal, to get 6.91 percent. They're like tourists who miss the best times on their vacations in other countries because they're chasing from money changer to money changer to get the best exchange rates. In choosing a bank, convenience and service are far more important than an extra smidgen of yield.

---------------- ***Summary*** ----------------

*Pros:*

- *Convenience.* It's relatively easy to make deposits and withdrawals.
- *Safety.* Federal insurance covers accounts up to $100,000.
- Yields on day-to-day accounts can go up, if interest rates rise.

*Cons:*

- Yields are low.
- You're locked in to a low yield, with a long-term CD, if interest rates rise.
- Interest is fully taxable.

*Recommendation:*

- Keep enough money for three to six months' worth of expenses in a day-to-day account. The greater your job security, the less you'll need.
- If you think you may have to tap retirement funds prematurely, keep a portion of your retirement plan in a day-to-day bank account.

---

# 2

# Stock Up on Cash: Combining Dividends with Growth Potential

Linda R. was the most conservative of investors. Her portfolio was concentrated in utility stocks. She liked the basic business. Customers got their bills every month, and they paid them. They had to, or they wouldn't have gas or electricity or telephone service. As a result, utility stocks paid respectable dividends, and those dividends often increased.

During the 1982–87 bull market, her stocks didn't keep up with the stock market measured by the Dow Jones Industrials and the S&P 500. That didn't bother Linda. She reinvested her dividends and watched her portfolio grow.

On October 19, 1987, Linda wasn't exactly laughing, but she wasn't jumping out the window, either. While the Dow fell 23 percent, and other stocks lost even more ground, Linda's utilities went down 15 percent, the same as the Dow Jones Utilities Average. A month later, while most stocks were still widely depressed, her utilities had rebounded to pre-crash levels.

## INVESTING, AND REINVESTING, FOR DIVIDENDS

We're not recommending that you load up on utility stocks. Indeed, utility stocks fared poorly in the 1970s, when inflation was greater than the ability of utilities to increase dividends.

19

However, stock market investors need to pay attention to dividends as well as to growth potential. Just as utilities' high yield softened the blow of the 1987 crash, so investing in dividend-paying stocks can give you more predictable, less erratic returns in the stock market.

After October 19, you may say, why invest in the stock market at all? There's enough stress to contend with. It's true that the stock market is increasingly volatile and thus increasingly risky. However, stock market performance, long-term, is just too good to pass up. Going back 60 years (which includes both the 1929 and the 1987 crashes) and adjusting for inflation, the stock market increased investors' money more than 60-fold! In the same period, gold values tripled while T-bills barely doubled an investor's money.

Whenever you see this type of comparison, the calculation assumes that all stock dividends have been reinvested in more stock. Thus, dividend reinvestment is a crucial factor in stock market success. Norman Fosback, whose Institute for Econometric Research prepared the graph on page 21, estimates that reinvested dividends account for nearly half the total return on common stocks.

To take a more recent perspective, look at returns for the 15 years through 1987. The Dow Jones Industrial Average went from just over 1,000 to nearly 2,000. The index rose only 90 percent, a compound growth rate of about 4.5 percent per year. But if you include all the dividends paid on those stocks and assume they were reinvested, the total return was over 300 percent! Counting reinvested dividends, the growth rate was nearly 10 percent per year.

Thus, when you invest in stocks, go for income as well as growth, and reinvest the dividends.

## Where the Cash Flows From

What are you buying when you invest in shares of common stock? You're buying a share—hence the name—in a business. That business may be anything from the world's largest producer of computers to a telephone utility to the corner takeout restaurant, provided the restaurant owner has sold shares in a public offering.

Whatever the business, it's run by managers who incur expenses and try to earn revenues. Any revenues in excess of expenses are *operating income*. From operating income, taxes are paid, as well as debt service to a bank or to bondholders.

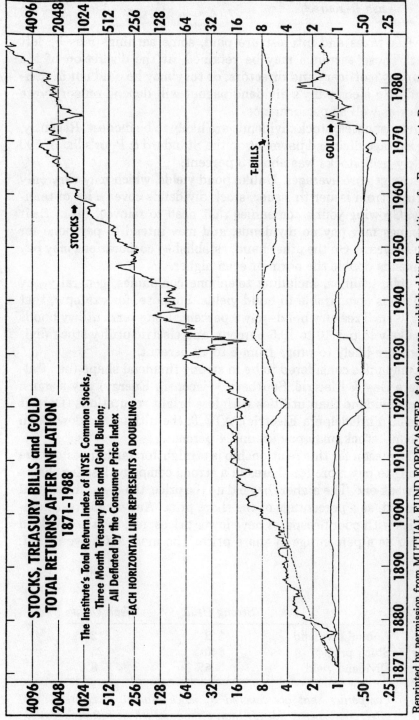

STOCKS, TREASURY BILLS and GOLD
TOTAL RETURNS AFTER INFLATION
1871-1988

The Institute's Total Return Index of NYSE Common Stocks,
Three Month Treasury Bills and Gold Bullion;
All Deflated by the Consumer Price Index

EACH HORIZONTAL LINE REPRESENTS A DOUBLING

STOCKS →

T-BILLS

GOLD →

Reprinted by permission from MUTUAL FUND FORECASTER, $ 49 per year, published by The Institute for Econometric Research,
3471 North Federal Highway, Fort Lauderdale, Florida 33306; telephone 800-327-6720.

After taxes and interest are paid, some earnings may be left over. Those earnings may be retained, at the discretion of the company's officers and directors, or they may be paid out in dividends. So a company's dividend payout will depend on corporate policy as well as performance.

In most cases, stock dividends are likely to be modest. Recently, the average dividend payment on the Standard & Poor's list of 500 widely-held stocks was about 3 percent.

Averages are averages. Unlike bond yields, which may vary only slightly from issuer to issuer, stock dividends cover a lot of territory. Growing young companies that need to reinvest all of their earnings may pay no dividends, and may intend to pay none for several years. On the other hand, established corporations may pay dividends double the norm or even higher.

Public utilities, including telephone companies, generally pay dividends comparable to bond yields. Suppose, for example, that long-term Treasury bonds pay 9 percent. Long-term utility bonds are likely to pay 10 to 10.5 percent, and electric utility stock dividends are likely to range from 6 to 12 percent.

Companies considered to be in strong financial shape (i.e., Baltimore Gas & Electric, Southern Wisconsin Energy) pay a much lower dividend than utilities with less bright reputations (Detroit Edison, Philadelphia Electric). AT&T, the ultimate widows' and orphans' stock, may pay around 4 percent.

The reason for this relationship is straightforward. Investors are willing to pay more for shares in a strong company, less for shares in a weak one. The higher they bid up the price, the lower the annual dividend, as a percentage of the share price. And vice versa. Companies with poor prospects have lower prices, making the dividend higher as a percentage of share price. The more safety you want,

|  | *Strong Utility* | *Weak Utility* |
|---|---|---|
| Annual dividend | $ 2 | $ 2 |
| Stock price | $40 | $25 |
| Dividend yield | 5% | 8% |

*Companies that are favored by stock market investors often pay lower dividends than companies whose future is in doubt.*

the lower the dividend you'll receive. If you are willing to sacrifice quality—own a company that's perceived by the market to be weaker—you can receive a higher dividend.

Sometimes a high dividend can be a red flag. The fact that the shares of a company trades at $30 and pays a 75-cent quarterly dividend ($3 per year) doesn't mean that it's a 10 percent investment. The stock may have fallen from $40 to $30 because of financial distress, and the next dividend may be 30 cents ($1.20 per year, or 4 percent), or the dividend may be skipped altogether.

## HOW STOCK DIVIDENDS DIFFER
## FROM BOND INTEREST

On the plus side, stock dividends can go up as well as down. That's not true of bond interest. When you buy a bond, you're locked in. You may pay $1,000 for a bond paying 8 percent; you'll get $80 in annual interest until the bond matures.

Stock dividends, however, can grow. If you invest $1,000 in a stock, you may receive only $60 (6 percent) a year in dividends at the start. But if the company prospers, it may increase its dividend each year—even each quarter—to $70, $80, $100, and so forth. Several studies have shown that stock dividends eventually catch and surpass bond interest, if held for the long-term. In addition, dividends usually increase when stock prices are rising, allowing one's investment to grow in value.

The 1986 tax law has accelerated the rate of dividend increases because corporations have found it in their best interest to raise dividends. Why? Companies are like merchants when it comes to their common stock. IBM wants to make its stock more attractive to buyers than GE stock or Treasury bonds. The greater the appeal to buyers, the higher the stock price. Higher stock prices make it easier to raise capital and they are the best protection against takeovers. Therefore, corporate managements will do what they can to make their common stock sell.

Since the 1986 tax law dramatically increased the rates on long-term capital gains, the purchase of stocks for long-term growth is less appealing. At the same time, the rate on ordinary income, including stock dividends, is much lower. Therefore, corporate managers have responded by increasing dividend payouts whenever possible.

## SHOPPING FOR UTILITY STOCKS

If you're interested in a high-dividend utility stock, find out if the company has been able to get regular rate increases in recent years. A rigid regulatory climate may make future dividend hikes hard to come by. Whenever interest rates and inflation come down, some regulators reduce the returns that a utility may earn. Boston Edison, for example, recently saw its ceiling for return on equity drop from 15.25 to 12 percent. In such circumstances, a utility may have to cut dividends.

On the other hand, utilities burdened with heavy debt to pay for new construction may be able to refinance the debt when interest rates fall. That will give them more cash to pay out in dividends.

If you're considering an electric utility, beware of commitments to new construction, especially in nuclear power. Most investors should avoid any company where nuclear power is a major concern.

## PLAYING THE RATINGS GAME

To receive a high cash yield from the stock market, look for stocks with a record of consistent dividend increases over the past ten or 15 years. Look at the "payout ratio" of dividends to earnings. The company should be earning enough to comfortably cover its dividend. If not, or if analysts expect a drop in earnings, be wary of future dividend cuts.

Before you invest, find out the company's bond rating. Why does a bond rating affect a stock investment? Because bond ratings, issued by independent rating companies, reflect a company's overall financial health. A company with a top AAA rating, for example, has virtually no clouds on its financial horizon. As you get lower, to AA or A or BBB, etc., companies have more debt on their balance sheets, legal headaches, and so on. So a bond rating is a short-cut evaluation of a company's fiscal health.

Bond rating services such as Moody's (Phone: 212/553-0300) or S&P (Phone: 212/208-8000) generally will give you this information over the phone. If it's B or lower, or if the rating has been dropped recently, you may be taking on more risk than the current dividend is worth. Most brokerage firms and public libraries have publications from Moody's and S&P, containing the information you need to evaluate a stock. Another valuable reference, the *Value Line Investment Survey,* may be available as well.

## DOING YOUR HOMEWORK

As you can see, choosing stocks—even high-dividend stocks—is a job that demands thorough research. If you consult a brokerage firm or a certified financial planner, you may have access to information about high-dividend stocks. Many brokerage firms, for example, publish research reports indicating which high-dividend stocks are likely to trim their payouts and which ones are likely to post increases.

Sometimes newspapers or magazines provide this information. Business Week and Forbes, in particular, regularly publish articles showing which companies have steadily increased dividends, for example, or which high-dividend companies are generating enough earnings that a future rise is likely. Such articles can be a handy place to begin your research.

## "BONDS" THAT CAN GIVE YOU STOCK
## MARKET PAYOFFS

From August 1982 to August 1987, in a roaring bull market, the leading stock market averages more than tripled. Even after Black Monday, the stock market was up over 150 percent in five years. Next to gains like those, 5 percent or 8 percent or even 10 percent a year from stock dividends doesn't sound like much. Many high-dividend stocks, including utilities, lag the overall market when stocks are rising rapidly.

Yet there is a way for investors to have their cake and eat it, too. You can get high current yields—immediate cash—and still participate in stock market growth.

You can do this by investing in *converts*—convertible bonds and convertible preferred stock. A convert is essentially a bond issued by a corporation. As a kicker, the investor has the option of converting this bond into that company's common stock. Thus, while a convert may be a bond, it's also a vehicle for investors to play the stock market while they receive high cash flow.

Let's say XYZ company sells a convertible bond for $1,000. Bondholders have the privilege of converting that bond to 50 shares of common stock. So, if XYZ's stock hits $30 a share in the future, a bondholder can cash in the convertible bond for $1,500 worth of stock. The higher the price of XYZ stock, the greater the return to the holder of convertible bonds.

Why is XYZ willing to offer this conversion privilege? To help sell its bonds. Typically, it can issue a convertible bond at an interest rate that's about one-third lower than it would have to pay on a straight bond issue.

Suppose XYZ has an "A" credit rating. Good but not great. To issue 20-year bonds, it may have to pay a 10 percent interest rate. By issuing convertibles, it might only have to pay 7 percent. On millions of dollars worth of bonds, the savings can be substantial.

Investors in convertibles are willing to accept the lower yield (7 percent rather than 10 percent) to get a stock market play in XYZ. But if they like XYZ's stock market prospects, why not just buy the common stock? Because converts usually pay a higher cash yield than common stock dividends.

Let's assume XYZ common stock currently sells at $15 a share, and the common stock dividend is 30 cents a year, or 2 percent. If this investor buys $1,000 worth of XYZ stock, he'll get $20 a year in dividends. If he buys a 7 percent convertible bond for $1,000, he collects $70 a year. Typically, convertible yields are much higher than the returns from common stock dividends. (See example at the bottom.)

Investors won't get as much appreciation when the common stock moves up, but they will get some. In our example, the stock moves from $15 to $30 a share (100 percent increase) but convertible bond

|  | *XYZ Common Stock* | *XYZ Convertible Bond* |
| --- | --- | --- |
| Price | $15/share | $1,000/bond |
| Number purchased | 66.67 | 1 |
| Amount invested | $1,000 | $1,000 |
| Yield | 2% (dividend) | 7% (interest) |
| Cash flow/year | $20 | $70 |

*Assume stock price doubles, to $30/share, and the Bond is convertible to 50 shares of XYZ Common Stock:*

|  |  |  |
| --- | --- | --- |
| Value of investment | $2,000 | $1,500 |

*Thus the Convertible Bond gives you more cash flow than the Common Stock, along with some appreciation potential. But the Common Stock will give you greater profits, if the price goes up.*

holders get only a 50 percent gain—their $1,000 bond now is worth
$1,500. To get the high yields of convertible bonds, you have to give
up some stock market upside.

## INCREASING YIELDS THROUGH COVERED CALLS

There is another strategy for generating high yields through stock
market investing. It's called *covered-call writing,* or *overwriting.*
Using this strategy, you buy shares in blue-chip stocks, the ones
for which stock options are listed. (You can easily get this information from your local newspaper.) Then, you "write" (sell) an option to someone else, giving them the right to buy this stock away
from you at a given price. You collect cash—a "premium"—for
selling the option.

For example, suppose you buy 100 shares of Black & Decker at
$18 per share, or $1,800, and you sell a call option at $20, expiring
in two months. Your call premium may be ¾, or 75 cents per share,
and you would receive $75.

After two months, the option expires. If it's not exercised, you
pocket the $75, which is more than 4 percent of your investment.
That's an annual rate of over 24 percent.

What does the option buyer get for giving you a 24 percent
return on your money? He can buy the stock away from you at $20
during the period of the option's life. Suppose the stock goes up to
$24. He'll exercise the option and acquire a $24 stock for $20. Your
total return is $275—$200 on your stock profit and $75 from the
option—for a 15 percent return, in two months. That's less than
the 33 percent profit you would have had, without selling the
option. So covered call writers are giving up potential upside in
return for current cash flow.

Investors pay transaction fees if they write call options, but they
also collect dividends while they own the stock. So it's possible to
wind up with more than 10 percent per year, perhaps even 20
percent per year with this strategy.

The risk, though, is that the stock you own will go down in
price. The money you collect from selling calls will act as a partial
offset, but you're still exposed to normal stock market losses. So
choose your stocks with care, rather than investing just because a
stock has a hefty call premium. Ask yourself, "Do I really want to
own this stock?"

| | |
|---|---|
| Price per share | $18 |
| Shares bought | 100 |
| Amount invested | $1,800 |

*Sell: Option to buy your shares at $20 per share,*
*within two months*

| | |
|---|---|
| Option premium | 75 cents/share |
| Amount received | $75 |
| Return on investment | 4%+ |
| Annual rate | 24%+ |

*Suppose the stock goes from $18 per share to $24*
*per share, within two months:*

| | |
|---|---|
| Option exercise price: | $20 |
| You receive: | $2,000 |
| Profit | $200 |
| Plus option premium | $75 |
| Total received | $275 |
| Return on investment | 15.3% |

*If you had not written a call, but merely sold your*
*stock at $24, you'd have received a 33% profit.*

## INVEST IN STOCKS, DON'T TRADE THEM

The stock market crash of October 1987 scared away many investors. Why invest in stocks when you can lose more than 20 percent of your principal in a single day?

The answer is that investors, not traders, profit from stocks. The in-and-outers, the options speculators, the arbitragers, the margin buyers—they were the ones who were hurt most by the crash. That's only fair. They were in the high-risk section of the market, to earn super-high yields, and they painfully learned why those strategies are risky.

Long-term stock market investors, on the other hand, can't complain. As we noted earlier, the market was much higher in 1987 than in 1982, even after the crash. Buy-and-hold works best as long as you buy the right stocks and hold them until their price gets too high. A basic rule of thumb is to keep 20 to 40 percent of your investment portfolio in stocks. The younger you are, and the more willing you are to take risks, the greater your stock market exposure should be. Lighten up a bit when inflation and interest rates are rising; increase your participation when rates come down.

In choosing the right stocks to buy, an emphasis on cash is helpful. Companies with a history of steadily increasing dividends are generally those whose basic business is sound and expanding. If you find such companies paying relatively high yields, it means that their stock prices are relatively low. They may well be attractive buys.

Dividend-paying stocks generate current income, and you will receive a cash return each quarter. They also provide more stability while the stock market becomes more volatile. You may miss out on the high fliers, but you won't come down to earth as violently.

─────── *Summary* ───────

*Pros:*

- Stock dividends, combined with stock-price appreciation, can add up to high long-term returns.
- Stock dividends may be increased if corporate profits improve.
- Some investments (convertible bonds, utility stocks) can provide relatively high cash flow while retaining some growth potential.
- High-dividend paying stocks may fall less than the general stock market in troubled times.
- Many companies offer automatic dividend reinvestment plans with no sales commissions.
- Paper profits, from stock appreciation, aren't taxed until they're realized.
- Covered-call writing can be a cash cow for sophisticated investors.

*Cons:*

- Most stock dividends are relatively low, compared with bonds, money market funds, or bank accounts. Many stocks pay no dividends at all.
- High dividends often reflect low share prices, which in turn may reflect investor disenchantment with the company.

- Stock dividends may go down as well as up. The highest-dividend stocks may reflect low-quality companies and may be the most vulnerable to sharp drops. (High dividends from weak companies are known as "hush money" to shareholders.)
- The stock market has become increasingly volatile and investing in stocks for cash exposes you to market risks.
- Stock dividends as well as gains from stock market profits are fully taxable when realized.

*Recommendation:*

Investors should have 20 to 40 percent of their portfolio in the stock market. The nearer you are to retirement, the lower your stock market exposure should be. Similarly, older investors should concentrate more on dividend-paying stocks and convertible bonds, paying less attention to speculative issues with no dividends.

# 3

# Treasury Trove: Collecting Federal Cash Flow

The year was 1974. Watergate was in the headlines, about to force President Nixon's resignation. In the wake of the 1973 oil shock, motorists endured long lines for the privilege of buying gas at over $1 per gallon. And the federal government issued Treasury notes bearing the astronomical interest rate of 9 percent.

Individual investors wanted those notes—who could pass up 9 percent on a government security? But most major brokerage firms refused to handle orders for the $5,000 investor.

For some financial professionals, this was an opportunity. Not only did they advertise in local newspapers, they literally walked the gas lines handing out business cards. Their offer: They would buy the Treasury notes for individual investors and charge only $25 per order, no matter the size. It was a loss leader, but it attracted investors. In retrospect, this was a "note-worthy" starting point for many financial advisers.

## LOW RISK, LOW REWARD

Why the demand for 9 percent Treasury notes? The yield was appealing, of course. But, most of all, this was a turbulent time in the economy. The stock market was plunging as inflation reached record levels. People were frightened, and they wanted safety in their investments. And safety, to many investors, means buying Treasury securities.

31

If you want safety, though, you have to accept lower returns. Securities issued by the U.S. Treasury may be the extreme in the low-risk, low-yield category.

All Treasury securities are bonds of some type. Investors are lending money to the U.S. government, allowing it to proceed with its various activities. In return for the loan, the Treasury provides the investor with a piece of paper promising to repay the loan with interest. This paper is a bond—a pledge—although it may be called a bill or a note or a bond.

Treasury paper generally is considered an ultra-safe investment. This may be somewhat confusing. Lending money to a borrower already trillions of dollars in debt and rolling up another $200 billion in debt every year may not seem like everyone's idea of safety.

However, the U.S. Treasury is not your average trillion-dollar debtor. It owns the printing press. When its bonds come due, it can exchange that paper for new paper, dollar bills in this case. The dollars are legal tender, readily exchangeable for goods and services.

Thus, when you invest in Treasury securities you eliminate the prime concern of all lenders: the risk of default. The lender knows that $1,000 invested today will be returned in full when the loan comes due. That's why Treasury securities are considered so safe.

Of course this safety has a price. You pay more for a Treasury security than you would for a security issued by a corporation. When you pay more, you accept a lower yield. For example, if long-term (30-year) Treasury bonds are paying 9 percent, top-rated utility bonds are likely to yield 10 to 10.5 percent on similar maturities.

The lower rates are perfectly acceptable for some investors. Let's say an investor has $50,000 in long-term bonds. Treasuries, at 9 percent, pay $4,500 in annual interest, whereas corporate bonds pay $5,250 at 10.5 percent. Some investors may prefer not to have to worry about a possible default and are willing to forgo $750 a year in interest income.

After taxes, the difference will be even less. In a 30 percent bracket, for example, corporate bonds pay only $525 more than the Treasuries. In addition, Treasury securities are exempt from state and local income taxes. An investor who pays a 10 percent state income tax effectively pays an extra 7 percent on corporate bond income. (The federal tax deduction for state income taxes accounts for the differential.) That knocks another $367.50 off the corporate-

|  | Treasury Bond | Corporate Bond |
|---|---|---|
| Amount invested | $50,000 | $50,000 |
| Yield | 9% | 10.5% |
| Annual interest | $4,500 | $5,250 |
| Tax @ 30% | $1,350 | $1,575 |
| Net to investor | $3,150 | $3,675 |
| Reward for assuming extra risk: |  | $ 525 |

*Effective state income tax (assume 10% state tax rate plus deductibility on federal tax return, at 30% federal rate):*

|  |  |  |
|---|---|---|
|  | $ 0 | $367.50 |
| Reward for assuming extra risk: |  | $157.50 |

Treasury yield spread. Since the investor winds up with only an extra $157.50 a year on a $50,000 portfolio by buying corporates instead of Treasuries, he may prefer the Treasuries to sleep better, unconcerned about default.

## BILLS, NOTES, BONDS

If you're interested in Treasuries, there are some basics you should know. Treasury securities are called bills, notes, or bonds. T-bills mature in one year or less, note maturities range from one to 10 years, bonds are longer-term. Minimum investments are $10,000 for T-bills, $5,000 for notes maturing in less than four years, and $1,000 for longer-term notes and bonds. Today, most banks or brokers will buy Treasury securities for you, often at a modest ($25–$75) fee. Or you can eliminate the fee altogether by buying direct from a Federal Reserve Bank.

T-bills are sold in three-month, six-month, and one-year maturities. They are bought at a discount. That is, to buy $15,000 worth of one-year T-bills, you pay, say, $14,000. One year later, the T-bill matures and you collect $15,000. The $1,000 difference is the interest income on the bills. All T-bill purchases are "book entry:" There's no delivery of the actual certificate.

T-bill interest isn't taxable until the bill matures. Thus, some investors try to buy T-bills that straddle two years. If you buy a six-month T-bill in July 1989 that comes due in January 1990, all of the interest is considered 1990 income, and taxes are not due until you file your return in April 1991. It's the same deferral strategy discussed earlier for bank CDs.

Treasury notes and bonds behave like any other bonds. You pay the face amount, say, $5,000 when you buy the bond. Suppose the interest rate is 8 percent, or $400 a year. The return is fixed over the life of the bond, and interest is paid semi-annually. Thus, you will collect $200 in interest every six months. When the bond matures, you get your $5,000 back.

In most cases, the interest rate on T-bills, notes, and bonds increases as the maturity gets longer. That is, a one-year T-bill may pay 6 percent, a five-year Treasury note 7 percent, and a 10-year Treasury bond 8 percent. This phenomenon (higher yields on longer maturities), generally applies to municipal and corporate bonds as well.

Why should interest rates rise as maturities lengthen? Because investors increase their risk as they stretch the maturities of bonds in their portfolios, and greater risk should bring greater rewards.

Didn't we just say that Treasury securities are riskless? Not really. While there is no risk of default, there is still the risk that plagues all bond buyers: inflation risk. Inflation erodes bond buying power and causes high interest rates, which, in turn, devalue bonds.

Inflation risk is small with short-term securities. Suppose you buy a three-month T-bill, which pays 6 percent when inflation is 4 percent. Over the three-month period, there is virtually no chance that inflation will shoot up. You are fairly certain of increasing your purchasing power by 2 percent (the 6 percent interest you collect minus the 4 percent increase in the price level), if you buy a string of four three-month T-bills.

But look what can happen if you invest $5,000 in 10-year Treasury bonds. Suppose they pay 8 percent, two percentage points (200 *basis points*) higher than the three-month T-bill. In the first year, if inflation stays at 4 percent, you increase your purchasing power by 4 percent, rather than 2 percent.

But 10 years is a long time. In that period, inflation may increase. It's not hard to find harbingers of future inflation: rising federal budget deficits, falling value of the dollar, turmoil in the Persian Gulf and a possible increase in oil prices.

Suppose inflation rises to 10 percent, the level of the early 1980s. Even though you are collecting cash regularly, you are actually losing buying power. Ten thousand dollars worth of goods and services cost $11,000 after a year of 10 percent inflation, but your capital will increase only from $10,000 to $10,800, since you are locked in at an 8 percent yield. And that's before taxes.

What's more, a new Treasury bond investor may be getting 12.5 percent on 10-year bonds when inflation reaches 10 percent. He paid $5,000 and collects $625 a year, while you are still collecting $400. Consequently, your bonds are worth less if you want to sell them. You might receive only $3,200 for bonds you bought for $5,000.

It's true that eventually you will get back your $5,000 outlay if you hold on for 10 years until maturity. But $5,000 in 1998 will be worth less than the $5,000 you invested in 1988. If we assume that inflation averages 7 percent over the period, for example, buying power will be cut in half.

## WHY BOND INVESTORS DEMAND HIGH YIELDS

Suppose we asked you to lend us $10,000, and we promised to pay you, say, $700 (7 percent) per year for the next 10 or 20 or 30 years, and, at the end of the period, we would pay you back the $10,000.

How would you feel about it? Chances are, you would chuckle a bit and ask if we had any bridges to sell. You would realize that the $10,000 we would return in the future would be worth a lot less than the $10,000 lent today. Yet, that's what investors do each time

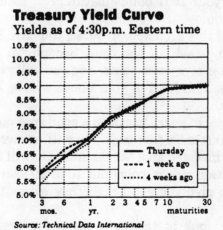

**Treasury Yield Curve**
Yields as of 4:30p.m. Eastern time

Source: *Technical Data International*

**Treasury Yield Curve** "reprinted by permission of *The Wall Street Journal*, © Dow Jones & Company, Inc. 1988. All Rights Reserved."

they buy a medium- or long-term bond. That's true for Treasury bonds, corporate bonds, or municipals.

The only way for bond investors to win is to get a high *real* interest rate (in excess of inflation) over the entire period. Suppose inflation stays at 4 percent for 10 years. The holder of an 8 percent bond gains 4 percent each year, and those earnings can compound. That's more than enough to make up for the 4 percent devaluation of your principal each year through inflation and income taxes.

Thus, long-term bond investors are gambling that their yields will be sufficient to outstrip inflation. They won't invest long-term unless they get a high enough yield. That's why the yield curve (p. 35) usually slopes up, with interest rates rising as maturities extend.

## RIDING THE YIELD CURVE

There is one strategy investors can use to make the most of the yield curve: stagger maturities. This strategy will work for municipals and corporate bonds as well as Treasuries.

Divide your bond portfolio into four equal portions. Suppose you wanted to invest $20,000 in Treasury bonds: you would put $5,000 in each portion.

Invest so that each $5,000 portion matures every two years. In 1989, for example, buy $5,000 worth of Treasuries maturing in 1991, $5,000 that matures in 1993, $5,000 in 1995, and $5,000 in 1997. When your 1991 bonds mature, roll them over into 1999 bonds. And so on.

What does all this accomplish? First, you have $20,000 worth of bonds generating cash all the time. Second, 25 percent of your portfolio matures every two years, and you will get your full principal back then. Third, all of your bonds will be bought at eight-year maturities.

Historically, eight years has been a good spot on the yield curve, and it's likely to remain that way. You will receive a higher return than if you had invested short-term. And you will have avoided the enormous inflation risk of going out 10 or 20 years. Buying eight-year bonds can give you good cash flow without a great deal of inflation risk.

For example, look at the yield curve for Treasury securities from early 1988. Investors in short-term T-bills earn about 6 percent. Going out to an eight-year maturity boosts the return to almost 9 percent—a significant difference. But going to 10-year Treasuries, or even 30-year Treasuries, provides scant extra return. Yield curves may change in shape (they may even turn negative, with short-term yields exceeding long-term yields, in chaotic times), but the curve pictured on page 35) is fairly normal.

What happens if inflation accelerates and interest rates pick up? Every time 25 percent of your investment matures, reinvest at the higher prevailing yields. By following this strategy, you have some protection against inflation. Disinflation—lower rates— usually doesn't worry bond investors, because the interest they receive represents real purchasing power. You will be happy to receive 8 percent on an eight-year bond if inflation falls to 2 percent.

## SAVINGS BONDS AREN'T JUST FOR BABY GIFTS

Any discussion of Treasury securities should cover EE Savings Bonds, even though they're not strictly cash investments. Savings bonds have all the advantages of Treasury securities, plus some unique tax advantages.

Like all bonds issued by the federal government, savings bonds are safe—there's no risk of default. They're easy to buy because they're sold at most banks. No fees are involved, and you can invest with as little as $25 at a time. They're exempt from state and local income taxes. The only real drawback is that no more than $15,000 can be invested in savings bonds per individual per year.

Yields are competitive. They float up and down with interest rates. But as long as you hold your savings bonds for at least five years, your yield won't be any lower than 6 percent.

The 1986 tax law has increased the use of savings bonds for college funding. (See Appendix B.) All unearned income of a child under 14 in excess of $1,000 per year will be taxed at his or her parents' tax rate, but use of EE bonds can reduce a child's tax bill.

|  | *CDs* | *EE Saving Bonds* |
|---|---|---|
| Amount invested | $40,000 | $40,000 |
| Assumed yield | 7.5% | 7.5% |
| Income | $ 3,000 | $ 3,000 |
| Current income taxes (Children under age 14) | $    675 | $    0 |

Baby Jane Smith, for example, received $20,000 from her grandparents when she was born in 1980. Her parents placed the money in bank CDs. by 1989, the money had grown to $40,000. By 1989, nine-year-old Jane will earn $3,000 in interest from her CDs.

Of that interest, $500 will be sheltered by the child's standard deduction, $500 will be taxed at the child's 15 percent rate ($75) and $2,000 will be taxed at her parents' 30 percent tax rate ($600), and Jane will owe $675 in taxes on $3,000 in interest income. And her tax bill will grow each year because she will be earning more compound interest.

Suppose Jane's parents cash in the CD and buy $40,000 worth of EE savings bonds instead. Taxes on savings bonds need not be paid until they're cashed in. The interest grows compounded, free of current taxes. Jane now will owe no taxes.

By the time she is 14, her savings bonds may be worth $60,000, depending upon interest rates. She could cash them in over two calendar years and repurchase CDs. If that's the case, she will have $20,000 in income ($10,000 per year for two years), from cashing in the bonds. Because she will be over 14, all of the income will be taxed at 15 percent. She will owe only $3,000 on the bond sale and have $57,000 to reinvest. Ongoing interest will be taxed at 15 percent.

Or, the money can be kept in savings bonds until Jane is 18 and needs the money for college. Taxes are postponed for four more years, and the tax-free buildup is increased.

### Safety or Growth?

The disadvantage to this strategy is the same for any bondtype investment: you are giving up growth. If you are content with a safe, 6 percent + compound yield on your college savings, EE bonds offer tax advantages. But they're not for everybody.

Betsy R., for example, has three young children. On each birthday, Betsy's parents give the child a $500 savings bond. Betsy thanks her parents, waits the required six months, and cashes in the bonds and invests the proceeds in a growth-stock mutual fund. She doesn't tell her parents because she doesn't want to stop the birthday gifts. But she believes that children's assets shouldn't be locked into low-yield investments.

In essence, Betsy is acting on the question that all bond investors have to ask: Is the yield high enough to make up for the likely loss of future purchasing power? The longer you extend bond maturities, the more likely you are playing a losing game.

## KEEPING BONDS IN PERSPECTIVE

Investors shouldn't overdose on bonds. As a very broad guideline, investors should keep 10 to 50 percent of their portfolio in bonds and bond-type investments. Younger investors (those under age 40) should keep bond holdings below 25 percent of their portfolio, and allow the proportion to increase as they approach and reach retirement. For all investors, maturities should be kept short, generally no more than eight years.

Bonds generally are less volatile than stocks, but they can produce surprising swings. Before the October 1987 stock market crash, for example, the bond market had been in a severe six-month slump, with Treasury issues absorbing some of the biggest losses. Inflationary worries and interest rate increases caused the decline in bond prices.

Treasury securities may be default-proof, but they are not inflation-proof, especially when the federal government is pursuing policies that contribute to inflation and devalue bonds.

 *Summary*

*Pros:*

- *Safety.* The issuer won't default.
- *Liquidity.* All Treasury issues can be bought and sold at any time.
- *Low cost.* They can be bought for little or no sales commissions.
- *Flexibility.* There is a choice from very short to very long maturities.
- *Tax benefits.* EE Savings Bond offer the choice of deferring income taxes. T-bills may permit year-to-year deferral. No state or local income taxes are due on any Treasury issues.

*Cons:*

- *Low yield.* Treasuries pay less than other bonds.

- *Inflation risk.* Whenever fears of inflation surface, Treasury bonds lose value. Investors were severely burned in 1987, for example.
- *No growth potential.* With a Treasury bond, or any bond, the yield can't increase over the years.
- *Federal taxes.* Interest on Treasury issues is taxable to the IRS.

*Recommendation:*

Fixed-income investments, including bonds, are a core part of any investor's portfolio. The 10 to 50 percent guideline is broad, but for the most part 25 percent is a good target. Among bonds, we favor Treasury issues for most investors, generally in short- and medium-term maturities. Staggering maturities is a helpful device.

Treasuries are best held in tax-sheltered retirement plans, including IRAs. Investors in high-tax states may consider holding them outside of retirement plans to take advantage of the state-tax exemption.

# 4

# Gentlemen (and Ladies) Prefer Bonds

Investors looking for the highest cash yields can consider corporate bonds. When you buy a corporate bond, you are lending money to that corporation. To corporation pledges to pay you interest and to repay you in full after a stated time period. As a bondholder, you are a senior creditor of that corporation: If things get rocky, your claims on the company's assets come before the claims of stockholders.

Bonds usually are issued in $1,000 denominations, and you can place orders through securities brokers. Interest is generally paid semi-annually. An investment of $1,000 in a bond that pays 8 percent yields $80 in interest each year, in two $40 payments. When the bond matures, the investor is paid back the original $1,000.

When you invest in a corporate bond, you have the same potential rewards as when you buy a Treasury bond. You will receive regular interest, and you have a chance for capital gains if interest rates fall. You bear the same risks, too. Your income stream can't grow, and your bonds may lose value if interest rates go up.

Corporate bonds, though, pose another risk: The company may not make all the interest payments it promises, or it may not repay the principal. To make these payments, a company must be generating enough cash from its business. It has no printing press to fall back on. And there must be enough cash on hand to repay that debt—or sufficient credit standing to obtain new loans—when its bonds mature.

41

To adjust for the higher risk, corporate bonds pay higher interest than Treasuries. If long-term Treasury bonds pay 9 percent, for example, high-quality corporate bonds may pay over 10 percent.

## BOND BUYERS RELY ON RATINGS

Corporate bonds also differ from Treasuries in that there's a wide range of issuers, with different financial strengths. Some blue-chip companies are in far better financial shape than Uncle Sam, judging by comparable balance sheets. You may like the idea of getting 10 percent from a solvent corporation rather than 9 percent from a debt-laden government.

The most creditworthy corporations are usually rated AA or AAA by Moody's or Standard & Poor's, the major rating services. These independent services evaluate a company's financial position and give a rating based on its ability to pay its debts. Corporations whose chips aren't quite as blue can issue bonds, too. Since their ratings are not as high, they are required to pay more to attract investors. The same page of the *Wall Street Journal,* for example, that lists a new issue of 30-year RJR Nabisco bonds, rated A and paying just over 10 percent, lists a 30-year bond from Textron rated Baa and paying almost 11.5 percent.

New issues of corporate bonds generally are issued at "par." You'll pay $1,000 for a $1,000 bond, and receive $1,000 back when it matures. Pretty straightforward.

Once bonds are issued, though, they fluctuate in price in a direction opposite from that of interest rates. Suppose Corporation C issues a 20-year bond, paying 10 percent, the going rate. That's $100 a year in interest. A year later, after interest rates have gone up, a comparable new issue yields 11 percent. Corporation C's bonds go down in price, to about $900, in order to make the $100 interest payment a competitive 11 percent.

Suppose that two years later interest rates have fallen and bonds yield only 9 percent. In this case, C's bond will go up in value to around $1,100 in order that the $100 in interest yields about 9 percent, the market rate. When C's bond sells below $1,000, it's a *discount* bond; above $1,000 it's a *premium* bond. You can check bond prices daily, in your newspaper, just as you can with stock prices. Many individuals who buy corporate bonds do so on the secondary market, where there's a wide range of maturities and issuers to choose among.

## THE RISE OF HIGH-YIELD "JUNK BONDS"

Until recently, the corporate bond market was fairly staid. Established companies generally had high ratings and paid interest around the banks' prime rate. Newer companies and those experiencing financial distress received lower ratings and paid higher interest. Overall, defaults were rare.

During the last few years, however, a *junk bond* market has emerged for investors willing to take on higher risks for higher yields. Technically, any bond rated BB or lower is a junk bond. But the upsurge in junk bonds in recent years is the result of the increase in corporate mergers and leveraged buyouts.

In a leveraged buyout, A uses borrowed money to acquire B. The borrowed money may come from an issue of new bonds; interest and principal on the bonds is to be paid from B's operations. Thus, B is saddled with more debt, and the chance of default is increased. In an alternative scenario, B takes on more debt ("poison pills") to weaken its balance sheet and make the takeover less attractive.

With these changes, the junk bond market has become especially perilous. Junk bond defaults, which averaged 1.5 percent from 1974 to 1985, reached 3 percent in 1986. LTV, one of the nation's largest companies, defaulted on $1.4 billion worth of junk bonds. (The 1987 figures were skewed by Texaco's troubles, but $9 billion worth of defaults were recorded.)

The junk bond market illustrates the risk-reward ratio in its extreme. Yields on junk bonds are often 4 or 5 points higher than Treasury yields: When long-term Treasuries pay 9 percent, junk bonds may yield 13 or 14 percent. It's hard to find a higher yield anywhere. In the past few years, junk bonds have done better than Treasuries, on average, because the default rate has been relatively low and the extra yield attractively high.

But junk bond yields are by no means guaranteed. Junk bonds are only for investors willing to run the risk of default; they're probably suitable only for investors who can afford a diversified portfolio of these issues. A suggested minimum investment is $25,000, spread among four or five different issuers. If one junk bond issuer defaults, you won't be totally wiped out because the other issuers will continue to pay the interest on their bonds.

## WHEN ZEROS ARE A PLUS

Some specialized types of corporate bonds have been introduced during recent years that appeal to some investors. There's the "zero-junk" hybrid, for example. These bonds are bought at a steep discount and pay no interest (zero) for several years. At the end of this period, interest payments are expected to kick in at a high level. Issuing these bonds may permit a company that has been acquired to get by the first few turbulent years after a merger because it won't have to pay debt service. Investors, of course, must be rewarded for giving up the early cash flow.

For example, Metromedia was involved in a leveraged buyout in 1984. Investors paid $350 for a bond with a $1,000 face value. The bonds pay no interest until 1989, when a $160 annual interest payment will begin. That's nearly 50 percent of an investor's original outlay. The bonds mature in 1998, at $1,000, almost three times the original outlay.

What about regular zero-coupon bonds? These bonds are not for cash investors because you get no cash. Instead, you get a fixed future return. Suppose you pay $1,000 in 1989; you might be promised $2,000 in 1996. That's a 10 percent compound return.

The advantage of buying zeros is that you don't have to worry about reinvesting all the interest payments, possibly at low rates. Thus, zeros may make sense when rates are high and you want to lock them in. When rates are low, you probably don't want to lock them in with zero-coupon bonds.

Also, corporate zeros are taxable each year, even though you receive no interest. You're paying taxes on "phantom income." The same is true of *CATS* and *TIGRS*—zero-coupon bonds packaged by securities firms and backed by Treasury bonds. If you want to accumulate money through zero-coupon bonds, outside of a retirement plan, you may want to select top-rated municipal zeros. (See Chapter 5.)

If you're interested in any type of corporate bonds, look carefully at their call features before you invest. Most corporations have the choice to call in their bonds after a specified date but before maturity. If this happens to you, you'll lose the yield that you were counting on. Call features are especially dangerous if you're investing in premium bonds: you're paying an above-par purchase price to get above-average yields. If those bonds are called in at par, for example, you will actually lose money because you paid a premium for them.

Some critics charge that corporations play "heads-I-win-tails-you-lose" when they issue bonds. If interest rates fall, they call them in and reissue new bonds at lower rates. If rates rise, corporations let you sit with paper losses.

Recently, the rules by which bonds are issued have become fairer. There are *put* bonds, for example. If interest rates rise and bonds lose value, they can be resold to the issuer, at par, after a certain time period. Or, there are noncallable corporate bonds that allow investors to enjoy any drop in interest rates without fear of early redemption. (Treasury bonds usually can't be called in before maturity.) Franklin Savings Association, an S&L in Ottawa, Kansas, has issued bonds that are not callable and that will be adjusted each quarter to keep ahead of inflation by 3 percent.

## WHAT INFLATION HAS DONE TO BONDHOLDERS

Be cautious about loading your portfolio with corporate bonds. History has not been kind to bond investors. If you purchased AAA-rated, 10-year corporate bonds in 1970, at redemption in 1980, each dollar you got back would buy the same amount of groceries as 40 cents would have bought in 1970. That's a tremendous loss of purchasing power. Investors were collecting money with their right hand with each interest payment they received, but at the same time losing money with their left hand as their principal eroded.

Junk-bond yields look tempting today, but there's a reason for the high yields. Risks of default are substantial, even for the knowledgeable investor. The issues are speculative, and investors who want to speculate have more profit potential in growth stocks or leveraged real estate than junk bonds.

Similarly, if you're investing on behalf of a corporation, you're probably better off buying preferred stock than bonds. Yields and risks are comparable, but corporations are entitled to an 80 percent income tax exclusion on stock dividends.

If you do want to own corporate bonds, remember that the interest has no shelter. Income is fully taxable at federal, state, and local levels. Even with a zero-coupon corporate bond, which is not paying interest currently, taxes are due on the "phantom income" received. Thus, corporate bonds may be more suitable for tax-exempt retirement plans, including IRAs, than for regular, taxable accounts. Plan on holding bonds until maturity: they're for investing, not for trading.

## Summary

*Pros:*

- High yields, especially in junk bonds.
- Relative safety—few corporations default on bonds.
- Low price volatility compared with stocks.
- Excellent hedge in times of low inflation or deflation.

*Cons:*

- Neither cash flow nor principal can grow if held to maturity.
- Price volatility has increased in recent years.
- The new breed of junk bonds is only a few years old, and defaults may exceed the historical norm.
- Call provisions may interfere with financial planning.
- Bond investments are especially vulnerable to inflation.
- All interest is fully taxable.

*Recommendation:*

As we said in Chapter 3 on Treasuries, it is okay for bonds to constitute 10 to 50 percent of an investor's portfolio. Those for whom a point or two in interest is important can focus on corporate bonds rather than Treasuries. Most investors are better off in Treasuries.

When interest rates are relatively low, and you're investing for the long-term, choose top-rated corporate bonds because they have slightly higher yields than Treasury bonds. When rates are high—over 10 percent–select a zero-coupon, Treasury-backed issue. Hold these bonds in tax-exempt retirement plans, if possible. Don't buy junk bonds.

# 5

# Tax-Exempt Cash

Whoops! You would think that a $2 billion default would cool investors' ardor. In 1983, the Washington Public Power Supply System, commonly known as Whoops, ceased paying interest on some of its bonds. As of this writing, the bonds still are in default. Thousands of investors, from major corporation to Mom and Pop saving for retirement, stand to lose virtually all of their investment in these tax-exempt issues.

But Whoops didn't kill the tax-exempt bond market. There have been adjustments, to be sure, since the massive default. Today, however, tax-exempt bonds are more popular than ever among individual investors.

What is a tax-exempt bond? It *is* a bond in the same sense as Treasury bonds and corporate bonds described in the last two chapters. Investors lend money and receive a security—a bond— as a pledge that their money will be returned at a certain time. In the meantime, the investors will collect interest.

The interest is exempt—not merely deferred—from federal income taxes. If you buy a $5,000 tax-exempt bond with a 10 percent coupon, you will receive $500 a year in interest income. You won't owe any federal income taxes on that $500, currently or in the future. (There are some exceptions to this rule, because of recent tax laws; these exceptions are covered later in this chapter.)

Why are these bonds tax-exempt? They get a break because they're issued by states, cities, other government bodies, and related agencies. Generically, they're called *municipal* bonds or *munis*, although not all are issued by municipalities. When the state of Kansas or the California Department of Veterans Affairs or the

Broward County (Florida) Expressway Authority needs to borrow money, they compete with the U.S. Treasury, AT&T, etc. Without a tax break, they would be forced to compete through higher interest rates. This would be costly for all government and quasi-government bodies.

During a period when the Treasury pays 9 percent interest to borrow money for 10 years, and AT&T pays 10 percent, thanks to the tax exemption Kansas or Broward County may pay only 8 percent.

## WHY INVESTORS LOVE MUNIS

If an individual investor in the 30 percent tax bracket invests in a Treasury bond and receives 9 percent, he pays 2.7 percent in taxes and takes home 6.3 percent. Buying AT&T bonds at 10 percent, he nets 7 percent after taxes. In both cases, he is better off with 8 percent from a municipal bond. He is willing to make a below-market loan—accept a lower rate of interest—because the interest is exempt from federal income taxes. In reality, the investor is pre-paying income taxes by accepting 8 percent on a bond investment rather than 9 percent or 10 percent. He hopes that the taxes he pre-pays in this manner will be less than the tax he would have paid on the interest from a taxable bond.

Although there are variations, muni-bond interest rates generally run about 85 percent of the rates on Treasuries of comparable maturity. That is, if T-bills yield 6 percent, short-term municipal paper yields about 5 percent. Sometimes, the spread narrows; munis have even had higher yields than Treasuries. When this happens, more investors are attracted to munis, driving up prices. This, in turn, reduces yields to more normal levels.

| | Treasury Bond | AT&T Bond | Municipal Bond |
|---|---|---|---|
| Amount invested | $50,000 | $50,000 | $50,000 |
| Assumed yield | 9% | 10% | 8% |
| Annual income | $ 4,500 | $ 5,000 | $ 4,000 |
| Taxes @ 30% | $ 1,350 | $ 1,500 | $      0 |
| Net to investor | $ 3,150 | $ 3,500 | $ 4,000 |

## MORE MUNI TAX ANGLES

There are other important tax aspects to municipal bonds. First, munis may not be exempt from state and local income taxes. A New York resident, for example, who buys Kansas bonds pays New York income tax on the interest he receives. Some investors seek out local bonds, which are double or triple tax-free. The New York investor, for example, can avoid New York as well as federal income taxes if he buys New York rather than Kansas bonds.

Second, any trading profits on municipal bonds are subject to federal income taxes. It's only the interest that's tax-exempt.

Third, borrowing to buy tax-exempts is not tax-exempt. Let's say you have a home equity line of credit that permits you to borrow money at 10 percent. In a 30 percent tax bracket, your after-tax borrowing cost is 7 percent. You could lock in a profit if you could use this money to buy munis paying 8 percent, except that the IRS won't let you deduct the interest on your loans. The 1986 tax act makes this issue much less appealing, because the lower tax rates diminish the arbitrage opportunities.

Further, the new laws make munis taxable in some circumstances. For example, Social Security income, which generally is tax-exempt, is partially taxable for affluent recipients. Tax-exempt bond interest is included in determining whether or not you're affluent for this purpose. If so, muni bond income increases your overall taxes.

The 1986 Tax Reform Act also makes investing in munis more complicated. The act divides newly-issued munis into two categories: public purpose and private purpose. In the latter category are bonds issued to finance apartment houses, airports, sewage plants, and many other uses. Interest from private purpose munis is now a "tax preference item." Investing in these munis can subject you to the alternative minimum tax and increase your tax burden.

Hence, some munis are no longer tax free. People on Social Security should consult with a tax advisor before investing in munis, and anyone should consult with a tax advisor before buying private purpose munis. Some private-purpose bonds, so-called *AMT* bonds, pay 0.25 to 0.5 percent per year more than non-AMT munis because of tax concerns. These munis may be good buys for the many investors who are not subject to the AMT.

In fact, tax reform has created a seemingly self-contradictory investment category: taxable munis. New convention centers and sports complexes are now considered "nonessential," and bonds issued to finance them are not tax-exempt. Therefore, issuers have brought out taxable bonds for such uses. These bonds are risky—who knows if a new sports complex will pay off?—and the yields are higher, perhaps one point or more above Treasuries. Unless there are some special credit enhancement features, though, investors probably are better off buying bonds issued by established corporations to get comparable yields.

Once past the tax angles, investing in munis is similar to investing in other types of bonds. The investor receives current income that's relatively secure. However, there is no growth potential, and the investor is vulnerable to inflation and rising interest rates and must be concerned with call protection. Munis generally are good candidates for the bond roll-over strategy discussed in Chapter 3.

If you decide to buy munis directly, a $25,000 portfolio is about the minimum to consider. This will enable you to invest $5,000 in each of five different issues. You will have diversification. If one of your bonds turns out to be a Whoops, you won't be wiped out.

## INSURING MUNIS FOR "BELT-AND-SUSPENDERS" PROTECTION

Another reaction to the Whoops fiasco has been the rise of insured bonds. Several private insurance companies cover specific issues. If the issuer defaults, the insurer will cover principal and interest.

Of course, the price of the insurance premium is borne by investors. If you want the increased security of insurance protection, you will have to settle for a lower yield. You may get a percentage point less than you would receive on a comparable but noninsured bond. On a long-term muni bond, that can be a lot of money.

Savvy pros look upon municipal bond insurance as little more than a marketing gimmick. It was created after the New York muni crisis in the mid-1970s and took off after the Whoops default. But insurers generally stick to high-grade, low-risk issues that don't need protection anyway. The insurers' major risk—repayment of principal—won't have to be faced for many years.

In fact, the muni-bond insurers have yet to be tested by a huge default, or a string of defaults. (Whoops was only partially covered.) It's by no means certain that the insurers will be able to survive a real crisis in the muni market. The five largest muni insurers at one point had less than $3 billion in capital to back $300 billion in principal and interest. Investors who buy munis direct probably will do better to skip insured issues and select a diversified portfolio of high-quality but noninsured bonds.

Insured bonds generally are rated AAA by the same agencies that rate corporate bonds. Noninsured bonds—still the majority of munis—are also rated to give investors an idea of relative safety. As you would expect, the higher-rated bonds pay lower yields.

Many small issues of municipal bonds, though, are not rated because of the expense involved. Included among them are good values and disasters. Liquidity tends to be limited. Before you invest in one of these, look for evidence that some professional, perhaps an analyst for a major brokerage firm, has taken a look at the issue.

## REAL RISK VS. APPARENT RISK

When assessing risks in muni bonds—or in any investment—keep in mind the difference between real risks and apparent risks. Apparent risks are those that are obvious to everyone. Once the news is out, the market prices securities accordingly. After the New York muni crisis, the prices of some bonds fell so low that they were yielding 17 to 20 percent tax-exempt. There was little real risk left. Investors who bought then wound up with handsome profits.

On the other hand, there was real risk in the muni market in the late 1960s. Prices were high, and investors weren't aware of the financial distress that lay ahead. Anyone who bought munis at the time was hurt by the inflation that followed in the 1970s.

## FINE POINTS OF THE MUNI MARKET

Municipal bonds may be either general obligation (g.o.) or revenue bonds. General obligation bonds are considered safe because they're backed by the full faith and credit of the issuer. A state or a city, for example, can raise taxes to pay off debt. To default would bar it from the credit markets.

Revenue bonds, on the other hand, are usually issued by a government-related agency; the bonds are backed only by the revenues from the project they finance. Dormitories must be occupied or sufficient expressway tolls must be collected to pay interest and redeem the bonds. These issues are riskier and should be analyzed more carefully. However, revenue bonds usually yield more than g.o. bonds.

Investors should be particularly cautious about retirement center and nursing home bonds. Congress gives these bonds special treatment, and they offer yields of 12 percent and up, tax-free. But the return usually is based on the success of the nursing home or retirement center, with no backing from a local government. Reportedly, over $1 billion of these bonds have defaulted in the past few years.

## NO CASH FLOW, NO TAXES

Some munis are zero-coupon. Zero-coupon bonds pay no interest until maturity, when all the compounded interest is due. With a muni zero, no taxes on "phantom income" are due during the life of the bond. It's one way to save for a future event, with no taxes. Parents, for example, can save for a child's college education without relinquishing control of the securities to the child.

However, a zero-coupon muni puts you totally at the mercy of the issuer. If the Firecracker Expressway proves to be a road to nowhere, you could be left with nothing when the bonds come due. The credit quality of the issuer is vital. It's encouraging to see that the state of Illinois is issuing tax-exempt, zero-coupon "College Savings Bonds" that pay extra to investors who use them to finance an in-state education. Perhaps other states will follow suit.

Another variation for muni investors is the lease/purchase agreement. The investor lends money to a local government to buy a specific item, anything from a fire truck to a computer system. The government agency buys the equipment by repaying the investor.

Typically, these arrangements are fairly short-term (three to five years), with a partial return of principal with each payment. This reduces the investor's exposure to rising interest rates. Because these transactions aren't easy to analyze—they're not rated—investors can expect a tax-exempt yield 10 to 25 percent higher than on a muni bond of a comparable maturity. During a period when three-year munis yield 5 percent, a lease/purchase agreement may pay 5.5 to 6 percent, tax-exempt.

## LOW TAX BRACKETS MAKE MUNIS LESS ATTRACTIVE

Who should buy munis? Only investors in high tax brackets should even consider tax-exempt bonds. Tax reform has made them less attractive relative to taxable bonds. An investor in a 40 or 50 percent tax bracket, under prior law, needed only 5 or 6 percent on a muni to match 10 percent on a corporate or a Treasury bond. Today an investor can keep around 7 percent, after tax, on a 10 percent taxable bond. Muni yields will have to nudge up near those of taxables to make them worth considering.

Before you buy munis, shop around. Get at least three different prices from different brokers before you invest. Take the same precautions before you sell. The muni market is not as formal as a stock exchange, and prices vary widely. Indeed, some brokers literally lost their licenses after the New York bond collapse: they purchased bonds from scared, naive investors for 40 to 50 percent below market and sold them at full value the following day.

Don't let muni investing become a mania. Michael B., for example, sold his business while he was in his early 40s. After taxes, he was worth several million dollars. He spent all of his time at his financial planner's office, going over the muni bid-and-asked prices, buying one $5,000 bond per day. It's good to be serious about investing, but not to the point where you're wasting your entire life.

## MIND YOUR OWN BUSINESS WITH MUNIS

Prior to recent times, privacy-oriented investors preferred munis. Municipal bonds were bearer bonds and thus truly anonymous. (A bearer bond belongs to whoever is holding it, no questions asked.) No records of ownership were kept; owners detached a coupon every six months and collected an interest payment from their bank. Some people's idea of estate planning was to tell their heirs where the key to the safe deposit vault was kept; the heirs could take the munis from the box at the owner's death before the authorities could seal it off.

That has changed somewhat. All municipal bonds issued since 1982 are registered bonds, and ownership is on record. Some older bearer bonds still are outstanding, but the supply diminishes as they're redeemed.

Some people still like bearer bonds—they like the idea of clipping the coupons and cashing them in. Some financial planners, in fact, have special coupon clippers they give as gifts to their clients.

Now, though, banks ask for Social Security numbers when they redeem coupons. To sell a bearer bond, you must show proof of ownership. In addition, the 1986 tax act requires everyone to report (not pay taxes on) all tax-exempt interest, beginning in 1987. Munis aren't the privacy havens they once were.

Some people say that munis are "the last real tax shelter" after the 1986 tax law. That's like saying the white rhino is "the last real dinosaur." Munis never sheltered income; rather, they provide income which is tax-exempt for most investors.

──────── *Summary* ────────

*Pros:*

- Interest income is exempt from federal income taxes.
- Investors in high-tax states generally can buy in-state bonds and escape state taxes, too.
- After-tax yields for high-bracket investors generally are higher with munis than with Treasuries or corporate bonds.

*Cons:*

- Muni investing has become more complicated. New laws on Social Security and the minimum tax make muni income potentially taxable.
- Information on many issues is hard to come by. It may be difficult to avoid defaults, such as Whoops.
- Individuals who trade munis tend to buy high and sell low because trading is relatively light.
- Because the market is relatively inefficient (as compared with Treasuries), trading prices are volatile. The recent exit of several major Wall Street firms from the muni market may reduce liquidity and increase muni price fluctuations.

- Munis have the typical bond drawbacks—lack of growth potential, vulnerability to inflation, bonds may be called prior to maturity.

*Recommendation:*

Munis fit into the 10 to 50 percent of your portfolio allocated to bonds. Low tax rates make munis relatively unattractive today. If you can net 6 or 6.5 percent on a Treasury, is it really worth the extra risks to earn 8 percent on a muni?

The only investors really suited for munis are those in ultra-high-tax localities, such as New York City, who face tax rates over 40 percent from all income taxes. Such investors should stick with double or triple tax-exempts. Hold munis in your personal account, not in a retirement plan, where the tax-exemption would be redundant. Plan on holding until maturity, rather than trading your bonds.

Of course, some investors are determined not to pay a nickel more than they must to the IRS. If you're in that category, you may get "psychic income" from owning munis rather than taxable bonds, CDs, or money market funds.

# 6

# Mortgage-Backed Cash

The last few chapters on different types of bonds discuss loans made to the best "credits," as borrowers are known. Money lent to the U.S. Treasury or to AT&T is certain to be repaid in full. The more creditworthy the borrower, the lower the interest rate he has to pay. The Treasury and AT&T pay close to the banks' "prime" rate—the interest rate for prime customers—or even lower. The state of Kansas also can borrow below prime because lenders owe no federal income taxes on the interest they receive.

Consequently, investors receive a relatively low yield when they lend money to the best "credits." On the other hand, if they are willing to make loans that are slightly more risky they receive a higher yield.

Such a loan is a home mortgage. Mortgage loan rates are generally a few points higher than prime rates. If you make a mortgage loan, you stand to get a higher yield.

To receive these higher rates investors do not need to go into the mortgage business. Mortgage lenders such as banks and S&Ls are often eager to sell off their loans. They are content to make some money on the sale and to collect servicing fees. They don't want to bear the risks of rising interest rates or defaults.

Various "packagers" buy mortgages from the original lenders and pool them. For example, five $100,000 mortgages and ten $50,000 mortgages are combined into a $1 million pool, and the pool is divided into $25,000 units.

If 40 investors each buy a $25,000 unit, each shares equally in 15 different mortgages. The monthly mortgage interest paid by the 15 homeowners is passed through the original lenders, through the packagers, to the investor who holds the *pass-through certificate.*

The holder of the mortgage-backed security, as the pass-through certificate is called, is the one who ultimately puts up the mortgage loan money. Via various fees and commissions, he is paying the middlemen for doing the paperwork, the credit checks, and for providing a diversified portfolio.

Not many investors, however, are eager to make a loan to 15 unknown homeowners for a couple of extra points of yield. Consequently, various private and public agencies guarantee or insure these loans to various degrees. Although "Fannie Mae" and "Freddie Mac" (as these loans are nicknamed) are familiar in the industry, by far the best-known name to individual investors is Ginnie Mae.

## GINNIE MAES ARE BACKED BY THE FEDERAL GOVERNMENT

Ginnie Mae is the nickname for the Government National Mortgage Association or GNMA. It's a federal agency that backs certain residential mortgages with the "full faith and credit" of the U.S. government. In case of default, investors are protected against loss of interest or principal. Thus Ginnie Maes are nearly as safe as direct Treasury issues. However, they have a slightly higher yield— usually ranging from one-half of a percentage point to two points— than the 10-year Treasuries to which they are usually compared. If 10-year Treasuries pay 9 percent, Ginnie Maes yield from 9.5 to 11 percent.

Why do Ginnie Maes have higher yields than Treasures when there's virtually no credit risk? There are a few important differences between investing in Ginnie Maes and investing in bonds of any kind. Although Ginnie Mae investing has become popular in recent years, Ginnie Maes are perhaps the most misunderstood investment by brokers as well as by investors.

When you buy a bond, you generally receive an interest payment every six months. When the bond matures, you get your principal back.

With a Ginnie Mae, or any other mortgage-backed security, you get a monthly check. That's because mortgage payments are due monthly. Monthly interest payments give you a higher compound yield compared with a bond that pays semi-annually because the money is received sooner. Each monthly check, though, is not pure interest—it's a combination of interest and principal. The two-payments-in-one-check feature is what makes Ginnie Maes so confusing.

## INTEREST PAYMENTS DECLINE AS PRINCIPAL IS PAID OFF

Let's say a homeowner owes $550 a month on his mortgage. At the beginning of the payment stream, 95 percent of the monthly payment is interest and 5 percent is a return of principal. After the various persons involved are paid, perhaps $500 is received by the investors holding the pass-through certificates. The $500 may consist of $475 in interest and $25 payback of principal. The investor with a 1/40 interest in the pool receives $11.875 in interest and $0.625 as a return of principal from the homeowner for the particular month.

As the months go on, the homeowner keeps paying $550. Each month, the share of interest goes down and the share of principal goes up. Of the $500 paid to investors, the interest portion gradually recedes to $450, $400, $300, and so on, and the return of principal increases to $50, $100, $200, and so on.

The problems are apparent. Investors have to recognize the difference between principal and interest in every monthly check. They need the discipline to reinvest at least the principal portion. If not, they gradually end up with no principal. With a mortgage-backed security, there's no return of principal when the loan comes due as there is with a bond.

Compounding the problem is the uncertainty of prepayments. When a house is sold, for example, mortgage loans commonly are paid off early, and the prepayment is passed through to the Ginnie Mae holder. Five or 10 percent of the investment may be returned at one time and will need to be reinvested. Often, it's hard to reinvest smaller sums and earn yields as high as the original Ginnie Maes were paying.

Another problem concerns movements in interest rates. With a bond, if rates go up, the value of the bond comes down. If rates go down, the value of the bond goes up.

A Ginnie Mae, too, loses value when interest rates go up. However, when interest rates go down, investors may not be able to profit because homeowners rush to refinance when interest rates drop. The investor is likely to experience more return of principal, leaving less capital with which to register a gain. Furthermore, he will have to reinvest the returned principal at a lower rate.

## COPING WITH DISCOUNT AND PREMIUM GINNIE MAES

Interest rate movements are especially important to investors who buy Ginnie Maes on the secondary market, rather than newly issued Ginnie Maes. Suppose new Ginnie Maes—the so-called "current coupon" variety—are priced to yield 10 percent. There also will be some Ginnie Maes outstanding with higher and some with lower coupons, reflecting past swings in interest rates.

If you buy a Ginnie Mae with an 8 percent coupon, for example, you will be able to buy the Ginnie Mae at a discount to compensate for the lower yield. When the mortgages are paid off, they will be paid off at full face value. If the mortgages are prepaid for any reason, the investor receives ahead of schedule the "built-in" profit—the difference between the face value and the discounted price. That increases the return on the Ginnie Mae.

On the other hand, an investor who buys a 12 percent-coupon Ginnie Mae must pay a premium to get the higher yield. If the mortgages in this pool are prepaid, the investor loses money every time from buying at a premium and selling at par. The sooner the prepayments, the lower the investment returns.

Consequently, it's virtually impossible to predict the true return on a discount or premium Ginnie Mae, even if held to maturity. Newspaper listings are misleading. Recently, for example, premium-priced Ginnie Maes were listed in published tables as yielding 11 or 12 percent, but true yields probably will be closer to 9 percent.

Some of the problems Ginnie Maes have for investors are addressed by a new type of security, called a *collateralized mortgage obligation* (CMO). In essence, the packager directs prepayments to different "tranches" or groups of investors. All prepayments go to the first tranch, until all the principal is returned, then to the second tranch, and so on.

This creates a series of mortgage-backed securities that are like bonds, with more certainty about the length of time until maturity. If you're in the first tranch, for example, you might expect your CMO to act like a three-year bond, while a third-tranch CMO may be similar to a ten-year bond.

However, most CMOs don't involve federally backed mortgages. Generally they are sold to institutions that can judge specific credit risks. The 1986 tax law created Real Estate Mortgage Investment Corporations, known as *REMICs,* to promote CMO-type investments. For now, though, these investments are not aimed at individual investors, especially those who want the full-faith-and-credit security of Ginnie Maes. If the uncertainty about prepayments bothers you, you're probably better off with a Treasury bond than a CMO.

## STICK WITH CURRENT COUPONS

Except for the most sophisticated investors, or those with the few advisers who really study the Ginnie Mae market, current-coupon Ginnie Maes are the best way to invest in mortgage-backed securities. Buy newly issued Ginnie Maes, paying the going interest rate, and you will avoid the complexities of discount or premium Ginnie Maes.

Ginnie Mae income is fully taxable at the state as well as the federal level, making them best suited for retirement plans. Owners of Ginnie Maes, either in a personal account or in a retirement plan, should be scrupulous about reinvesting the bits and pieces of principal that constantly are being returned. The best strategy is to park the returned principal in a money-market fund and roll it over into another investment (possibly more Ginnie Maes) when enough has been accumulated.

Direct Ginnie Mae investments generally require a $25,000 minimum. You may buy into an older pool for less money, because these pools often have been reduced in size through mortgage prepayments. The $1,000 or $5,000 investor, however, can participate in Ginnie Maes only through mutual funds (Chapter 11) or unit trusts (Chapter 14).

--------------- *Summary* ---------------

*Pros:*

- Federal guarantee protects investors against principal loss.

- Yields are 0.5 to 2 percent higher than medium-term Treasury bonds.

- Interest is received monthly rather than semi-annually.

- A constant return of principal reduces exposure to rising interest rates because the returned principal can be reinvested at higher rates.

- A large, active trading market makes it easy to buy and sell Ginnie Maes.

*Cons:*

- A constant return of principal demands more investor effort to reinvest in order to avoid dissipation of invested capital.

- If premium or discount Ginnie Maes are acquired, uncertainty of principal repayment makes it impossible to predict a true yield.

- There's less upside, compared with a bond, because falling interest rates lead homeowners to refinance resulting in a faster return of principal for Ginnie Mae holders.

- Ginnie Maes are fully taxable.

*Recommendation:*

Although Ginnie Maes are not true bonds, they can be considered as bonds for purposes of portfolio allocation. Thus, they belong in the 10 to 50 percent of your portfolio reserved for bonds. Over time, Ginnie Maes provide higher returns than Treasury bonds, with less volatility and virtually the same lack of default risk. Therefore, investors who are willing to take time to understand Ginnie Maes and reinvest returned principal, should hold Ginnie Maes instead of Treasury issues. Newly issued, current coupon Ginnie Maes are appropriate for most investors, who should hold them in tax-exempt retirement plans.

## CREDIT MARKET COMPARISONS

In the last four chapters, we have discussed different types of bonds: Treasuries, corporates, municipals, and mortgage-backed securities (primarily Ginnie Maes). For purposes of asset allocation, you should combine these four types of securities into one group. Suppose one investor holds 5 percent of his portfolio in Treasuries, 5 percent in junk bonds, 5 percent in munis, and 5 percent in Ginnie Maes. He has 20 percent of his assets in bonds. Similarly, another investor with 15 percent in Ginnie Maes and 5 percent in munis also has 20 percent in bonds.

The guidelines we mentioned in our chapter on Treasuries are worth repeating. Bond investors should stay short—don't buy anything that will mature in more than eight years. (Current-coupon Ginnie Maes are an exception. Although the estimated maturity may exceed eight years, the ongoing principal repayment effectively shortens the maturity.) Plan on holding until maturity. Younger investors, who don't mind being locked in for long-term growth (in stocks and real estate), should not hold more than 25 percent of their assets in bonds. Older investors may want to be a little heavier in bonds, up to perhaps 50 percent for retired investors who need the interest income to live on.

Here is a recap on the different types of bonds:

1. *Treasuries.* These bonds are for investors who want absolute safety from default. Yields are low. They are best suited for investors in high-tax states because they're exempt from state and local income taxes.

2. *Corporates.* These bonds are for investors who are determined to get the highest possible yield. The credit risk must be recognized. They belong in tax-exempt retirement plans (including IRAs), especially for investors in high-tax states.

3. *Municipals.* These bonds are for investors in the top tax brackets. Investors in high-tax states should buy local issues. Credit risks must be recognized. Don't put munis in retirement plans.

4. *Ginnie Maes.* These investments are for investors who are willing to work a little harder. They have practically the same safety as Treasuries and they offer higher yields, but prepayments must be constantly reinvested. They work best in retirement plans.

# 7

# Real Cash: The New Rules for Investing in Real Estate

Ask someone you know about the "best investment" he or she ever made. Chances are, the answer will be real estate. It's hard to argue with the person who paid $50,000 for a house (putting down $10,000) and sold it for $200,000 (collecting $160,000 after paying off the $40,000 mortgage.)

There are people with the same kinds of stories about income-producing real estate (properties owned and rented out to others). George H., for example, began his investing career buying shells of run-down buildings in a poor New York neighborhood. He rehabilitated the buildings and rented the apartments. George never collected rents without a German shepherd in tow, and he frequently heard the ring of gunshots as he made his rounds. He worked seven-day weeks, taking calls from tenants at all hours of the night.

When one of his buildings was on a sound footing, George would sell the building and buy more shells. Before taking his profits as a real estate investor, George owned 15 buildings at one time.

Today George is still involved in real estate. He owns a turn-of-the century mansion, designed by architect Stanford White, that now is an office building and appraised for over $4 million. Today's tenants generally pay their rent without any persuasion from German shepherds.

## COLLECTING RENTS FROM REAL ESTATE

Such success stories lure investors to income-producing real estate, such as a small apartment house or office building, or even a warehouse, factory, or retail block. When the value of the property is great, investors can form partnerships with a small group of friends.

It's easy to see where the cash comes from in this type of investment. As long as the monthly rent collected from tenants exceeds the monthly carrying costs, the excess goes right into the investor's or partnership's pocket.

This type of cash is more like a stock dividend than bond interest. The cash return is not fixed. If rents increase more than expenses, cash income rises, and the value of the rental property is likely to increase.

Owning real estate, though, is much different from owning corporate stock. If you buy stock, you need only to decide whether to sell or to hold on, and perhaps how to reinvest the dividends. If you buy real estate, your efforts have just begun. You now own an operating business, which must be managed if you are to receive an investment return.

The conventional wisdom is that the three most important words in real estate are location, location, location. Buy property in the right place, and you will be able to attract tenants. Your building will inexorably go up in value.

Although location is important, there are other words that have to be in the real estate investor's vocabulary: for example, *existing* and *new construction.* If you buy a property in the construction stage, you can only make rough guesses about future revenues and expenses. If you buy an existing property, however, you can see the operating history. An office building may have tenants in place, with leases that won't run out for several years. A beach house may have a five-year record of renting out every summer, giving you an idea of how much you can expect to collect and how much it costs to keep up the property.

Usually, you are safer buying existing properties. Since new properties are riskier, investigate the properties carefully before buying.

## HOW TO CALCULATE "CAP RATES"

Evaluation of rental properties requires familiarity with other concepts: *net operating income,* or NOI, and *cap rates,* short for capitalization ratios. Net operating income is calculated from adding together a property's total income (all of the revenues from tenants) and subtracting all the costs of actually operating the property (insurance, maintenance, taxes, and management fees). The difference is a property's NOI.

Assume you are looking at an office building with four tenants. One pays $1,000 a month in rents, two pay $2,000 a month, and one pays $3,000. That's a total of $8,000 a month in rents, or $96,000 a year in total revenues. Assume that all tenants have stable businesses, and their leases extend for several years, so chances of vacancies are slight.

By examining the owner's records, you calculate how much he has been paying for operating costs, and project that in the next 12 months he is likely to pay $46,000. Subtract the $46,000 from the $96,000 estimate of total revenues to obtain an estimate of $50,000 in NOI.

Note that the NOI remains constant, whether or not the property has a mortgage. Once you have the NOI, you can calculate the cap rate. A cap rate is simply the cash return to a free-and-clear owner. It's a way of comparing real estate to other investments.

Let's say the owner of the building is asking $500,000. If you buy it for that price, the $50,000 NOI is 10 percent of the purchase price. That's a cap rate of 10, or a "10 cap."

Suppose, after some negotiation, you buy the building for $450,000. The NOI remains the same—$50,000—but now it's 11.1 percent of the purchase price. The cap rate is 11.1. As you can see, the higher the cap rate, the lower the price, and the better the deal for investors.

| Annual rent revenues | $96,000 |
|---|---|
| Subtract: Annual expenses | $46,000 |
| Net Operating income (NOI) | $50,000 |

| Purchase Price | Capitalization Ratio (Cap Rate) |
|---|---|
| $600,000 | 8.3 |
| $500,000 | 10.0 |
| $450,000 | 11.1 |
| $400,000 | 12.5 |

Now look at the investment from another perspective. You have $450,000 you want to invest. You could invest in long-term Treasury bonds and receive a 9 percent yield, absolutely free of default risk and requiring no further effort. Or you could take your money and buy an office building, free and clear of all debt. The cash yield on the office building will be higher—11.1 vs. 9 percent— and you have the potential for making even more money. However, you need to be more actively involved, and you bear the many risks involved in running a business.

## ADDING LEVERAGE TO THE EQUATION

Suppose you can't write a check for $450,000. You might invest $100,000 in cash (about 22 percent) and obtain a mortgage for the $350,000 balance. To keep the example simple, assume that the mortgage is a "12 percent bullet loan." That is, you will pay 12 percent interest each year without having to repay any principal. At the end of the loan period, the entire $350,000 will be due.

At 12 percent, you'll owe $42,000 a year on a $350,000 mortgage. Of the $50,000 in cash from operations, you will use $42,000 to pay off the debt service, leaving you with $8,000 a year in cash income from the property. However, because you only invested $100,000 as a down payment, your "cash-on-cash return," as insiders put it, is 8 percent.

Why did your return drop from 11.1 to 8 percent? You borrowed at 12 percent to buy a property paying 11.1 percent. You have "negative leverage" of nearly 1 percent. Does it make sense to use leverage in this way? Yes, if the property appreciates by more

|  | *All Cash* | *Leverage* |
|---|---|---|
| Purchase price | $450,000 | $450,000 |
| Down payment | $450,000 | $100,000 |
| Mortgage | 0 | $350,000 |
| Interest (@ 12%) | 0 | $ 42,000 |
| Cash from operations | $ 50,000 | $ 50,000 |
| After interest payment | $ 50,000 | $  8,000 |
| Cash-on-cash return |  |  |
| ($50,000/$450,000) | 11.1% |  |
| ($8,000/$100,000) |  | 8% |

than 1 percent. As long as your total return—current cash plus appreciation—is greater than the interest you're paying for borrowed funds, you come out ahead with leverage. When properties are appreciating, leverage can increase your profits.

## INCREASING LEVERAGE INCREASES YOUR RISKS

It is important to understand that the more leverage you use, the greater your risks. You are giving up a bird in the hand—the higher current yield—for two in the bush—possible appreciation. In the meantime, your mortgage interest puts a heavier burden on the property. Suppose one of your $2,000-a-month tenants has a business reversal and disappears overnight. You're out $24,000 in annual revenues, with no appreciable decrease in operating costs.

If you can't re-rent the space, the NOI drops from $50,000 to $26,000, but you still have to cover $42,000 a year in mortgage interest. Either you cover the remaining $16,000 a year out of your own pocket, or the mortgage lender will foreclose on the property. The owner who buys for all-cash has no risk of foreclosure. The all-cash buyer, moreover, can add a mortgage later to get most or all of his cash back. He doesn't have to find a buyer—a "greater fool"—to get him out of a troubled deal.

If you decide to use leverage, you will find yourself having to choose among all the varieties of mortgages available today. In general, you should use fixed-rate financing for investment real estate. That locks in one cost of doing business—the mortgage payments—and removes one uncertainty.

Real estate buyers who use leverage may have to make a decision about "points." Each point is a pre-payment of 1 percent of the loan amount. Two points on a $100,000 loan equals $2,000, paid up-front. The effect is to reduce the actual loan proceeds and increase the interest rate. Some banks will compete on terms: They will offer a lower rate if you will pay points. It's usually worthwhile to pay as long as you get at least a quarter-of-a-point break on the interest rate for each point paid to the bank. Paying two points, for example, might reduce a mortgage from 11 to 10.5 percent. If you own the property long-term, the interest-rate savings will outweigh the initial cost of the points.

## REAL ESTATE STILL OFFERS A FEW
## TAX BREAKS

There's another major difference between owning real estate and buying stocks or bonds: taxes. Investors who take the risks of real estate ownership are entitled to tax benefits.

In real estate the prime tax benefit is depreciation. When you buy a property, an allocation must be made between how much you paid for the building and how much you paid for the land. The land portion is nondepreciable, but on the amount paid for the building, you are entitled to a paper (non-cash) tax deduction for depreciation. Real estate has a strange characteristic—it usually appreciates while the tax rules allow you to say it's depreciating.

Under the 1986 tax law, buildings are depreciated over 31.5 years. Apartments get a break because Congress wants to encourage new housing. Apartments can be written off slightly faster, over a period of 27.5 years. Also, some items in the building can be written off faster because they are considered *personal property* rather than *real property*. These refinements are rather technical, and best left to your accountant. For your purposes, figure a depreciation deduction of 3 percent a year, or 4 percent a year with an apartment house.

In our previous example, depreciation will be about $12,000 a year on a $450,000 office building (assuming $50,000 allocated to the land). With a NOI of $50,000, the all-cash investor has a $38,000 profit, for tax purposes, after deducting the depreciation. If he is in a 30 percent tax bracket, he will owe $11,400 in taxes (30 percent

|  | All Cash | Leverage |
|---|---|---|
| Cash down payment | $450,000 | $100,000 |
| NOI (cash from operations) | $50,000 | $50,000 |
| Subtract: Depreciation | $12,000 | $12,000 |
| Subtract: Interest | 0 | $42,000 |
| Taxable income | $38,000 | ($4,000) |
| Taxes (@ 30%) | $11,400 | 0 |
| After-tax cash flow |  |  |
| (minus taxes) | $38,600 |  |
| (minus interest) |  | $8,000 |
| After-tax cash-on-cash return |  |  |
| ($38,600/$450,000) | 8.6% |  |
| ($8,000/$100,000) |  | 8% |

of $38,000), and will be left with $38,600 after paying his taxes. On a $450,000 cash investment, that's an 8.6 percent after-tax yield.

What happens in the case of the leveraged investor? His loan interest is considered business interest and is deductible. He also gets the full amount of depreciation deductions, even though he has bought the property mainly with borrowed money.

In our example, the $42,000 in interest and $12,000 depreciation deductions are subtracted from the $50,000 NOI. For tax purposes he has a net loss of $4,000 from the property, even though he has received $8,000 in cash. The investor owes no tax at all from his real estate. The $8,000 cash distribution, 8 percent of his $100,000 cash investment, is his to keep. His after-tax yield is the full 8 percent.

By comparison, a Treasury bond investor earning 9 percent gets to keep only 6.3 percent, after-tax, in a 30 percent bracket.

## SETTLING UP LATER, WITH YOUR TAXES

Depreciation deductions sound great—they shelter some or all of real estate income from taxation. However, depreciation allowances provide a way of deferring taxes, not avoiding them.

Suppose the investor holds the property for five years, taking $60,000 worth of depreciation deductions, and sells the property for the same $450,000 he invested. Has the investor broken even on the deal? Not as far as the IRS is concerned. The $60,000 in depreciation deductions have reduced his *basis* in the property to $390,000. Thus, a sale for $450,000 represents a $60,000 taxable gain. In a 30 percent bracket, he would owe $18,000 in taxes, even though he made no money on the deal. He would be repaying the taxes he deferred over his five-year holding period. The same is true for the leveraged or the unleveraged investor.

Under prior law, investors in this situation received a tax break because the sale was treated as a long-term capital gain, and less taxes were due. That break was repealed, however, in the 1986 tax act. Now, a sale of real estate is taxed the same as any other income you earn.

What happens to the $4,000 loss reported by the leveraged investor? For a purely passive real estate investor—an individual in a limited partnership, for example—the loss probably can not be deducted. Instead, it must be "carried forward" to future years, when it can be used to offset taxable income from the property.

However, investors who actively participate in real estate get a special tax benefit. To actively participate, you must own the property outright or in a general (not limited) partnership in which your interest is at least 10 percent. It's all right to hire a management firm, as long as you personally make certain decisions on hiring repairmen, approving tenants, setting rental rates, etc.

If you meet this *active participation* test, you can deduct up to $25,000 a year worth of losses from other income. So our leveraged investor with a $4,000 loss gets to subtract $4,000 from his taxable income. If he's in a 30 percent tax bracket, reducing his income by $4,000 saves him $1,200 in taxes.

Altogether, our leveraged investor gets $8,000 in cash distributions plus $1,200 in tax savings. His total cash yield is $9,200, or 9.2 percent of his $100,000 outlay. His after-tax yield in this example is actually greater than the all-cash investor's, because of the tax benefits.

However—there always seems to be a "however" with the 1986 tax law—the $25,000 loss allowance applies only to investors with adjusted gross income (AGI) of $100,000 or less. If the AGI is over $100,000, the loss allowance for actively managed real estate shrinks by $1 for every $2 of extra AGI. For AGI of $150,000, no losses are deductible. In our example, the investor would have to have an AGI of $142,000 or less, to fully utilize the $4,000 tax loss. However, losses that can't be used immediately may be "banked," and used to offset future taxable income from the venture.

The tax break for investors with $100,000 or less of AGI definitely is the exception. For the most part, the tax act of 1986 took away tax benefits from real estate. Many commentators have said that real estate values will collapse with fewer tax benefits. If that's the case, why invest in real estate?

## SUPPLY AND DEMAND IS NOW ON YOUR SIDE

Generally, real estate prices are lower than they otherwise would have been because of the 1986 tax shock. That's fine for those considering investments now. The effects of tax shock are factored into real estate pricing. If you do it right, you can buy low today, and sometime in the future—don't forget that real estate is a long-term investment—you may be able to sell high.

There's a maxim in economics: If you subsidize something, you get more of it; tax something, you get less of it. For years real estate has been subsidized by the federal tax code. As a result there has been more construction than would have occurred without the tax benefits. More construction has led to more buildings and relatively low rents.

Tax shock has knocked out many real estate subsidies. Looking at it from another perspective, taxes on real estate have gone up. Either way, there will be less real estate than there would have been under the old tax system.

This may or may not be a desirable result, depending upon your political and economic outlook. But it certainly means more demand for existing real estate from tenants. The increased demand will push rents higher than they would have been under the old tax system. Higher rents are likely to mean higher returns for real estate investors.

People have made money in real estate over the years, and they likely will continue to do so. For most investors, real estate belongs in your portfolio. Plan on investing 10 to 30 percent of your portfolio in real estate in addition to your principal residence. If you own income-producing real estate directly, and take an active interest in its management, your dollar commitment likely will be so large that you'll be nearer 30 percent than 10 percent.

Does it make sense to own real estate directly? It can, provided you know what you're doing, and you do it right. However, the special tax break for "actively managed" real estate will spur investing in this area—small apartments, offices, etc. The demand from investors will likely push cash yields down to minimal levels, as those investors depend on tax savings for their returns, while they wait for inflation to push up real estate values.

To succeed in this market, you have to work at it. You have to find the right property in the right location, and you have to make sure you buy at a good price. Afterwards, you have to keep a close eye on operations. Even if you hire a property manager or a rental agent, you have to make sure they are working for you and not just for themselves. The biggest mistake most "do-it-yourself" real estate investors make is to underestimate the effort that's required. If you have the time and inclination to work at real estate investing, go to it. You'll probably do better than most investors in terms of the ultimate return.

There is another important distinction between real estate and other investments. Bank CDs, bonds (except municipal bonds), and Ginnie Maes are all appropriate choices for tax-exempt retirement plans, including IRAs. Stocks may be suitable for some investors. But real estate, especially leveraged real estate, may

produce "unrelated business taxable income." If this happens,
your tax-exempt retirement plan could wind up owing taxes.
Check with your tax adviser before making any real estate investments for a retirement plan.

### ———— *Summary* ————

Pros:

- Cash flow can increase over time if rents go up.
- Increasing cash flow can drive up the value of the underly-
  ing property.
- Leverage may be used to increase total return.
- Cash flow may be fully or partially tax-sheltered.
- The 1986 tax law will reduce real estate construction, in-
  creasing demand for existing properties and causing rents
  to be higher than they otherwise would be.
- Real estate can be an excellent inflation hedge.

*Cons:*

- Real estate requires active management. More effort is required by investors, compared with putting money into
  stocks or bonds.
- Real estate rents can go down as well as up. Factors beyond
  your control—a statewide slump, for example—can produce disappointing results.
- Leverage makes real estate riskier. You may even lose your
  entire investment through foreclosure. (That has happened
  in Houston, for example.)
- Future tax law changes may reduce property values.
- Real estate is not liquid—you can't buy and sell easily, as
  you can with stocks and bonds.

*Recommendation:*

Investors should hold 10 to 30 percent of their portfolio in income-producing real estate. Younger investors, especially those
who don't own their own homes, should have a higher concentra-
tion. Plan on holding real estate for the long-term. In general, real
estate is more suitable for a personal investment rather than in a
tax-exempt retirement plan.

## PUTTING TOGETHER YOUR PORTFOLIO

In the preceding seven chapters, we have covered the basic ingredients of an investment portfolio, especially for the investor who wants steady cash flow. We've set some portfolio guidelines, but they are pretty broad: 10 to 50 percent in bonds, 20 to 40 percent in stocks, 10 to 30 percent in real estate, plus some emergency money in bank accounts or T-bills.

Our guidelines are broad because there is no such thing as the "right" mix. That varies from individual to individual, and each individual's mix will vary over the years. Speaking very generally, younger investors should gravitate more toward stocks and real estate while older investors may want more emphasis on bonds. But even that rule is made to be bent, and possibly broken.

Let's say, though, that we have Mr. or Ms. Average Investor. Neither old nor young, neither conservative nor aggressive. He or she wants a competitive return, long-term, with no special circumstances. All likely economic scenarios should be covered.

This "typical investor" might start with a mix of 30 percent in bonds, 30 percent in stocks, and 20 percent in real estate. Such a mix may generate cash flow of around 6 percent per year, with about 4 to 5 percent to keep after taxes. The investor will be about even with inflation, or nearly so, just from after-tax cash flow. And there would be good prospects for additional growth from stocks and real estate. The real estate probably provides the best inflation protection while bonds stand out in disinflation, and stocks should perform well if the economy has slow, steady growth.

How would Mr. or Ms. Average Investor allocate the other 20 percent? Cash equivalents should be included, and a "miscellaneous" category probably should include natural resources, including gold and oil.

| Hypothetical $100,000 Portfolio | | | | |
|---|---|---|---|---|
| Category | Allocation | Amount | Yield | Cash flow |
| Bonds | 30% | $30,000 | 9% | $2,700 |
| Stocks | 30% | $30,000 | 3% | 900 |
| Real estate | 20% | $20,000 | 6% | 1,200 |
| Cash (bank) | 10% | $10,000 | 6% | 600 |
| Natural resources (Oil/gold) | 10% | $10,000 | 6% | 600 |
| Total | | | | $6,000 |

Later on in this book, we'll show you some investments that can shade a basic portfolio. Take, for instance, a participating mortgage income fund, which we'll explain in Chapter 15. Such investments are part bond, part real estate. So an aggressive investor, mainly concerned with inflation, may substitute such a mortgage venture for some of the bonds. A conservative investor, on the other hand, who values current cash flow most of all, may prefer to invest in participating mortgages rather than in a straight real estate deal.

Don't get hung up on percentages. There's not a great deal of difference between having 18 or 22 percent of your portfolio in bonds. The most important thing is to know how each type of investment works, how it likely will perform in different economic environments, and to feel comfortable that the overall portfolio makes sense for you and your family.

In Appendix D, at the end of this book, we'll show you some real-life examples of how investors have put together diversified portfolios.

# SECTION II

## Managed Cash

Up to now, we have shown how you, as an active investor, can earn cash returns. You can make basic, safe investments in bank accounts or Treasury bills. Or you can try for higher yields with stocks, bonds, or real estate. Cashing-it-yourself requires time and effort on your part to make the most of the available opportunities.

Even a seemingly simple investment choice, such as putting money in the bank, requires thought and planning. First, pick the right bank. All banks do not offer the same deals. Second, decide which type of bank account suits you best. If you choose a time deposit (a CD), you have to choose the right maturity. If you think rates are going up, stay short-term. If you think rates will fall, go longer term. Every time a CD matures, you will need to make these decisions all over again.

Choosing the right bank account is simple compared with stock market investing. Even if you limit yourself to high-yield stocks, there are hundreds of issues to choose among. How can you tell which companies have cash flow strong enough that their dividends will be maintained and even increased? Which companies may have to cut their dividends because of troubled times? Utilities, for example, may run into unexpected construction costs.

You can do it, if you're willing to work at it. All the research information you need is available from companies, securities firms, and paid publications. There are courses on personal finance that you can take. If you have the time to read the materials and the aptitude to evaluate them, you can make intelligent decisions.

Investing in real estate can be more difficult. There's little information readily available compared with the stock market. You often have to generate your own information and negotiate purchase prices. And you need to run your property after you buy it.

Some investors love to take an active role in their investments. They subscribe to and devour stock market newsletters; they buy options on properties and haggle over purchase price. Often they reap high investment returns.

Other investors aren't so enthusiastic. They would rather work or play or watch TV. Yet they don't want to accept low bank yields on their entire portfolio, and they don't want to squander their money through careless investments.

## HIRING A MONEY MANAGER

One obvious solution, if you are a more passive investor, is to hire somebody to manage your investments, just as you hire an accountant to prepare your tax returns. If you have $250,000 or more to invest, you can hire a bona fide "money manager."

Your money manager likely will be a "gunslinger" with a reputation for piling up huge stock market returns. This person makes a full-time job out of studying investments. They not only read the relevant reports, but they have a sophisticated computer system to help them compare one stock with another.

Remember the saying, "God gave us the nuts, but He did not crack them." Money managers must seek out opportunities that other people fail to recognize. To do so, they meet with corporate executives to get the inside story on how companies are doing. An executive who intentionally lies about projected earnings will be discovered before too long. Once burned by a misleading forecast, a money manager will place the offending company into portfolio exile.

If you can afford a money manager, he or she will sit down with you to determine your goals and risk tolerance. This manager will custom-design (or tell you that he/she is custom-designing) a program just for you. A money manager will try to "time" the market, moving into stocks when bullish, into cash equivalents when bearish.

A money manager wants to perform because their record is very visible, and there are lots of other hot-shot gunslingers you can turn to if you're displeased. You will probably be charged 1 to 2 percent of the total assets in your portfolio each year for these efforts. As long as your money manager is successful, you will gladly pay for the superior performance as well as the peace of mind. After all, management is getting other people to do all the work.

## MUTUAL FUNDS OFFER MONEY MANAGEMENT FOR THE MASSES

But what about the investor who doesn't have $250,000 in a securities portfolio? Does he have to go it alone?

No. Millions of individuals get money management through mutual funds. These funds sell shares, just as corporations sell shares of common stocks. The money raised by selling shares is invested by professional money managers working full-time for the fund.

Consequently, an individual can hire professional money managers by going through a mutual fund, often for as little as a few hundred dollars. In addition, he can acquire a diverse portfolio. Suppose 1,000 investors each contribute $1,000. The fund can buy $1 million worth of stocks. It can buy many issues, far more than each individual would likely buy if he or she directly invested $1,000 in the stock market.

In the next four chapters, we will discuss specific types of mutual funds. In general, they relate to the categories covered under direct investments. Instead of buying stocks or bonds on your own, you hire someone to make those decisions.

## LOAD FUNDS VS. NO-LOADS

When you hire someone, you pay him. Whenever you invest in any type of mutual fund, part of your investment goes toward compensating the people who manage and administer the fund.

One important distinction is between *load* and *no-load* funds. A *load,* in this case, means a sales charge. If you buy a mutual fund through a broker, or any financial adviser who accepts commissions, you will probably pay a load. That's how the broker or financial planner makes his living. There's nothing wrong with paying commissions, as long as you get a fair return for your money. (For more on choosing money manager, brokers, and financial planners, see Appendix C.)

Historically, the standard load has been 8.5 percent. Suppose you invest $10,000 in a mutual fund with an 8.5 percent load. The salesman collects $850. This leaves $9,150 to work for you.

Suppose a bond is priced to pay 10 percent, and an individual pays the same commission rate as a mutual fund. If he invests $10,000 in the bonds, he will receive $1,000 a year. However, if he places the $10,000 into a full-load bond fund, which then buys the same bonds, he will receive only $915 a year because the fund has only $9,150 to invest after paying the sales load.

In practice, the spread may be slightly smaller, because the fund uses its market clout to negotiate a lower trading commission to buy the same bonds. But the fund also charges various fees that investors won't incur by doing it themselves.

In response to investor unhappiness over having their investment return diluted, no-load funds have become popular. In these funds investors buy shares directly rather than through a broker. Eliminate the broker, eliminate his commission. The fund can put more of an investor's dollars to work for him.

In response to this competition, load funds have been restructuring their charges. Some funds now are *low-load*, charging only 2 or 4 percent sales commission. Others have *back-end* charges, levied against investors when they sell their shares rather than when they buy. In some funds, the back-end charge diminishes and eventually disappears after a few years; the object is to keep investors in the funds rather than skipping in and out. Even some no-loads these days have sales charges—the so-called "12b-1" plans to cover distribution costs. In some cases, a load fund with a low management fee charges less than a no-load fund with high management fees.

It sounds confusing, and it is. Some critics say funds now have "snow loads," to mislead investors. In 1988, mutual funds—at the insistence of the SEC—began including "fee tables" in all prospectuses, to illustrate the impact of all the charges.

When you think of loads and no-loads, remember the story of the sales rep who was caught in the rain and bought a trenchcoat. He put it on his expense account, but his boss wouldn't pay. Next month, when he handed in his expense account, the sales rep told the boss, "The trenchcoat is in there—try to find it."

The bottom line: If you want someone to work for you, you will have to pay him. If you have a reliable broker, and he selects a mutual fund for you, you will have to pay him a commission in some fashion. If you want to make your own selection, you can cut out the broker, buy a no-load, and save the commission. Publications such as *Barron's, Forbes, Financial World,* and *Money* regularly report mutual fund performance, and there are specialized newsletters and directories. You will have to decide whether the lower cost (and the increased cash flow) is worth the increased effort on your part.

## PRICING MUTUAL FUND SHARES

Most mutual funds discussed here are *open-ended.* They keep issuing new shares, as long as you send in the money. Suppose a fund begins life with $1 million in assets, and arbitrarily places a par value of $10 on each of its shares. It will issue 100,000 shares. An investor sends in $1,000, and the fund issues the newcomer 100 shares. At this point, the fund has $1,001,000 in assets and 100,100 shares. The net asset value (NAV) per share is still $10.

If there is a market reversal, and the fund's holdings drop by 10 percent, the fund's assets are $900,900, and each share is valued at $9. If another investor sends in $1,000, he will get 111.1 shares (most funds issue fractional shares). On the other hand, if the fund's assets increased 10 percent, and the price per share has risen to $11, a newcomer sending in $1,000 will receive only 90.9 shares.

The price per share fluctuates, leaving you open to capital gains or losses. Money market mutual funds use a different structure, with the price fixed at $1 per share while the yield fluctuates.

## PASSING CASH THROUGH TO YOU

How do you get cash from an open-end fund? As far as the IRS is concerned, a mutual fund acts as a conduit, or a pipeline, and the fund itself is not taxed as long as certain technical requirements are met. In essence, a fund buys securities, collects the dividends or interest, and passes them through to the fund's shareholders on a proportional basis.

If you own 1 percent of a bond fund, you're entitled to 1 percent of the interest payments. Various expenses and incentive fees come out before the money is passed on to you. That's the price you pay to the mutual fund management. In most funds, total expenses are around 1 percent of total assets. If a fund generates 10 percent in interest or dividends, it will pass about 9 percent through to investors. (Even in a bond fund, where all the income is from interest, payouts to shareholders are technically dividends.)

Funds also may distribute capital gains if they sell securities at a profit. They are passed through in the same way as interest or dividends.

If you don't need the cash right away, you can choose a distribution reinvestment plan from most funds. Instead of paying you dividends or interest, the fund uses the money to automatically purchase new shares on your behalf at the going rate. (And, in some funds, at the going commission rate on reinvested dividends.)

For example, you have 100 shares of a fund, valued at $10 per share. The fund pays quarterly dividends. It declares the equivalent of a 10 percent annual dividend for the current quarter. A 10 percent annual dividend is $1 a share, and the quarterly payout is about 25 cents. With 100 shares, you are entitled to a check for $25.

That's fine if you want pocket money, but not so handy if you want to reinvest. To make things easier, you can choose the automatic reinvestment plan, which will credit you with an extra 2.5 shares, instead of sending you a $25 check. Now you have 102.5 shares. If the situation is the same the next quarter, you will be entitled to a dividend of $25.625, and another 2.5625 shares would be added to your account, bringing the total to 105.0625 shares. And so on.

| | |
|---|---|
| Price per share | $ 10.00 |
| Shares purchased | 100 |
| Dividend rate | 10% |
| Annual dividend/share | $ 1.00 |
| Quarterly dividend/share | 25 cents |
| Total quarterly dividend | $ 25.00 |
| Dividend reinvestment | 2.5 shares |
| New total shares | 102.5 |
| New annual dividend | $102.50 |
| New quarterly dividend | $ 25.625 |
| Dividend reinvestment | 2.5625 shares |
| New total shares | 105.0625 |

## TAXING PROBLEMS

Over the years, this can be a convenient way to build up your assets, as long as you don't need the income. However, the IRS treats each distribution reinvestment as if you had received a check and purchased additional shares, and you will incur tax liability on the full amount of distributions received.

When you want to cash out of an open-end fund, partially or in full, you sell your shares back to the fund at the current per-share price, and you will owe taxes on any gain. The rules of mutual fund taxation are confusing—the best advice is to keep good records of every share you buy, by direct purchase or distribution reinvestment, and every share you sell. With good records, your accountant will be able to make the computations.

There's a tax trick to mutual fund investing. Ask your broker, or the fund itself, when distributions usually are made. Invest after that date, not before. Try by all means to invest after a fund's annual capital-gain distribution, which usually occurs at year-end or the beginning of the next year. If you invest at the wrong time, you will acquire an entirely unnecessary tax bill.

Here's an example: Suppose a mutual fund has a strong first half, resulting in an increase in share price from $20 to $30. You buy in September, and the price retreats to $26 by December. So far, so bad. You have lost $4 per share.

At year-end, the fund distributes $6 per share from the earlier successful trades. To reflect this, the price goes down $6. Your shares are worth only $20 apiece, and you have to reinvest the $6 distribution. Worse, you owe taxes on the $6 payout, even though you didn't enjoy any of the gain. The result: you have a loss on the value of your shares, and a taxable capital gain—insult added to injury. So check on any fund's distribution situation before investing.

## BUYING DISCOUNT STOCKS AND BONDS
## THROUGH CLOSED-END FUNDS

A few funds are closed-end funds. Such a fund might raise $1 million when it's formed, and issue 100,000 shares. No additional shares will be sold, and no shares will be redeemed. The 100,000 shares will trade, just like shares of common stock. If you want to buy, you buy from a current stockholder rather than from the fund. If you want to sell, you sell to another investor rather than to the fund. Share prices fluctuate according to the demand from buyers and sellers.

Closed-end funds may offer high cash flow. Often, they sell at a discount from NAV. That is, a fund may have enough assets to justify a $10 price per share, but shares may sell for only $8. Investors are able to buy $10 worth of stocks or bonds for $8, and increase their current yield.

Investing in closed-ends is not for the novice. A few analysts follow closed-ends, and they know why they trade at a discount. These experts may help you select among closed-end funds.

## ALL IN THE FAMILY

Some companies (i.e., Fidelity, T. Rowe Price, Vanguard) offer "families" of mutual funds, mainly open-ended. These families have many types of stock, bond, and money market funds. Usually, you can switch from one fund to another with just a phone call as long as you're staying in the family. Charges are minimal (i.e., $5), if any. So you can do your own "market timing," quickly and inexpensively. However, every switch may cause you to owe taxes.

Besides investing in mutual funds, there are other ways for investors to get professional investment management. Insurance companies have various vehicles. There are different types of trusts, in which a trustee is responsible for your money. Later, we will take a look at unit investment trusts and real estate investment trusts, two popular forms of trusts.

No matter which version you pick, the principle of managed money is the same. You're hiring someone else to invest your money for you. The manager will make loans (buy bonds or T-bills or mortgage securities) or purchase assets (shares of companies or interests in real estate). The manager will do the same things that you could on your own, but you pay because you think a manager can do it better.

Investing through a professional manager doesn't mean abdicating all responsibility for your personal finances. You should "plant your seeds and tend your garden." That is, learn all you can about the basics of investing. Evaluate your money managers as you would evaluate any professional that you hire. If you are not satisfied with that performance, switch your assets to another manager. Nobody will pay attention to your investments if you don't do so yourself.

——————— *Summary* ———————

*Pros:*

- Managers can devote more time to learning about possible investment choices.
- Managers may have special expertise, access to information, and clout in seeking reduced sales commissions.
- More diversification is possible when your funds are pooled with those of other investors.

*Cons:*

- Sales charges reduce your return right from the beginning.
- Annual management and administrative fees will lower your returns.
- You lose control when someone else manages your buy/sell investment decisions.

*Recommendation:*

Most investors should invest through mutual funds and trusts if only for the added diversification. Although there is no such thing as a no-load managed investment, some programs have lower costs than others.

Again, there's a trade-off between money and effort. If you are willing to do some research, it's possible to pick out the low-cost funds and choose the ones that best suit your needs. Otherwise, you may be better off paying a broker or planner to help you make selections.

But no investor should let a broker or planner make unquestioned decisions. If you put all of your eggs in one basket (one money manager), keep you eye on the basket. You need to monitor all of your financial advisers, and take your business away from those who don't perform well for you.

# 8

# Cashing In on the Money Market

You can have the VCR, the speakerphone, the mini-floppy disk. For our money, nothing has changed the face of the United States in the past 10 years as much as the money market mutual fund, known not by nickname or acronym but as the "money market fund."

Money market funds are essential to cash-flow investing. The advantage for investors is a fairly predictable stream of cash flow, every month or quarter or six months. You reduce your dependence on long-term appreciation, such as growth stocks offer, where your profits may never materialize.

Cash-flow investing enables you to build wealth through reinvesting distributions, especially with today's low tax rates. Compound interest is working for you, with constant reinvestment. But it's not easy to find a good home for a series of relatively small checks. The answer is to sweep your distributions into a money market fund, let them commingle and multiply, and then reinvest them in a higher-yielding vehicle.

## THE GROWTH OF MONEY MARKET FUNDS

Until the 1970s, there were no money market funds. Throughout that decade, inflation varied from uncomfortably high to scary. As inflation went from peak to peak, so did interest rates.

Investors, though, had to lock up their money if they wanted to realize higher yields. They had to buy a CD or some type of bond.

If they wanted day-to-day access to their funds, they had to settle for passbook accounts, where interest rates were kept artificially low by federal law. If they wanted the convenience of checkwriting, they generally received no return at all, and may even have had to pay for the privilege.

Enter the money market fund. As its full name—money market mutual fund—suggests, it is a variety of mutual fund. Some of the pioneers were mutual fund companies. They raised money from investors and promised them the previously unattainable benefit of high yields plus complete access to one's own money.

## HOW MONEY MARKET FUNDS WORK

Money market funds use investors' money to make short-term loans. Although it varies from fund to fund, average loan maturities usually are in the 30- to 45-day range.

Many of those loans are made to borrowers who also borrow from banks. Money market funds loan money by buying T-bills and short-term federal agency issues. They buy commercial paper (unsecured corporate loans) and banker's acceptances (loans secured by merchandise). They even buy CDs from foreign and domestic banks.

As with any mutual fund, all of these loans are pooled, and the interest, after taking out fees, is passed through to investors. In the late 1970s and early 1980s, when banks offered 5.5 percent (passbook) or 0 percent (checkbook), money market funds, unaffected by bank regulations, offered yields as high as 15 percent along with checkwriting privileges. Money market fund deposits, less than $4 billion in 1977, soared to $45 billion in 1979 and to over $180 billion in 1981. Today over $300 billion is invested in money funds.

## COMPETITION FROM BANKS

The banks struck back. In 1982, they received federal permission to offer money market deposit accounts, virtually the same as money market funds. There are some minor differences among the various bank accounts and funds: Some require smaller initial deposits or minimum balances; some have wider checkwriting privileges.

Essentially, though, money market funds and deposit accounts are the same. They make safe, short-term loans, so your principal is not at risk. They credit you with interest on each business day. You can place money in or out, whenever you wish, penalty-free.

Although individual accounts or funds vary, average yields are about equal. Your money market fund or deposit account probably will pay about the same as T-bills purchased directly, reflecting the fact that you're making short-term, low-risk loans. Money market funds invest heavily in commercial paper, which may yield a point or so higher than T-bills, but the fees paid to the fund's management generally are about 1 percent, negating the difference. Most money market funds are no-load. However, the fund's expense ratio is important. Some funds charge well over 1 percent per year, reducing their yield. In 1987, for example, low-expense funds paid around 6.5 percent while high-expense funds paid little more than 5 percent.

## PAID PARKING

Banks have a major advantage over money market funds. A money market deposit account is like any other bank account—federally insured for up to $100,000. There is no risk of losing money as long as you keep your accounts within limits.

Why invest in a money market fund when you can be in a fail-safe money market deposit account? Because money market funds have assumed a unique role: the investor's parking lot.

Most mutual fund families now include a money market fund. Suppose you want to take profits from one of your funds, or you think the market has reached a peak. After you sell, it's convenient to shift the proceeds into the related money market fund. You can keep it there earning money in a form easily accessible until you're ready to go back into a stock or a bond fund.

You don't have to invest through a mutual fund family to use money market funds. Many investors own securities that pay a relatively small amount in interest or dividends. In the case of Ginnie Maes or equipment leasing income funds, the cash flow includes principal that should be reinvested. That's simple if a fund or a corporation has a dividend reinvestment plan. However, many types of investments don't offer automatic reinvestment. In such cases reinvestment of the principal is more cumbersome, especially when it comprises checks for $25 or $250.

Therefore, most securities firms and financial planners urge investors to establish companion money market funds. Brokers often have money market funds with no required minimum balance. In these funds investment cash flow can automatically "sweep" into the money market funds where the funds earn interest, although at a relatively low rate. When enough money is accumulated in the fund, you can easily write a check to make another investment.

Some major brokerage firms, and their registered representatives, fought the advent of money market funds. No commissions are involved, so why bother? Then they found out that controlling an investor's money market fund is like having captive money. They know how much their clients have to invest when they recommend other types of securities.

## HOW SAFE ARE MONEY MARKET FUNDS?

Money market funds have an excellent safety history. Some funds stretch out their maturities to gain an extra point or so in yield. Even these longer-term funds, holding paper for as long as a year, have not run into defaults.

If you're truly concerned about safety, some money market funds invest exclusively in T-bills and other U.S. government paper. These funds stretch maturities out to about one year to generate competitive yields. Some government-only money funds are structured to pass through the exemption from state and local income taxes.

Longer maturities also are a characteristic of tax-exempt money market funds. These funds loan money to local governments and related agencies; they have average maturities of about one year. Interest on these obligations is exempt from federal income taxes, just like the interest on municipal bonds. There are even specialized tax-exempt money market funds which loan money solely to one particular state or city in order to provide fund investors exemption from all taxes on the fund's income.

Tax-exempt money market funds have lower yields than taxable ones. Recently, when taxable funds were paying 6 percent, tax-exempts were paying around 4 percent. After-tax, though, the high-bracket investor may be better off in a tax-exempt fund.

Taxable or tax-exempt, the advantages are clear. With scant risk, you can have your money earning interest all the time.

If interest rates rise—disaster for most lenders—money market funds will receive a return of principal, when the loans are due, and will be able to reinvest at the higher rates. You're set to cash in on rising interest rates. All the while, you have total liquidity; you can get at your money when you need it.

Most investors should have some type of money market fund, whether the balance is $500 or $5,000. They're unmatched for flexibility. You don't want to keep all of your money in these funds, but you should keep some there.

## Summary

*Pros:*

- Money market funds provide protection against loss of principal.
- They provide liquidity or ready access to your money.
- They provide protection against inflation. If interest rates go up, so will your yields.
- They provide convenience. Distributions from other cash-generating investments can be swept into money market funds until they can be reinvested on better terms.

*Cons:*

- Money market funds have low yields. Except in times of rampant inflation, money market yields lag most alternative investments.
- They are fully taxable except for the low-yield tax-exempt funds.
- They are not backed by government guarantees.

*Recommendation:*

Every investor should have a money market fund. That's especially true for individuals who invest in cash-generating vehicles. Arrangements can be made that automatically sweep all distributions into a money market fund to assure immediate reinvestment.

Money market funds are considered cash equivalents, along with bank accounts and T-bills. Thus, they can be used to keep the recommended three to six months' of cash reserves, as mentioned earlier, in addition to distributions from other investments.

# 9

# Bond Funds: Beware the Yield Curve

While the stock and bond markets boomed, during the period 1982–87, growth in mutual funds was incredible. From 1981 to 1987, net investment in mutual funds, excluding money market funds, rose from $2 billion a year to over $100 billion a year. During that time, the number of funds increased from 800 to over 1,800.

Surprisingly, most of the growth was in bond funds rather than high-flying stock funds. Even before the October 1987 market crash, about 75 percent of all new mutual fund money went into bond funds.

Why the popularity? In a word, cash. Many investors became accustomed to double-digit yields from money market funds and CDs in the early 1980s. When those yields plunged, investors looked elsewhere. "If I can't get 10 percent, can I at least get 8 percent?"

Bond funds seemed to be the answer. They offer the convenience, diversification, and professional management of all mutual funds—plus the high current yields. Moreover, many bond funds offer dividend reinvestment plans that allow you to reinvest bond fund distributions at 8 or 9 percent, rather than "sweeping" them into a money market fund paying 5 or 6 percent.

You should reinvest your bond fund dividends—provided you don't need the cash for living expenses and payment of tax obligations. Franklin Income Fund, for example, says that an investor who put in $10,000, in 1972, would have held shares worth $9,814, at the end of 1987, without reinvesting dividends. But that same investor, reinvesting all dividends, would have held shares worth $57,548!

## MORE RISKS THAN MONEY MARKET FUNDS

Unfortunately, many investors don't fully appreciate the risks in bond funds. Portfolio managers, after all, are not wizards. There's a reason why some bond funds can yield 12 to 13 percent while money market funds are yielding 5 to 6 percent.

Bond funds can act in two ways to increase yields. They can extend maturities, reduce credit standards, or both. Bond funds with exceptionally high yields specialize in lending money to low-rated corporations, usually for 10 years or more.

Bond markets follow the yield curve illustrated in Chapter 3. The longer the time until the bond is due, the higher the yield. Typically, this relationship holds true up to about 10 years, after which the yield curve levels off.

Why do longer-term bonds have higher yields? The high yield is a premium to bond investors for waiting for repayment. The longer the wait, the more than can go wrong. And there is more of a chance for interest rates to rise, devaluing outstanding bonds.

## CHOOSING THE RIGHT BOND FUND

Bond fund investors can pick their spot on the yield curve. There are short-term, intermediate, and long-term bond funds. The longer the maturity, the higher the current cash flow. But there's also a greater chance for losing a portion of the principal if interest rates go back up.

For example, the first nine months of 1987 were dismal for bonds and bond funds. Yields on long-term Treasuries rose from 8 to 10 percent, other rates moved in sync, and bond prices tumbled along with prices of bond fund shares. Investors were shocked to see losses on their monthly brokerage firm statements. Even after a fourth-quarter rise, bond fund prices were down for the year. The average bond fund returned only 1 percent in 1987—cash flow from interest payments just compensated for principal losses. (Stock funds actually had a higher return in 1987—2 percent—despite the October crash.)

In this generally weak market, the Federated Short and Intermediate Government Fund, which holds short maturities, posted a gain of over 5 percent, while Benham Target 2010, which holds only bonds maturing that year, lost over 15 percent. But in 1986, a bull market for bonds, the opposite occurred: Benham Target 2010 was up over 50 percent, while Federated Short-Intermediate had a below-average 9 percent gain.

## BOND FUNDS VS. DIRECT BOND PURCHASES

Yield-oriented investors may remove some interest-rate risks by buying bonds through a fund. A $1,000, 8 percent bond yields $80 a year in interest. If interest rates go up to 10 percent, the bond declines in value to $800, yielding 10 percent, based on current market value. The 10 percent yield is scant consolation to the investor who is receiving only 8 percent on his original investment and has a 20 percent capital loss to boot.

Suppose you had invested the $1,000 in a bond fund. You might start out receiving only 7 percent because of fees. When interest rates rise you may hold on to your fund shares, but other investors won't. Some will sell their shares, and some will make new purchase. The fund is constantly buying and selling bonds. In times of rising interest rates, it will be acquiring bonds paying 8, 9, 10 percent, and so on. If you hold on, your current cash flow will rise. You still will be vulnerable to capital losses, but at least your current yield can move up with rising rates.

If you think there's no free lunch, you're right. If you buy a bond directly, and hold on until maturity, you will eventually get a full return of principal, assuming no default. With an open-ended bond mutual fund, there's no maturity because bonds are constantly bought and sold. The only way to get a return of principal in times of rising interest rates is to hold on and hope that rates will, ultimately, return to the level when you bought the bond fund.

## FROM TREASURIES TO JUNK

Yields also are affected by the credit quality of the borrowers. Some funds invest only in Treasury bonds, or obligations of federal agencies. As you might expect, these funds have low yields because there is no risk of default.

At the other end of the spectrum, *junk bond* funds invest in low-grade corporate bonds. Yields are higher, but there are definitely risks of defaults. Some of this risk is reduced by diversification, but what if several junk bond issues fail? Indeed, junk bond funds are subject to the vagaries of the stock market, because a falling stock market may lead to a weak economy and defaults by junk bond issuers. These funds were hard hit by the stock market crash, while other bond funds rallied.

## BATTLE OF THE BUY-WRITES

Another way for a bond fund to increase distributions is to sell options on its holdings. This is similar to the covered-call writing strategy for stocks discussed in Chapter 2.

A number of so-called *enhanced* bond funds have been created in recent years, enhancing their cash flow by selling options, usually on government bonds. Insiders call these funds *buy-writes*, because they buy the bonds and write (sell) call options against them.

In the mid-1980s, buy-writes became the hottest of the hot, raising billions of dollars. The funds advertised distributions of, say, 12 percent (surrounded by asterisks and footnotes) when the Treasury bonds they were holding in their portfolio were paying, say, 9 percent. No wonder investors flocked to these funds. In mid-1988, though, the rules on mutual fund advertising were changed. Option premiums can't be promoted as "yield." Therefore, buy-writes aren't as big a factor as they were in bond funds. Buy-write funds virtually are forced to hold long-term bonds because those bonds command the highest option premiums. Other bond funds, on the other hand, can cut maturities as interest rates go up in order to cut losses.

Thus, buy-write funds are the closest thing available to pure long-term government bond funds. The option-writing makes them less volatile than long-term Treasuries if the Treasury bonds are held directly, but buy-write funds are more volatile than other government bond funds. In recent years buy-writes have done well in good markets, compared with other bond funds, but not as well during bear markets.

Over a long period buy-writes can be expected to generate higher total returns, but they will also show more price volatility compared with other government bond funds. That's because long-term issues go up and down the most with interest-rate swings.

## GOING GLOBAL

Another variety of fund growing in popularity is the international bond fund, which buys bonds issued overseas, mainly by foreign governments. An increasing number of such funds are offered to U.S. investors.

In some respects, international bond funds are similar to domestic funds. You can buy funds that specialize in top-quality issues (such as Japanese bonds) but pay low yields. Or, you can choose a fund that holds high-yielding bonds issued in countries such as New Zealand or Denmark, which don't have the same perceived safety. Some analysts say that international bond funds are better than U.S. funds because overseas economies, particularly in Europe, are likely to have slow growth and low inflation. And European central banks are more likely to intervene to hold down interest rates.

International bond funds also have a wild card: the currency play. If the dollar falls, bonds denominated in foreign currencies go up. In 1987, for example, while domestic bond funds just about broke even, some international bond funds were up as much as 20 percent. The difference was the fall in the value of the dollar. Of course, if the dollar moves up, those international bond funds will lose value. In the worst of all possible worlds, rising interest rates will be combined with a stronger dollar, giving investors a double whammy. For U.S. investors, international bond funds have higher risks as well as the chance for higher returns.

Another recent development is the *global* bond fund, which holds 25 to 50 percent U.S. bonds and the rest from various other countries. Such funds hedge against currency risk through diversification, and yields may be a point or two higher than Treasury bond funds because high-rate currencies are included.

Going one step further, closed-end global funds are emerging as a popular category. Closed-end funds trade like stocks, without redeeming existing shares or selling new ones. Because no cash needs to be held for redemptions, more money can be invested in bonds compared with open-end bond funds.

## LOOKING BEHIND PERFORMANCE CLAIMS

Finally, there are municipal bond funds. They come in the same varieties as taxable bond funds: short- or long-term, good credits and junk. Interest from these funds is exempt from federal income taxes, and certain funds offer exemption from state and local taxes as well.

No matter what type of bond fund you are investigating, you should ask about past performance. The Securities and Exchange Commission (SEC) instituted new rules in mid-1988, to standardize claims. Under these rules all funds must quote yields based on the most recent 30-day period. At the same time, yield claims must be accompanied by figures for average annual compound total return for the latest one-year, five-year, and 10-year period. *Total return* includes principal gain or loss as well as distributions. It doesn't help investors to get a 12 percent current yield, if a fund is losing 20 percent of its principal because of rising interest rates.

Another new wrinkle is the *all-purpose* bond fund, a mix of Treasuries, junk, and international bonds. The pitch of these funds is that you get high yields plus diversification. Actually, what you are buying is a bet that portfolio managers will be skillful in three very different markets. If you really want bond diversification, look for three proven performers, one in each category.

## PORING OVER THE PROSPECTUS

Be sure to read the fund prospectus before you buy. That's true for any investment, but especially bond funds. The prospectus tells you whether a fund is going short or long, what kinds of bonds it's buying, and whether or not it will sell options. A list of current holdings will be included. You'll know what you're buying.

Besides the present—the portfolio—look at the past. The prospectus will show how the fund has performed. Ideally, look for a fund that has been in existence for several years, to cover down and up markets. Look for consistency, in dividend distributions as well as in total annual returns. Also look at the latest 12-month performance to see how a fund has performed in today's investment climate. Some funds have changed portfolio managers, and the new ones may not be able to match the prior performance records.

——————— *Summary* ———————

*Pros:*

- Diversification.
- Inflation protection. You're not as exposed in a bond fund as you are holding bonds directly. Managers can shorten maturities, reducing losses, as rates rise. And your cash flow can grow as interest rates go up.
- High yields. Government bond funds yield 2 to 3 percent above money market funds. Junk bond funds have yields that are 3 to 5 percent higher than governments. Municipal bond yields lately have been nearly as high as the yield on governments, tax-exempt.

*Cons:*

- Fluctuations in principal. Be prepared to see your shares go down in price if rates rise.
- No repayment at maturity. If you buy a bond fund when rates are at low levels, you may never get a full return of capital.

*Recommendation:*

For the 10 to 50 percent of your portfolio you should keep in bonds, bond funds work best for most investors. Buy from a mutual fund with a strong record over several years. Wait until rates are relatively high—over 9 percent on long-term Treasuries—before buying.

Don't believe the MBA salesman who tells you, "You make money in bonds through appreciation." You don't. No one, not the smartest Wall Street Ph.D. with the most powerful computer, knows where interest rates are going, year-in and year-out. Over time almost all bond funds wind up earning the coupon rate, with no capital gains or losses.

Government bond funds are fine unless you have a fanatical devotion to tax avoidance (buy muni funds) or need every penny of extra yield (buy high-rated corporate funds). For most investors, a slight addition to after-tax yield is not worth the loss of quality.

Ginnie Mae funds (Chapter 11) offer virtually the same credit quality, along with higher returns and more long-term stability. So Ginnie Mae funds may be a better buy than Treasury bond funds.

Global or international bond funds should be considered for part of your bond holdings, as long as you are comfortable with the quality of the issues to be held.

Short- and intermediate-term bonds work best for most investors, and you should seek funds that emphasize such maturities. Only if you plan to hold for the long term should you invest in long-bond funds, including buy-writes. Subscribe to dividend reinvestment plans where available. Except for municipal funds, bond funds work best if they are held in a tax-exempt retirement plan, including an IRA or Keogh plan. If you put munis into an IRA or Keogh, you'll make them taxable, because you'll owe taxes when you withdraw your money.

# 10

# Stock Funds:
# Mixing Growth with
# Income

Walt S. is a lucky young man. When he was born, his grandmother invested $2,000 in his name, in a mutual fund that buys stocks. As he grew up, his grandmother retained the shares and received the statements. Walt didn't know about the account, so he was never tempted to sell.

On his twenty-second birthday, Grandma turned the shares over to Walt. Except, they weren't worth $2,000: They had grown in value to $44,000. "It was like winning the lottery," says Walt.

## LESS CASH, MORE GROWTH

For growth, most investors should have stock funds, even if they give up some current cash. There's no question that bond funds provide more cash flow than stock funds. According to *Forbes,* bond funds passed through investment income (bond interest) averaging 9.4 percent, in a recent 12-month period. During this same period, stock funds paid only 1.7 percent in investment income (stock dividends).

But there is more to the comparison than current yield. Bond funds have the drawbacks of any investment in bonds. They lose value if interest rates rise. Appreciation potential is limited. Over the long term, the total return from stock funds is higher than the return from bond funds, just as stocks generally beat bonds.

Over a 15-year period, 1972 through 1987, stock funds averaged a total return over 340 percent, assuming dividend reinvestment. In the same period, bond funds were up less than 225 percent. That's a compound returns of about 10.5 percent per year for stock funds, versus 8 percent for bond funds. And those figures include the stock market crash in October 1987.

Investors would be foolish to pass up this kind of potential return, just because current yields are low. On the other hand, there are advantages to cash-oriented investing. Is there a middle ground? Can the investor who wants current cash use stock funds? Definitely. To start, you need to differentiate among available stock funds.

## AIMING FOR GROWTH AND INCOME

Stock mutual funds usually are separated into four categories: aggressive growth, growth, growth and income, and balanced funds. The first two categories—growth and aggressive growth—are not for investors who want cash returns. These funds hope for big scores. Often, they invest in companies that pay little or no dividends. Thus, there are no dividends to pass through to the mutual fund shareholders.

The third category—growth and income—may be the most appropriate for investors who want to play the stock market while receiving current income. Funds in this category also are known as *total return funds* or *equity income funds*.

Don't let all the names scare you off. No matter how the marketers dress up these funds, the premise is basic. These funds buy shares in companies that pay above-average dividends. Typical holdings include utilities, banks, insurance companies, large chemical companies, automakers, and major oil companies. These dividends are collected by the funds and passed through to fund shareholders. During recent times, while the average stock fund was yielding 1.7 percent, many of these growth and income funds were paying 4 or 5 percent, with some as high as 8 percent.

Fund portfolio managers don't focus solely on current yield. They look at the prospects for future dividend increases, and they try to avoid companies where the dividend may be cut. In addition, they look for companies where the common stock has growth potential.

Such funds tend to hold established, well-capitalized companies. Their stocks may not run up as much as the high fliers in bull markets, but they tend to slide less when times are bad. The presence of a respectable dividend helps to maintain the stock price.

As a result, growth and income funds tend to be more stable than pure growth funds. The tortoise even can beat the hare, over the long term. For the 1972–87 period, growth and income funds posted a total return of 350 percent on average. That's better than the average for all stock funds and markedly better than growth funds (310 percent).

Some growth and income funds enhance their income by selling calls: options to buy the stocks they hold. The premiums they receive from selling options increase their current cash distributions. However, since those stocks will be called away if they shoot up in price, these funds are giving up appreciation potential to get the extra immediate return. Giving up potential gains is much more important to a stock fund, where long-term growth can be expected, than it is in a bond fund (see Chapter 9) where there's scant reasonable prospect of long-term gains. If you go into a buy-write stock fund, you may give up a lot of your upside in return for a little extra current cash flow.

## COVERING THE OTHER CATEGORIES

The final major category—balanced funds—consists of funds that own bonds as well as stocks. Yields in these funds fall in the middle: While stock funds averaged 1.7 percent in dividends, and bond funds paid 9.4 percent, balanced funds averaged 4.8 percent in dividends. Long-term total returns tend to be higher than bond funds but lower than stock funds. Funds that specialize in convertible bonds or convertible preferred stocks also split the difference between stock funds and bond funds.

There are a few other categories, although most stock funds fit into the four groups mentioned above. *Sector* funds have become popular. These are stock funds that invest in one specified industry. Fidelity, for example, offers mutual funds in chemicals, computers, energy, health care, and so on, through the alphabet to telecommunications and utilities. Sector funds generally pay little or no dividends—they're for the investors who think they can hop nimbly from one hot category to the next.

International funds are similar. These funds invest in overseas companies. They are oriented to growth far more than to current income. International funds all have an inherent currency play. If the dollar sinks, values of foreign holdings will rise, but the reverse will happen if the dollar rises.

Another class of funds—precious metals—really belongs in the growth and income category. These funds invest in companies that mine gold or silver; such companies often pay high dividends. Some of the highest-yielding funds are in this category. There is also a built-in inflation hedge, because mining company share prices rise along with precious metals prices. Precious metals funds boast extraordinary returns when the price of gold rises, but they are serious laggards when gold prices decline.

Lately, *index* funds have gained prominence. Such funds are structured to follow major stock market indexes, usually the S&P 500. These funds won't give you the best performance, but they won't be the worst. If you buy a fund indexed to the S&P 500, you're buying blue-chip, established stocks. Dividend payout will be around 3 percent, which the fund will usually reinvest. In the 1980s, blue-chip stocks have led the market, and index funds have done well. It remains to be seen how they'll perform in the future, that is, whether blue-chip stocks will continue to appreciate faster than small growth stocks?

How can you tell which funds fall into which categories? In some cases the name says it all. It's not too difficult to figure out where to put the Scudder Growth & Income Fund, for example.

More often, you'll have to read the fund's prospectus. There's generally a statement of purpose, spelling out the fund's objectives. There also should be a listing of what types of stocks the fund holds, and a history of recent cash distributions. The ratio of net investment income to the average net asset value per share, as revealed in the fund's financial statements, indicate the current yield.

## DIGGING INTO APPRECIATION FOR CASH FLOW

What if 3.5 percent from a growth and income fund—or even 5.5 percent— isn't good enough for you? You need a higher current yield to pay your bills. Does that mean you have to go to a bond fund?

Not necessarily. Here's a strategy for earning bond-type yields while retaining stock-type appreciation: You can arrange for fixed distributions from your stock fund.

As of this writing, most Treasury notes and bonds are paying 8 to 9 percent. Straight government bond funds—those that don't enhance their yields with specialized trading strategies—pay a bit less. Suppose you have $100,000 to invest in a mutual fund, and you would like to earn 8 percent current income, or $8,000 per year.

Invest in a growth and income fund, one that has a history of steadily rising distributions from all sources (investment income plus capital gains). Let's say you buy 10,000 shares at $10 apiece.

During the first year, total distributions from the fund equal 40 cents a share, or 4 percent on your $10 purchase price, and you collect $4,000. To make up the difference—the other $4,000— you sell some of your shares in the fund. Many funds will arrange some sort of automatic distribution system to save you the headache.

Suppose the share price averages $11 in the first year you hold them. To raise your $4,000, you need to sell approximately 364 shares. This leaves you with 9,636 shares at the beginning of Year Two.

Suppose distributions increase from 40 cents a share to 45 cents in the next year. You will collect $4,337 in dividends from the remaining 9,636 shares. To get the remaining $3,633 that you need for

| | |
|---|---|
| Original price per share | $ 10 |
| Amount invested | $100,000 |
| Number of shares | 10,000 |
| Dividend rate | 4% |
| Dividend amount | $ 4,000 |
| Current income desired | $ 8,000 |
| Shortfall (to be covered by selling shares) | $ 4,000 |
| Number of shares to sell (assume price rise to $11) | 364 |
| Remaining shares | 9,636 |
| New dividend rate | 4.5% |
| New dividend amount | $ 4,337 |
| Current income desired | $ 8,000 |
| Shortfall (to be covered by selling shares) | $ 3,663 |
| Number of shares to sell (assume price rise to $12) | 302 |
| Remaining shares | 9,334 |
| Current value (@ $12) | $112,008 |
| Gain | $ 12,008 |

$8,000 in annual income, you have to sell more shares. If the share price has averaged $12 in Year Two, you need to sell an additional 302 shares, leaving you with 9,334 shares.

What's the point? After two years, you would have received $8,000 per year, just as you would have if you had invested in a bond fund. But you own 9,334 shares of the stock fund, worth $12 a share, for a total of more than $112,000. In your bond fund, your holdings would be worth no more than $100,000 unless interest rates have fallen.

There's no magic at work. This strategy is simply based on the idea that the total return from a stock fund—dividends plus appreciation—will, over a long period, probably be more than the total return from a bond fund. Your actual experience probably won't be as smooth as in the above example, but the result is likely to be obtained over 5 or 10 years. The cash-now investor can take advantage of stock fund ownership by selling some shares and dipping into his unrealized profits as he goes along.

## WHY STOCK FUNDS MAKE SENSE

Whether or not you have a pressing need for instant cash flow, stock funds belong in your portfolio. The October 1987 crash undoubtedly reduced the stock market's appeal for many investors, especially if they had trouble reaching their fund or their broker with sell orders. But don't overreact: Even after the crash, the market was still up well over 100 percent since the start of the bull market 1982. When you double your money in five years, you have earned 14 percent per year, crash or no crash.

For most individuals, the best way to invest in the stock market is through a mutual fund. You get some big players on your side, in a market that's dominated by the big and the bigger.

## CHOOSING THE RIGHT STOCK FUND

The tough questions are what type of fund to choose, and which specific funds in that category. Since the Tax Reform Act of 1986, growth funds are less appealing. When there was a maximum 20 percent tax rate on long-term gains versus rates up to 50 percent on dividends, it paid to give up current yield and wait for stocks to rise in price. Today, when all of your income is taxed at 28 percent or 33 percent, investors may want to look for funds that deliver dividends today, even if the appreciation outlook is more modest.

If precious metals appeals to you, because they often provide current income plus an inflation hedge, keep in mind two types of funds that have emerged. One type of fund is worldwide; the other type avoids all South African shares, concentrating on North American and perhaps Australian companies.

Investors should not be so shortsighted as to think the United States has the world's only healthy stock market. In the 1980s, the American market has generally been strong but the Japanese, Hong Kong, and Singapore markets, to name a few, have outperformed ours. Well-diversified investors will put 5 to 10 percent of their assets offshore. It's very difficult for individual Americans to intelligently invest in overseas companies, and international stock funds are often the best choice.

Whichever type of stock fund you're considering, look for a consistent long-term and short-term track record. Also, pay attention to the size of a fund. The most successful funds attract the most money, but the bigger a fund gets the more its personality changes. Big funds often have found it hard to stay on their original track and consistently pick undervalued companies.

———————— *Summary* ————————

*Pros:*

- Diversification.

- Professional money management.

- Variety. You can select the types of stocks in which you wish to invest. If you want meaningful cash flow, you can choose growth-and-income funds. You also can use stock funds to give you exposure to gold (precious metals funds), oil (natural resource funds), or overseas economies (international funds), to name some possibilities.

- Growth potential. Stock funds can increase dividends, as well as grow in price-per-share.

- Long-term track record. Stock funds have been good performers, on average, over the years. Many of them have performed well enough, in bull and bear markets, to give you confidence that they will continue to gain.

*Cons:*

- Cash flow is generally lower than you will earn from bond investments or cash equivalents. Most of your return is expected to come from appreciation, which might not materialize.

- Volatility. As recent events have shown, stock fund prices can rise and fall sharply, along with the stock market.

- No guarantees. You can lose most of your money in a bad market.

- Reliance on the fund manager. If you pick the wrong fund, you may do worse than the stock market as a whole.

- Fund proliferation. This is the flip side of variety. There are so many funds around, particularly stock funds with unique strategies, that it can be difficult to pick the appropriate fund.

*Recommendation:*

For the stock market allocation of your portfolio (20 to 40 percent), stock funds are better than doing-it-yourself, for most investors. Choosing stocks is a more difficult decision than choosing bonds (how can you make the wrong decision if you want to buy a 10-year Treasury bond?), because there are so many different issues. You really need to invest through a fund in order to earn a competitive return in the institution-dominated stock market.

Cash-oriented funds, especially in the growth-and-income class, look increasingly attractive. They have held their value better, in sharp stock market drops, than pure growth funds. Investors should look for funds where the expected dividend payout is at least 3 percent.

Give stock funds a chance. Don't agonize over every turn in the Dow. After a year, though, if your fund has done much worse than its rivals, start looking for a different stock fund. You don't marry a stock mutual fund for life.

Especially if you hold a diversified portfolio, keep stock funds outside of your retirement plan while you put vehicles that generate higher cash flow in these plans. A large portion of your stock fund's profits will be unrealized capital gains (stocks have gone up in value but haven't been sold yet), and you don't need shelter if you don't have taxable income.

# 11

# Ginnie Mae Funds Make Reinvestment Easy

Cliff and Claire Huxtable, yes. J.R. and Sue Ellen, no. Some marriages work better than others. Right up at the top of the list is the union of mutual funds with Ginnie Maes.

In Chapter 6 we explained how Ginnie Maes work. Investors become mortgage lenders, generally loaning money to finance single-family homes. Just as homeowners repay a little principal, with each monthly payment, the Ginnie Mae investor collects a little return of his original capital along with his monthly interest income. Plus, whenever a home in a "pool" is sold or refinanced, the mortgage is prepaid and the Ginnie Mae investor gets a larger return of principal.

Therefore, anyone who owns a Ginnie Mae directly faces several problems. First, each month's check will contain a return of principal that may be almost miniscule. With diligence and a good broker, these small sums can be swept into a money market fund. There, they will earn relatively low yields until there is enough to make a new investment. If the return of principal is commingled with interest payments, you may spend some of your capital each month.

There is also the matter of unpredictability. You never know for sure when the mortgages in your pool will be prepaid and you will have a sizable chunk of principal to reinvest. When you receive a prepayment, you'll have to make a major reinvestment decision or risk spending your capital.

## THE MUTUAL FUND SOLUTION

Mutual funds solve these problems. Most Ginnie Mae mutual funds have automatic reinvestment of principal. Let's say, for example, that a homeowner makes a monthly payment of $100. The payment consists of $90 worth of interest plus a $10 return of principal.

A Ginnie Mae mutual fund will collect the $100 and automatically reinvest the $10 in more Ginnie Maes. The $90 will be passed through as interest to shareholders, after the fund takes its cut. Similarly, money from prepaid mortgages will be reinvested by the fund. If you choose, the interest can be reinvested as well. You will be spared a lot of the headaches of owning Ginnie Maes directly.

Ginnie Mae funds give you the advantages of Ginnie Mae investing while eliminating the main drawbacks. You get a high yield, backed by a federal guarantee against loss. It's true that many Ginnie Mae funds are load funds, which tends to reduce the yield, but the Ginnie Mae market is so specialized that a skillful portfolio manager may provide yields equal to or better than a small Ginnie Mae investor can earn on his own.

Indeed, Ginnie Mae funds are almost the only way the really small investor can participate. A basic "piece," or pass-through certificate, sells for $25,000. And the one-piece investor lacks diversification because his pool contains similar mortgages in one geographic region. Ginnie Mae funds, on the other hand, give investors diversification and professional management for as little as a few hundred dollars.

Ginnie Mae funds tend to be more stable than most bond funds. They may not perform as well in bull markets, when interest rates are falling, but they hold their value better when interest rates go up.

Why? Because principal is constantly being returned and reinvested. When interest rates are falling, the rise in value of the underlying securities is offset by the continual reinvestment at lower rates. In fact, people tend to prepay mortgages as rates drop, increasing the amount that's reinvested at low rates. Therefore, when falling interest rates drive up the value of all bond funds, the rise of Ginnie Mae funds is tempered by reinvestment.

But when rates rise, returns of principal work to a Ginnie Mae fund's advantage. The reinvestment is at a higher rate, bringing in more income and partially offsetting the fall in share value.

Even though prepayments slow during a period of rising rates, they don't stop altogether because people still buy and sell houses.

In 1986, for example, interest rates fell. Counting cash flow and share-price appreciation, government bond funds were up 14 percent, on average, and municipal bond funds gained 18 percent. Ginnie Mae funds lagged, returning an average of 10 percent.

But, in 1987, when interest rates rose, municipal bond funds lost 1 percent, on average, because the fall in share prices outweighed the cash income. Government bond funds barely broke even. Ginnie Mae funds outperformed them and most other bond funds, averaging a 2 percent total return.

## NO ESCAPE FROM BOND BAD NEWS

Just because Ginnie Mae funds are a good way to buy Ginnie Maes, don't consider them a perfect investment. They're still bond funds, subject to loss of principal when interest rates rise. You may buy shares of a Ginnie Mae fund at, say, $10 a share, only to find those shares selling for $8 or $9 a few months later, if there's a steep rise in interest rates. Your total return will depend on share price movement as well as current yield.

You have to be particularly careful when shopping for Ginnie Mae funds. There really are two categories of such funds. *Ginnie Mae* funds invest primarily, almost totally, in Ginnie Maes.

There also are *Government Securities* funds. These may invest in Ginnie Maes plus Treasury issues, or in Ginnie Maes plus issues from other federal agencies such as Fannie Mae or Freddie Mac. If the emphasis is on Treasury issues, yields will be a bit lower. If there are other agency issues, the yield may be a bit higher but you won't have the ironclad credit guarantee that you have with Treasuries and Ginnie Maes.

## GETTING THE NUMBERS RIGHT

You also have to be wary of Ginnie Mae funds' newspaper advertising. Some Ginnie Mae funds are guilty of misadvertising. Recent SEC regulations (see Chapter 9) on mutual fund advertising may help rein in abuses, but you still have to be careful.

Quite often, these funds hold "premium" Ginnie Maes. Suppose a $100,000 Ginnie Mae has been paid down to $83,000. A mutual fund buys it for $89,000. That's approximately a 7 percent premium.

Why would a fund pay a premium? Because the Ginnie Mae, which was issued during a time of higher interest rates, has a 12.5 percent coupon rate. The Ginnie Mae will pay over $10,000 a year in interest, about 11.7 percent on an $89,000 purchase price. Thus, the fund might advertise an 11 percent or an 11.5 percent yield while new Ginnie Maes are yielding 9 or 9.5 percent.

Is there a catch? You bet. If interest rates fall, homeowners will swap their old 13 percent mortgages for new 9 and 10 percent loans. Every time a mortgage is prepaid, the fund gets $1 back for $1.07 invested. And it will have to reinvest the prepaid mortgage money at falling interest rates. The ultimate yield could be as low as 7 or 7.5 percent if prepayments are extremely high.

To avoid this trap, check the fund's portfolio before investing. It's unrealistic to try to avoid all premium Ginnie Maes, but you should look for a balance of low-yielding and high-yielding coupons. Outstanding Ginnie Maes have coupons ranging from 5 to 17 percent, representing interest-rate volatility in the past two decades.

### Summary

Pros:

- Safety. Although the funds are not guaranteed, the securities they hold—Ginnie Maes—are backed by the federal government.
- High yields. Ginnie Mae funds typically pay 1 to 2 percent more than funds that hold Treasury bonds.
- Convenience. Returned principal is automatically reinvested, eliminating a major drawback to owning Ginnie Maes directly.
- Small investment size. A Ginnie Mae fund may require less than $1,000 while a new Ginnie Mae costs at least $25,000 if bought directly.
- Stability. The constant reinvestment of principal means that Ginnie Mae funds won't fall as much as other bond funds in bear markets.

*Cons:*

- Principal risk. Like all bond funds, Ginnie Mae funds lose value when interest rates rise.
- Reduced profit opportunity. When rates fall, Ginnie Mae funds gain less than other bond funds, because prepayments increase.
- Confusion. Uncertainty of prepayments makes yields hard to determine.
- Taxation. All Ginnie Mae fund distributions are fully taxable.

*Recommendation:*

Ginnie Mae funds are an excellent substitute for Treasury bond funds. Yields are higher, year-to-year fluctuation is smaller, but safety is nearly as great. Since their rise in popularity during the early 1980s, Ginnie Mae funds have outperformed Treasury bond funds.

The combination of safety and high yields is hard to beat for the fixed-income (bond) segment of your portfolio. If you do invest in a Ginnie Mae fund, pick one with a good record over several years. The Ginnie Mae market is specialized, and you need a skilled manager. If possible, hold Ginnie Mae funds in a tax-exempt retirement plan.

# 12

# Tapping Life Insurance's Cash Value

Life insurance isn't a subject we like to read about. In fact, life insurance isn't a subject we even like to think about. We know some is needed to fulfill family obligations. After that, we prefer more pleasant topics.

However, without adequate life insurance any personal financial plan may be worthless. The same holds true for disability coverage, which many people overlook. If you die or become disabled, without sufficient coverage, your family may have to sell all the investments you've accumulated, just to maintain its living standard.

Once you've built a solid base of life insurance and disability protection, you shouldn't forget about life insurance. Some policies make good investments that can provide cash when you'll need it.

## INSURING A COLLEGE EDUCATION

Take Edward Collins, a 55-year-old actor who remarried a few years ago and now has a four-year-old son. He wants to provide for the boy's college education, but he knows his earnings may fluctuate from year to year.

Edward is currently starring in a hit Broadway show. He and his wife are able to place $20,000 in a single-premium variable life insurance policy, which they give to their son.

The concept of single-premium variable life insurance is best understood by breaking out the components. In insurance jargon, a *premium* is the amount paid for coverage. You pay only once for a "single-premium" policy. There's no need to make ongoing annual, semi-annual, quarterly, or monthly payments. In Edward's case, the $20,000 payment is no accident. That's the maximum a couple can give to a child in a given year without incurring a gift tax. Next year, if finances permit, Edward and his wife may give the boy another $20,000 policy.

"Variable" means that the payoff from the policy will vary depending on how the premium dollars are invested. We'll discuss this later in the chapter. For now, all you have to know is that the death benefit—the payoff to the beneficiary when you die—is not fixed. Neither is the cash value, the policy's investment account.

Finally, we get to "life insurance." Because Edward invested the $20,000 in life insurance, that money can build up without any tax penalty. Suppose the policy earns 10 percent in the first year. The cash value will be $22,000 at the start of the second year. Without the shelter of life insurance, Edward might owe $800 in federal, state, and local income taxes (40 percent of the $2,000 earnings), leaving him with only $21,200 in his investment account at the beginning of the second year.

## LEARNING THE RULE OF 72

Over a period of years, tax-free compounding produces some spectacular results. The "Rule of 72" illustrates how long it takes for money to double. If you earn a steady 6 percent, for example, it takes about 12 years for $20,000 to become $40,000 (72 divided by 6 equals 12).

### *"Rule of 72"*

| If You Earn a Constant | Your Principal Will Double in About |
|---|---|
| 3% | 24 Years |
| 4% | 18 Years |
| 6% | 12 Years |
| 8% | 9 Years |
| 9% | 8 Years |
| 12% | 6 Years |

If you earn 8 percent each year, money doubles after 9 years. At 9 percent, it takes just 8 years. And, if you can earn a compound 12 percent, $20,000 becomes $40,000 in just 6 years. In Edward's case, his financial planner expects to earn about 10 percent per year. If successful, the $20,000 will double in about 7 years, and quadruple in about 14 years. The $20,000 original premium is projected to reach nearly $80,000 by the time the boy is 18, ready for college.

At 18, the boy will be able to take policy loans to pay for college. He might borrow $20,000 the first year, leaving $60,000 in the account. By the time he's ready for the second year's $20,000 loan, the cash value may be up to $66,000, if 10 percent growth continues. All of those loans, moreover, will be tax-free.

What happens if 55-year-old Edward fails to live another 14 years to see his son enter college? The policy will pay about $80,000 in death benefits. The money will be exempt from income taxes because it's life insurance proceeds and will be available for college costs.

Edward may realize other benefits from this investment. He has approximately $80,000 in life insurance coverage and can reduce his previous insurance coverage by $80,000, cutting his annual premiums.

Moreover, life insurance cash value is, at the present time, not considered a family asset for purposes of college financial aid. When Edward's son applies to college, the insurance policy won't hamper his ability to receive grants or loans.

## THE BENEFITS OF HIGH-COST COVERAGE

Don't be confused. Single-premium life insurance is a special type of policy for special needs. Basic family protection is available for a much smaller annual outlay. So why buy a policy with the least coverage rather than a policy with the most coverage?

Because the money that's not needed for insurance can go into the policy's cash value. The less premium diverted to insurance, the more that goes into the cash value. But because the policy is legally life insurance, as defined by Congress, it qualifies for all the tax benefits of life insurance. The 1986 Tax Reform Act did not affect these benefits. Therefore, life insurance has a competitive advantage over all the investments hurt by tax reform.

## PLAYING THE MORTALITY TABLES

Suppose a 50-year-old man pays $50,000 for a policy, naming himself as the insured and his daughter as the beneficiary. The policy earns 10 percent each year, for the next 15 years. During this time, the $50,000 virtually quadruples in value to $200,000.

He dies at age 65. His daughter receives a death benefit of $250,000, free of income taxes. Where has this money come from? The first $50,000 is a return of the original premium. The next $150,000 is the money the $50,000 premium has earned, at 10 percent, over the 15 years. No income tax has ever been paid on this money, and none ever will be. (Estate taxes need to be planned for, though.) The remaining $50,000 is the money the insurance company actually has to pay out, as its part of the bargain. It's easy to see how single-premium life insurance is an effective way of transferring investment income to heirs, free of income taxes.

For another example, suppose you're 40 years old with a 65-year-old parent. You could buy a policy and name your parent as the insured (of course, the death benefit would be smaller, relative to the amount of the single premium). You could be the beneficiary. Some single-premium policies don't require a medical exam.

As long as your parent stays alive, your single premium will grow free of income taxes. Assuming he dies before you, you'll collect the death benefit and get back your investment income without ever having to pay income taxes.

There are any number of games you can play, determining who'll be the insured or the beneficiary. Such concerns generally fall into the area of estate planning. But what if you're interested in single-premium life as an investment to generate cash while you're still alive?

## GET CASH, OWE NO TAXES

The earlier example about Edward the actor shows how to tap the cash value of insurance investment through tax-free policy loans. Suppose you have a $100,000 cash value in your policy, and the policy earns 10 percent a year. Each year you can borrow the $10,000, tax-free. You can spend the money as you like, and you never have to repay the loans.

Here is a simple example of how such loans may work. You have

| | Policy Loan | No Policy Loan |
|---|---|---|
| Investment | $100,000 | $100,000 |
| Growth rate | 10% | 10% |
| Income | $ 10,000 | $ 10,000 |
| New cash value | $110,000 | $110,000 |
| Loan | $ 10,000 | 0 |
| Loan interest rate | 6% | N/A |
| Interest paid | 0 | N/A |
| Amount earning 10% | $100,000 | $110,000 |
| Amount earning 6% | $ 10,000 | N/A |
| 2nd Year income | $ 10,600 | $ 11,000 |

$100,000 in cash value, growing to $110,000 after earning 10 percent for one year, and you take out a $10,000 loan. The company will divide your cash value account into two sections.

One section consists of the $10,000 you borrow. The company may charge you 6 percent interest on the loan. At the same time, it credits that section of your account with 6 percent income. The charge and the credit wash out, and you would owe nothing.

At the same time, the other $100,000 of your account continues to earn income on the same basis as before, 10 percent in our example. Insurance companies call this an interest-free loan. As you can see, however, the loan really costs you 4 percent in this example. That's the amount lost from transferring money from a 10 percent account to a 6 percent account.

Most single-premium insurance policies permit this type of "interest-free borrowing" as long as you're taking out the money you have earned. Once you start to borrow your original premium payment, the interest rate may be a couple of points higher than the money with which you're credited. The insurance company is charging you for borrowing back your own money.

When you borrow from an insurance policy, there's no repayment requirement. However, any outstanding policy loans reduce the amount paid in death benefits.

Policy loans open up some possibilities for getting your hands on tax-free cash. You might, for example, take money you currently have in taxable CDs, Treasury bills, or money market funds and transfer it to a single-premium life policy. You let the money build up, tax-free. When you want or need the money, you can get it by borrowing.

Suppose you buy a $50,000 policy at age 50. By age 65, at 10 percent compound growth, you'll have a $200,000 cash value. Suppose you retire then and borrow $20,000 per year, tax-free, for living expenses. That's a 40-percent annual after-tax return on your original investment. And, if you continue to earn 10 percent a year, you'll be borrowing only the annual earnings. The cash value will remain at $200,000.

## SINGLE PREMIUM COMES IN TWO VARIETIES

Where will the earnings come from? Insurance companies, once they collect your premiums, have the same investment alternatives as you do. They can make loans, to companies or to governments, and thus generate a fairly certain return on their investments. Or, they can buy things, mainly stocks in other companies, and take more risks in search of a higher return.

This leads to the two basic types of single-premium policies. One is called simply single-premium whole life. With this type of policy, the insurance company promises a fixed return, for a year or two years or five years. This return usually is about the same as the return on long-term municipal bonds. Once the period expires, a new yield will be announced for another set period. If the company sets its subsequent rates too low, it risks your switching to a competing, high-yield policy.

In a variation, some policies guarantee an indexed yield. For example, the account might earn interest that's always two percentage points more than T-bills yield. Thus, the return rises and falls with fluctuations in interest rates. Most single-premium whole life policies, indexed or fixed-rate, guarantee you against any loss of your original principal.

Another type of single-premium policy, growing in popularity, is single-premium variable life. Your return—your cash value and your death benefit—will vary according to your investment acumen.

Most variable life policies contain several types of mutual funds. A stock fund, a bond fund, and a money market fund are standard. Some policies also offer zero-coupon bonds, government securities, and specialized stock funds. You, the policyholder, determine how you want your money to be split among those funds. You can switch among the various funds as your investment outlook changes.

For example, high interest rates usually dampen the stock market. So when interest rates are in double digits, you may want to put money into bond funds to lock in high yields, and in money market funds to realize current returns. As interest rates fall, you might want to switch your money to stocks which should start to perk up.

It's not as simple as that, of course. Not every investor will adroitly hop from fund to fund. You can actually lose money if you're in the wrong fund at the wrong time. And, just as you can play the stock and bond markets without paying taxes, through variable life insurance, you also realize no tax advantages when you take capital losses inside a life insurance policy.

Some mutual fund families offer related variable life policies. If so, you probably can switch into the company's variable life plan at no charge. Your investment income now will be tax-free and you'll acquire extra insurance protection. However, your yield will probably be two or three points lower each year to pay for the insurance policy expenses.

## A LIFETIME COMMITMENT

Single-premium life insurance isn't for everyone. Along with the tax benefits, there are definite risks.

First, there's the sheer inconvenience. No matter how hard the insurance companies try, getting money into and out of an insurance policy isn't the same as relying on a bank or a money market fund.

There's also the illiquidity. Once you're in one of these policies, you're in it forever. You can switch from one policy to another. You can take out policy loans. But if you ever terminate one of these policies, all of the built-up income is recognized immediately, and taxes will be due.

There's also the investment risk. Single-premium whole life policies are sold on the high quoted yield. To deliver those high yields, insurance companies generally put your premium money into lower-quality investment grade bonds or perhaps into junk bonds. Thus, you're an indirect bond investor.

If interest rates go up, bond investors will suffer. You may not suffer directly if the insurance company's financial strength is sufficient to provide you with the promised return. However, you'll lose the opportunity to reinvest your principal at the higher interest rates. And there's always the risk that the insurance company itself will be hurt so much, from bond portfolio losses, that it won't be able to fulfill its promises.

In a variable life policy, the investment risks are more obvious. Such policies generally have performed well in the 1980s, with interest rates trending down, pushing up stocks and bonds. But the stock and bond markets can reverse quickly, as we've learned. If we have a re-run of the 1970s, with high inflation and interest rates, investors who don't move into money market-type investments may suffer serious losses.

Relying on policy loans as a means to gain access to cash has its drawbacks. There is a cost, as we've seen above. You pay to borrow your own money. In some policies, overborrowing may lead to a policy termination unless you put some cash back in.

Also, policy loans reduce the death benefit. You pay for life insurance all along. In most single-premium policies, the annual costs come to 2 to 3 percent a year. Does it make sense to borrow money and negate the benefit you're paying for?

Another risk involves the financial ability of the insurance company to make its payments when they're due. To reduce this risk, you can invest through an insurer that's based in New York state, where the regulatory climate is strict and large reserves are required. Whether or not you're a New Yorker, if you buy a policy from such a company you'll be protected. Ask about the insurance company's financial strength: a rating of A or better from A.B. Best and Co., which rates insurers, is a good sign.

The other major risk is legislative. More changes in tax law are likely. Next time around, some of life insurance's tax benefits may be cut back. In the past, changes in life insurance taxation haven't been retroactive. That is, owners of existing policies were entitled to their anticipated tax benefits. But the 1986 law had retroactive elements, especially in the tax shelter area, so nothing is certain. You may buy a single-premium insurance policy in 1989, only to have Congress take away some of the benefits in 1990 or 1991. Nothing has done more to reduce Congress' credibility, among financial advisers, than this recent trend to change tax law retroactively.

In fact, as this book went to press, Congress was considering a law to reduce the tax advantages of single-premium life insurance. Passage is likely, in 1988 or 1989. The outcome, now uncertain, probably will mean that payments have to be made over several years and that you'll have to wait several years before receiving tax-free policy loans. If you buy an investment-oriented insurance policy, find out if there's a bail-out feature, on this issue, before you invest.

## ONLY BUY INSURANCE IF YOU NEED IT

Ultimately, single-premium life only makes sense for people who place some value on the life insurance component. That doesn't mean you need this life insurance for your basic financial planning. It means that the death benefits you paid for should be welcome to someone you hold dear, including yourself.

If you're totally alone in the world, you might be better off with a single-premium deferred annuity. The idea is the same, but the tax-free buildup will be greater because there's no need to pay for life insurance. Annuity payouts can be structured to last your entire life, no matter how long you live.

These policies are truly for those with a long-term perspective. The longer you can leave your money untouched, compounding tax-free, the greater your capital buildup. The dangers of terminating these policies and the disadvantages of policy loans makes then unsuitable for investors who need ready cash.

If you have truly long-range goals—retirement income, college funding, transfer of tax-free investment income—single-premium life insurance can be for you. The availability of policy loans gives you access to your cash in an emergency. And the life insurance benefits can be a valuable "kicker."

--------- *Summary* ---------

*Pros:*

- Tax-free buildup. Your premium income compounds, tax-free.

- Tax-free policy loans. You have access to your money. Loans call for little or no interest; they need never be repaid.

- Death benefits. Insurance proceeds provide extra family protection. There are no income taxes due on this money.

- Versatility. By adjusting the insured, the beneficiary, and the policy owner, you can maximize the financial benefits.

- Safety. Single-premium whole life comes with an insurance company guarantee against loss of principal.

- Growth potential. Variable life lets you play the stock market, tax-free.

*Cons:*

- Illiquidity. You can switch policies, but cashing one in triggers a tax obligation.

- Policy loan temptation. If you borrow too heavily, you can wipe out your death benefit and may force a termination of your policy.

- Inflation risk. With single-premium whole life, your guaranteed yield may not keep up with the inflation rate.

- Investment risk. You actually can lose money with variable life policies.

- Cost. You pay for life insurance, whether or not you really need it.

- Taxation. Congress may reduce the tax benefits, and may even do so retroactively.

*Recommendation:*

Single-premium life doesn't fit neatly into our system of portfolio allocation. Only invest if you need such coverage. Ideally, you should be a stock or bond investor with long-term goals, and someone else that you'd like to protect through life insurance. If you fit, invest no more than you're prepared to let sit for at least 10 years, gathering interest, before taking out any loans. Choose a life insurance company in sound financial health and work with an investment pro who's familiar with these policies.

Single-premium whole life may be a good substitute for the bond sector of your portfolio. Single-premium variable is more flexible, because you can hold stocks as well as bonds.

One investment strategy that's appropriate for many investors is to choose a variable life policy that offers zero-coupon bonds as an alternative. You can put half your money in stocks, half in a money market fund. If the money market fund averages a 6 percent yield, it will double in 12 years. Thus, you'll have a complete return of your original principal in the money market fund. You can't lose, even if your stocks are totally wiped out, but you can earn much more, in a strong stock market.

If interest rates ever reach the point where you can earn 9 percent on zero-coupon bonds, move from the money market fund to the zeros. At 9 percent, the money will double in eight years. This strategy gives you no downside with plenty of upside, plus tax shelter.

# 13

## Real Estate the REIT Way

In previous chapters, we have discussed the different types of mutual funds. In each case, you pay someone else—the mutual fund companies' employees—to manage your investments. The investments held by mutual funds usually are securities—corporate stocks and various kinds of bonds.

There are also a few mutual funds that claim to specialize in real estate, but they really offer securities. These funds usually buy the common stocks of companies with operations in the real estate industry. Fund performance will reflect corporate performance, not the value of specific properties.

For a managed investment in "pure" real estate, you can turn to real estate investment trusts, commonly called REITs (rhymes with sweets). These trusts are similar to the closed-end mutual funds described in a previous chapter. Money is raised when the fund is formed, and investors are given shares. These shares trade like common stocks on an exchange or over-the-counter. If you want to buy shares, you buy from existing holders rather than from the fund. If you want to sell, you sell to other investors. The share price rises and falls, depending on supply and demand among buyers and sellers.

REITs differ from closed-end mutual funds in what they do with the money that's raised. Most of the money has to be devoted to real estate activities. REITs do what you would do if you decided to invest in real estate on your own. REIT personnel analyze cap rates, loan-to-value ratios, and all the factors discussed in Chapter 7. They hire people to take care of day-to-day property management.

The main difference between a REIT and the local real estate investor is that a REIT has a staff of full-time employees with more money to invest. Investing in a REIT gives you the usual mutual fund advantages—diversification and professional management—combined with a real estate investment.

Virtually all of a REIT's earnings (at least 95 percent) have to be passed through to shareholders. By doing this, a REIT avoids the corporate income tax leaving more cash to be passed through to the shareholders.

## THREE KINDS OF REITS

Where do the earnings come from? *Mortgage REITs* make loans to developers and property buyers. A REIT may raise $10 million from the public and, for example, make 10 $1 million loans. After paying all the management expenses, loan interest may be 10 percent. The 10 percent will be passed through to the REIT shareholders in proportion to the number of shares they own.

*Equity REITs* buy properties rather than make loans. An equity REIT may raise $10 million, borrow another $10 million, and spend $20 million to purchase properties. It collects rents from tenants, pays operating expenses and loan interest, and passes through any excess cash to shareholders.

*Hybrid REITs* lend some of their funds and use the rest to buy properties.

Why should investors consider REITs? Investing in a REIT is like owning a high-dividend stock with a direct real estate play. It's about the only way a "little guy" can include real estate in his portfolio.

REIT shares commonly are priced at $10 or $20 a share. For as little as a few hundred dollars, investors can participate in diverse, professionally managed real estate. If you need cash, you can sell your shares. This is generally easier than selling a share in a local office building or an apartment house.

Mortgage REITs usually offer high yields because they make mortgage loans. Recently, for example, while money market funds were yielding around 6 percent, and 10-year Treasury bonds were priced to yield about 8 percent, many mortgage REITs were paying 12 percent or more. Increasingly, mortgage REITs make *participating* loans. That is, if the property on which they make a loan goes up in value, the REIT shareholders participate in the appreciation.

Equity REITs have slightly lower yields than mortgage REITs. Usually the current yield on equity REITs lies between the rates on money market funds and long-term Treasuries. In equity REITs, investors have direct property ownership. If rents go up, cash flow to shareholders rises. Increasing cash flow is likely to push up the price of the shares. Some equity REITs have records of 15 percent annual dividend growth over the past 10 years.

Hybrid REITs provide a slightly higher yield than an equity REIT plus more growth potential than a mortgage REIT.

## REITS LOOK SWEETER AFTER TAX REFORM

The 1986 Tax Reform Act contains many provisions inimical to real estate investment, but REITs were spared. In fact, some technical provisions of the law make it easier for REITs to conduct their operations. Cash flow from mortgage REITs are fully taxable. After tax reform, the lower tax rates favor mortgage REITs.

The taxation of equity REITs is a bit more complicated. The taxable income from a real estate property may be less than the cash income because of depreciation deductions. The same is true of an equity REIT. You may receive 7 percent in cash distributions but your share of the REIT's taxable income may be only 5 percent.

Let's say you invest $10,000 to buy 1 percent of an equity REIT. Shares are priced at $10. In the first year, the REIT distributes

|  | Total REIT | Your 1% Interest |
| --- | --- | --- |
| Share price | $10 | $ 10 |
| Total shares | 100,000 | 1,000 |
| Distributable cash | $70,000 | $700 |
| Yield | 7% | 7% |
| Depreciation | $20,000 | $200 |
| Taxable income | $50,000 | $500 |
| Taxes @ 30% |  | $150 |
| After-tax income (cash distribution minus taxes) |  | $550 |
| After-tax yield ($550/$10,000 invested) |  | 5.5% |

$70,000 in cash, after paying all of its expenses. Your share is $700, or 7 percent of your $10,000 investment.

Because of depreciation, though, the REIT's properties have only $50,000 in taxable income. The share passed through to you is $500. You pay taxes on $500, not on the $700 you receive. You're getting the benefit of the equity REIT's depreciation deductions. If you're in a 30 percent tax bracket, you pay $150 in income taxes. That leaves $550—a 5.5 percent after-tax yield.

Before tax reform, some real estate deals were structured so that property owners actually received tax losses, rather than income, because interest and depreciation deductions were so huge. REITs, even equity REITs, were unable to pass through losses. Thus, they never were "tax shelters," and they weren't hurt by anti-shelter legislation. They have always been income generators, the type of investment favored by the new law.

## MARKET DISCOUNT PLAGUES REIT INVESTORS

For real estate investors, though, REITs pose some disadvantages. They trade like stocks, and they're priced like stocks. And stock-market pricing isn't always rational.

Suppose you buy a local office building at market value for $1 million. Its neighborhood enjoys a real estate boom. Based on sales of comparable buildings in the vicinity, the building is worth $1.2 million after two years. You could sell it for that amount if you wanted to. Or you could get some tax-free cash by borrowing against the increased valuation.

Now suppose you had invested in a REIT instead. The REIT took your money along with money from other investors and issued shares at $10 apiece and bought 10 office buildings, just like the one in the example above.

Their office buildings, too, appreciate 20 percent in two years, and the properties now are worth $12 million.

Unfortunately, the message may not have gotten through to Wall Street. Perhaps the leases in the 10 office buildings did not expire during the two years, and rent increases have not been realized. Cash flow to investors remains at the original level.

The flat cash distribution may cause the stock price to stay at $10, or even to drop a bit if sellers exceed buyers. In the example, the net asset value (NAV) per share may be $12, meaning that the value of the REIT's assets justify a $12 price. Yet the REIT shares may sell for only $10—a 16.7 percent discount from NAV. Historically, most equity REITs sell at a discount to NAV, although the size of the discount varies from time to time, and from REIT to REIT. Discounts usually are in the 10 to 30 percent range.

Mortgage REITs, too, are subject to stockmarket vagaries. REITs enjoyed a boom in the early 1970s, mainly among mortgage REITs that made loans to developers. After the recession of 1974–1975, some of their loans went bad. The stockmarket, though, did not discriminate between healthy REITs and sick ones. All REIT stocks took a terrible pounding—an index of REIT stocks fell from 103 in January 1973 to 35 in December 1974. That's a loss of two-thirds' of shareholders' equity. It took more than 10 years—until April 1983—for the index to climb back to its 1972–1973 highs.

## MAKING THE PAYOUT MORE CERTAIN

Investment promoters have come up with a technique that's aimed at reducing REITs' dependence on stockmarket pricing. They have created the finite-life REIT, sometimes known as a FREIT. FREITs come in all varieties: equity, mortgage, hybrid. The difference is that FREITs go out of business after a set time period, usually 12 to 15 years (standard REITs have perpetual lives). At that time, all loans will be due and all properties sold. The proceeds will be distributed to shareholders.

With a FREIT, investors can see they will actually realize the properties' real estate values in the not-too-distant future. Take our example, where a REIT with assets worth $12 per share is priced at $10. Let's say that the REIT was certain to sell all of its properties tomorrow, collect the sale proceeds, and distribute $12 per share to investors. The share price will be bid up to $12. Proponents say that FREITs will help to eliminate the traditional discount from NAV and make REIT values more directly related to the underlying real estate.

Not everybody is convinced about the virtues of FREITs. The most common complaint is that FREITs tie the hands of management. Suppose a FREIT formed in 1985 has a 15-year life. All the properties will have to be sold by the year 2000. This places the REIT in a poor negotiating position because buyers know it must sell.

Even worse, the year 2000 may fall in the midst of a recession, forcing the REIT to sell when real estate prices are low. If there was such a thing as a 15-year FREIT back in 1972, it would have been forced to sell its properties in 1987, a year in which many markets were overbuilt and tax reform disrupted the market. It was not a good time to be a forced seller of real estate.

The FREIT concept is still relatively new, having first gained popularity in 1983. So it's difficult to say whether or not FREITs have succeeded in eliminating the discounting that has plagued REITs. Many FREITs have not fared well in the secondary market, but this may have been due to reasons other than their finite-life structure.

## NO NEED TO BUY BLIND

The REIT explosion in recent years is dizzying. There are nearly 200 REITs from which to choose. They range from one-property REITs (Rockefeller Center) to REITs that specialize in hotels to REITs that make loans to affiliates of the sponsor. They vary widely, and you shouldn't just go and "buy a REIT."

First, you should differentiate between mortgage and equity REITs. Mortgage REITs pay higher current yields; equity REITs have more growth potential. In either case, you should ask your broker or financial advisor if the REIT's distribution is covered from earnings. If the cash is coming from property sales, the current distribution level may not be maintained.

In general, it's better to choose a REIT that has a track record. You can see what's in its portfolio and how it has performed over the past. Newly issued REITs often suffer from a share-price drop shortly after issue. Some new REITs even are "blind pools"—you don't know what properties you'll be buying. Why do that when you can invest in a REIT with a long and successful past performance history?

The greatest problem with REITs is their strength—liquidity. Because REITs trade like stocks, investors who own REITs focus on short-term, sell-or-hold decisions. In October 1987, for example, REITs crashed along with the rest of the stock market, losing 14 percent of their value in a month. Certainly, the real estate owned by REITs didn't go down in value by 14 percent in a month. Real estate ownership is generally a medium- to long-term affair, and you may not get to cash in fully if you choose a vehicle—a REIT—where you can go in and out, from day to day.

## Summary

*Pros:*

- Pooling of funds. You can invest in real estate on a small scale, with diversification and professional management.
- Convenience. You avoid all the headaches of operating your own investment real estate.
- Liquidity. REIT shares trade like common stocks.
- High yields. Mortgage REITs have exceptionally high distributions, perhaps several points higher than bonds or Ginnie Maes. Cash flow from equity REITs is extremely high for an investment with growth potential.
- Track record. When you buy an existing REIT, there's a past performance to study. You know what you're getting.
- Tax-favored position. Congress has put limited partnerships on its "hit list," as we'll see later. REITs seem to be the "good guys" now. So there's no corporate tax to worry about, depreciation and interest deductions can pass through, and any taxable income from REITs is taxed at low personal tax rates.

*Cons:*

- Loss of purity. When you buy a REIT, you don't have a direct real estate play. It's real estate combined with a stock or a bond, which can work against you in bear markets.
- Price volatility. Not only can prices go down, they can go down quickly.
- Lack of inflation protection. One reason to own real estate is to provide an inflation hedge. REITs don't always come through. In 1973–74, for example, when inflation reached double digits, REITs suffered a calamitous fall.
- Portfolio income. Income from REITs can't be offset by *passive losses* from old tax shelters.

*Recommendation:*

Differentiate between mortgage and equity REITs. Mortgage REITs pay extremely high yields, and may also offer a real estate play, if the mortgages are "participating." Aggressive investors can use them, instead of straight bonds, while conservative investors can use them instead of direct real estate ownership.

Equity REITs, on the other hand, are really high-yield stocks. They pay excellent dividends and have growth potential. Some equity REITs have performed well long-term. So investors can consider equity REITs as another option, besides utilities, for getting high cash flow from the stock market.

It's difficult to think of a reason for buying a REIT—any REIT—on the initial offering. Instead, buy existing REITs that have traded for a while. For example, VMS Realty Partners is a REIT sponsor with a good record and excellent financial strength. Recently, it sold a new REIT on the promise of a 12 percent guaranteed yield for the first two years. The REIT was part-specified, part-blind pool. At the same time, VMS had five other REITs, fully invested and publicly traded, all priced to pay around 13 percent.

# 14

# Unit Trusts: Know When to Hold 'Em

Unit investment trusts, also known as unit trusts, have lost ground in recent years to mutual funds. But these trusts have their place in the investment world, especially when interest rates are at or near their peak.

Back in the mid-1970s, for example, inflation and interest rates climbed to double digits. New York City was in financial disarray to the point that the city, a huge player in the municipal bond market, threatened default. The entire muni market reacted. Prices of muni bonds went down; that is, interest rates went up. Long-term tax-exempt bonds paid 12 percent, an unheard-of figure at the time.

This was bad news to Harry, an investor holding hundreds of thousands of dollars worth of New York City bonds. He panicked. What should he do with all of his devalued bonds?

His financial planner advised him to sell his New York City issues, giving him a large capital loss. The loss was sufficient to offset some capital gains from other investments and to reduce his current tax bill.

The planner also told Harry to lock in the high interest rates while they were available. How? Harry could buy other long-term municipal bonds, but if he stuck to a few issuers, he risked another New York City disaster.

An alternative, the one Harry's adviser recommended, was to buy a municipal bond unit trust. A unit trust adds safety because investors get a diverse portfolio of bond issues. They are often more convenient, because checks are sent monthly or quarterly or semi-annually. There's no need for investors to clip bond coupons and cash them in at a local bank.

Harry took the advice, more than 10 years ago. Harry has passed away, but his heirs still receive 12 percent, tax-free, from Harry's investment. If they wanted to, they could cash out at a huge gain.

## A ONE-DECISION INVESTMENT

With a unit trust, money raised from investors is used to buy a portfolio of securities. The securities are placed into a trust. Shares of the trust, called *units,* are distributed to investors in proportion to the money they have contributed.

That's it. The securities are held, with no buying or selling. Interest income is passed through to unit holders. When the trust expires, proceeds are returned to investors.

Most unit trusts hold fixed-income securities. That is, they hold some type of bonds. Usually a particular trust will hold bonds of a similar maturity. They will all come due at about the same time, giving investors a return of capital in addition to periodic interest payments.

A few years ago, Ginnie Mae unit trusts were popular. However, the uncertainty regarding prepayments poses problems for unit trust investors. Open-ended mutual funds seem to be more suitable for Ginnie Mae investing because they are constantly buying new securities. Prepaid and repaid principal can be reinvested in more Ginnie Maes. Today, unit trusts are used mainly for medium- and long-term municipal bonds.

## CERTAIN RETURN AT A LOW COST

Unit trusts offer some of the same advantages as mutual funds. The required investment is generally small, usually $1,000. For that sum, you get diversification because you own a portion of the trust's many securities. Professional managers select the securities. You have liquidity because the sponsor will buy back the units if you need to cash out. As in mutual funds, the longer the maturity you choose, the higher the yield. If a trust maturing in 25 to 30 years yields 9 percent, a trust maturing in 6 to 7 years may yield 7 percent.

What are the reasons for choosing a unit trust over a mutual fund? First, there's the certainty of return. If you invest $1,000 in a unit trust holding securities with an average 9 percent yield, you are fairly sure of receiving $90 per year for the life of the trust. By contrast, mutual fund yields will drop if interest rates go lower, because new money is being invested at the lower rates.

Unit trusts, then, provide a way to lock in an interest rate before an anticipated drop. In times of low rates, you probably won't want to lock them in with a unit trust.

The other major advantage is lower cost over a long period. It's true that unit trusts generally have sales charges while many mutual funds claim to be no-load. In practice, the spread is narrowing as unit trust loads drop to the 2 to 5 percent range, and no-load funds add various charges.

In addition, mutual funds need to be constantly managed. As an investor, you pay for that management. Unit trusts charge minimal ongoing administrative charges. Over the long haul, unit trusts are likely to have the lower cost—and the higher yield—even if the initial expenses are higher.

## NO FLEXIBILITY

The disadvantages of unit trusts mirror the advantages. There's no flexibility: You can't switch from a unit trust to a money market fund or a stock fund, for example.

Unit trust management expenses are lower because there's virtually no management. A skilled mutual fund manager may enhance the original portfolio through savvy trading. With a unit trust, you must be right to begin with because that's all there is. The original bonds are yours, in good times or bad.

Similarly, mutual funds are able to generate higher yields when interest rates rise because they buy bonds at the new, higher rate. The rise in yield offsets the loss in value when interest rates rise.

For unit trust investors, there's no silver lining when interest rates rise. Rising interest rates generally are a sign of inflation, and your fixed return is worth less. The sponsor will buy back your unit, but the buyback price falls if interest rates go up. If you want a full return of principal, you may have to hold on until the bonds are redeemed.

Some unit trusts offer a *reinvestment option* in addition to monthly or quarterly checks. However, it's usually not possible to reinvest in the original trust. The money is swept into a mutual fund or money market fund in most instances. Or your interest may be reinvested in a future trust.

Besides the interest-rate risk, there's also the chance that one or more of the securities in a unit trust will default. Some trusts advertise that the bonds they hold are insured. That is, private insurance covers the risk of default. In truth, bond insurance is primarily a marketing gimmick. The insurers only cover bonds that are insurable—highly unlikely to default.

Meanwhile, you will be collecting about 0.5 percent less on an insured portfolio because of the cost of the insurance. The price you pay for the insurance may not be worth the added comfort. Your real safety comes from the diversification and professional selection of the securities in the trust.

Unit trusts are appropriate only for investors who are in for the long haul. You must have other assets in your portfolio to provide growth. Most of all, what you see is what you get. You must feel that the prevailing yields are worth locking in for the coming years.

If you hold unit trusts that you have bought in the past, and you feel interest rates are near bottom, you may want to sell them and take profits. The trusts aren't managed, and there's nowhere to go but down in times of rising interest rates. If you take your profits, you can switch into a money market fund or a short-term government bond fund where you are likely to do better.

Similarly, if interest rates go up, and you think the time is right to buy unit trusts, ask your broker or planner for price quotes on UITs that were issued in the past. The math is complicated—you need to find out if you would be paying a premium for the bonds in the portfolio, and how many years it will take to amortize the premium, but the result may be a yield that's significantly higher than the yield available on new UITs.

## WHY PUT STOCKS INTO UNIT TRUSTS?

There's another wrinkle in unit trusts: stock trusts. These trusts generally buy a fixed portfolio of stocks and hold on for a given period, anywhere from 3 to 25 years. At that point, the stocks will be sold.

Some trusts, for example, hold utility stocks. Sponsors say that your income will grow as utilities increase their dividends, and there is likely to be long-term growth in share prices as well. Other stock trusts try to focus on emerging small companies. Still another variation combines a stock unit trust with zero-coupon bonds. The bonds assure a return of capital while any stock appreciation is gravy.

Whatever the sales literature says, it's hard to think of a good reason for locking in an unmanaged equity portfolio. Investors should stick to basics when it comes to unit trusts. If you want to lock in today's interest rates for the long-term, a unit trust is a good vehicle. For other investment goals, look elsewhere.

─────── *Summary* ───────

*Pros:*

- Certainty of return. Your total return, long-term, is predictable.
- Low cost. Administrative charges are extremely low if the bonds are held long-term.
- Disinflation hedge. It's hard to beat unit trusts if you buy when interest rates are high. You will lock in high yields and be able to sell at a profit, if you wish.

*Cons:*

- Lack of flexibility. You have to live with any mistakes the manager buys when the trust is formed.
- Inflation risk. If interest rates rise, your interest income loses buying power, and you'll suffer a loss if you sell before maturity. If you hold on to maturity, your return of principal will buy far less than the money you put in.
- Reinvestment risk. Because you can't reinvest interest in the same trust, you have to make other arrangements for relatively small amounts.

*Recommendation:*

Unit trusts that invest in bonds may be attractive at times of extremely high interest rates. When municipal bond yields reach

10 percent or higher, for example, it probably makes sense to lock them in with a unit trust. Check the trust's maturity, and don't go out too long. If you have 15 years until retirement, for example, don't invest in a 25-year trust. Invest money you can be fairly certain of putting away for the long-term. You're probably best served by having your interest swept into a money market fund.

Don't buy equity unit trusts. Managed mutual funds give you the flexibility you need, especially in times of increased stock market volatility.

---

# SECTION III

# Partners-in-Cash

During the 1980s, mutual funds registered huge sales increases. Not so coincidentally, the mutual fund boom mirrored the surge in the stock and bond markets, during the period 1982–87 while interest rates were falling. Most mutual funds prospered, and investors flocked to them.

Investors now can choose among an incredible array of mutual funds. Tax-exempt bonds for California residents? Savings & loan stocks? Non-South African gold stocks? If that's what you want, there's a mutual fund for you.

But with all of their variety, virtually all mutual funds have common features. Most are interest-rate sensitive. Fixed-income (bond) funds rise when interest rates fall, but they lose value when rates rise. Stock funds fluctuate with the stock market, which has become highly sensitive to interest rates.

In late 1981, interest rates peaked, with the banks' *prime rate* (for the most creditworthy borrowers) topping 20 percent. By early 1987, the prime rate was down to 7.5 percent. No wonder most mutual funds boasted lucrative returns at that point.

But rates began climbing again in 1987, breaking a five-year downtrend. Then the stock market crashed. And what happened to mutual funds? Out of 1184 funds tracked by Lipper Analytical

135

Services, 444 lost money for investors. Only 328 earned at least 4.5 percent, the inflation rate for the year.

What will happen if interest rates head further north, to the levels of the late 1970s and early 1980s? Stock and bond funds likely will report painful losses.

## MORE RED FLAGS ON MUTUAL FUNDS

With fixed-income funds, you usually know what you're getting. A junk bond fund, for example, invests in low-rated corporate bonds. You know you'll receive a higher yield today, in return for accepting high risks (interest rates may rise, or the companies that issued the bonds may default).

Stock funds, though, are basically "blind pools." That is, the fund takes your money and does whatever the manager likes. It's true that you can check a fund's portfolio before you invest, but the list of current holdings may be out of date by the time it's printed. The fund manager can sell all of those stocks and buy new ones. Or, if he decides the market has reached a peak, he may move out of stocks into money market funds, waiting for a new buying opportunity.

Mutual fund proponents argue that investors are liquid. If they don't like the direction a fund is taking, they can sell their shares and switch to another one. But that may lead to a tax obligation; it certainly will lead to a new decision about where to invest.

If interest rates shoot up and everyone heads for the exit at the same time, who knows how long it will take to process all the sell orders? Or what kind of a price investors eventually will receive? On October 19, 1987, many mutual fund investors were unable to reach their funds on the phone. Liquidity is a great benefit for investors, but a security is only as liquid as its ability to attract an acceptable price from a buyer.

Taxes are another issue. Despite publicity to the contrary, the 1986 tax act did not remove tax considerations from investing. Whenever you get a distribution from a mutual fund, the money is considered ordinary income, taxed at the highest marginal tax rate. State and local income taxes may also take their bite. The only way to avoid these taxes is to invest in mutual funds through a tax-exempt retirement plan, including an IRA.

For stock fund investors, the tax picture is even bleaker. The fund owns common stocks of various corporations, all of which have to pay a corporate income tax; the 1986 tax act requires corporations to pay billions more. Only after these taxes are paid can corporations pay the dividends that eventually will be passed through by mutual funds. No wonder stock funds distribute only around 2 percent! And then you have to pay taxes on your distributions. Economists refer to this phenomenon as double taxation: first at the corporate level, then on your personal return.

Some investors, therefore, prefer to reduce their participation in mutual funds. They like the idea of hiring someone to manage their money for them. But they like investments that may prosper in times of inflation and rising interest rates. They like to have a more certain idea of how their money will be invested.

Some investors are willing to forgo some liquidity and make a medium- or long-term commitment. Historically, buy-and-hold investors have outperformed in-and-out traders. In addition, they like to avoid full taxation on every penny they receive and the double taxation of corporate dividends.

## PUTTING PART OF YOUR PORTFOLIO
## IN PARTNERSHIPS

Investors with these goals can go into limited partnerships. But isn't limited partnership synonymous with tax shelter? And didn't the new tax law kill tax shelters?

No, and no. A limited partnership is simply a structure for business ventures, such as a corporation or a regular ("general") partnership. In a limited partnership, there are two classes of partners: limited partners (*limiteds*) and general partners (*g.p.s*). There may be any number of limited partners, up into the thousands.

Typically, most of the money comes from the limiteds. They're called limited partners because their financial liability is limited to the amount of cash they contribute, plus any notes they personally sign. If you invest $5,000 in a limited partnership, and don't sign any notes, you can't lose more than $5,000, no matter what happens to the venture. In this regard, you're on the same footing as any other purely passive investor.

The general partner is the one who runs the partnership's business. If it's real estate, for example, he's responsible for acquiring properties, arranging the financing, managing the properties or hiring a manager, maintaining the properties, refinancing the mortgages if necessary, and ultimately selling the properties. The general partner also is responsible for all paperwork and for sending reports to the limited partners.

The general partner's liability is not limited. If the partnership runs up excess debts, the lenders may proceed against him. A general partner may be an individual, a corporation, another partnership, or some combination thereof.

Limited partners pay the general partner for running their business. In most cases, there's an upfront fee for putting the deal together, an ongoing management fee, and a "back end" fee that's based on the performance of the business (i.e., profitable sales of real estate). As a general rule, limiteds do better if the fees are weighted to the back end because the general partner has an incentive to produce strong results.

In limited partnership investing, a good rule of thumb is that at least 80 percent of the money raised should go "into the deal." All the upfront costs should be 20 percent or less, with the remainder going to buy real estate, drill for oil, and so on.

## ONE TAX INSTEAD OF TWO

The main advantage of limited partnership investing is that the corporate income tax can be avoided. Under the 1986 tax law, with its stiff increase in corporate taxes, this is increasingly important. The limited partnership itself pays no taxes. All income is passed through to the limited partners, who pay taxes at their personal rates, which are lower than corporate tax rates.

Another advantage is flexibility. Partnership agreements can be drawn up to allocate the proceeds in any way the partners wish, as long as the IRS "distortion" rules aren't violated. A partnership agreement might call for the limiteds to receive 99 percent of all profits, losses, and cash flow, and the general partner 1 percent, until a certain point is reached. This point might be the return of the limiteds' capital. After that point, the split may change to 80 percent for the limiteds and 20 percent for the general partner.

Suppose a partnership registers a $100,000 loss in a given year. The loss will be passed through to the partners in proportion to their stake in the deal. The limiteds may get $99,000 of the loss. If there were nine limited partners, with equal shares, each would get an $11,000 loss. If there were 990 equal limiteds, each would get a $100 loss.

Until tax reform, the loss could be deducted against the

investor's other income. That's where the tax shelter came in. In fact, some limited partnerships intentionally loaded up on non-cash expenses (depreciation, deferred fees, accrued interest). In many cases, the paper losses exceeded the investor's cash contribution, putting the investor ahead from tax savings alone.

That's all in the past. With a few exceptions, losses from limited partnerships can be deducted only against income from other limited partnerships. Now, limited partnerships are structured to provide cash flow rather than tax shelter.

Suppose a limited partnership makes $100,000 in cash, after paying all of its expenses. No corporate income taxes are due, and the $100,000 can be passed through to investors. If there are nine equal limiteds, and they're entitled to a 99 percent share, each limited receives $11,000 in cash.

Non-cash expenses still may be used in moderation. Depreciation and accrued interest may drop taxable income to zero in our example. No tax obligation will be passed through to the partners, and each investor will keep the entire $11,000.

## PAY TAXES LATER, RATHER THAN SOONER

The limited partnership promoter may tell you that this represents $11,000 in tax-free cash. That's not really the case. Your cash flow is tax-deferred, not tax-free. You'll pay the tax eventually, generally when the limited partnership sells its properties and ceases operations. Limited partnerships usually last for 10 to 15 years.

To understand how the deferred taxes will be paid, let's say you buy a stock for $10 a share. A year later, you receive a $1 per share dividend. However, you don't owe any taxes on the dividend. Instead, Big Brother changes all the records of your purchases, inserting "$9" a share for "$10." (Technically, it's a "basis adjustment.")

Then you sell the stock for $10. You think you've broken even—bought for $10, sold for $10. Big Brother, though, says you really paid only $9 for the stock. All the paperwork says $9. And you owe taxes on a $1 gain.

That's what can happen in a limited partnership. Some of your cash flow may be tax sheltered. The taxes you don't pay now will be paid later. However, if there is inflation in the interim, you'll pay the taxes in devalued dollars. It's better to pay tax on $1 of income in 1998 than in 1988.

## PARTNERSHIP INVESTMENTS ARE SMALLER, MORE TARGETED THAN MUTUAL FUNDS

Consequently, limited partnerships still can provide some tax shelter by throwing off cash flow that's not immediately taxable. There may be other advantages, too.

Most limited partnerships are more specified than mutual funds. You're buying a given cable TV system or two specified nursing homes, for example. You can analyze the business before you invest. Even "blind pool" limited partnerships tend to be fairly restricted in terms of operations. The general partner may intend to develop new miniwarehouses, for example, and his experience in developing miniwarehouses is spelled out in a prospectus or an offering memorandum. Although there are some exceptions, limited partnership investments tend to be smaller, more targeted, and less open-ended then mutual funds.

In addition, limited partnerships often provide a direct play in an operating business. The partnership may be drilling for oil or raising an orange crop. Higher inflation and rising interest rates may not be as disastrous as they are likely to be for mutual funds.

For example, suppose you invest in a limited partnership that buys a shopping center. Some of the money used to buy the property is borrowed through a long-term, fixed-rate mortgage.

A few years from now, interest rates rise steeply. This doesn't concern your partnership because it already has locked in a long-term loan at a fixed interest rate. The rising interest rates probably reflect increased inflation. If so, the stores in the shopping center will be charging higher prices. Some of the higher prices will be passed through to you in higher rents from the stores. Therefore, inflation may drive your returns up rather than down.

Not all limited partnerships thrive during inflationary periods, just as not all businesses survive. But many limited partnerships, especially those in real estate and oil and gas, and perhaps equipment leasing, are likely to outperform mutual funds if prices jump up.

## TWO FACES OF LIMITED PARTNERSHIPS

There's a difference between *public* and *private* limited partnership. A public program is just that—available to the general public. There may be suitability requirements for investors, but the standards tend to be low. Investors who earn as little as $30,000 a year can qualify for many public partnerships.

The low suitability standard ("warm and breathing") indicates relatively low risks. Public partnerships often acquire properties with little or no leverage, or they make well-secured loans. They are large—a $50 million "raise" is common, and some raise as much as $500 million. Consequently, they are well-diversified. Some public partnerships are "blind pools," as we described above.

Private placements, on the other hand, tend to have higher suitability standards. In many private deals, investors need a $200,000 income or a $1 million net worth to qualify. The tougher requirement indicates a high-risk investment. Prior to tax reform, most tax shelters were private placements. Today private placements aren't as tax-oriented, but they tend to be speculative. Investors take high risks—perhaps they help finance a new restaurant chain—in return for the chance of earning rewards a public deal is not likely to provide.

## A LOOK AT THE DARK SIDE

Limited partnerships are neither better nor worse than mutual funds. Although they have advantages (no corporate income tax, direct business participation), there also are disadvantages, especially illiquidity and high loads.

Limited partnership investors are routinely warned that there is no secondary market for their interests. You can't sell your piece of a limited partnership in the same way you can sell a share of IBM or Fidelity Magellan. However, if your limited partnership has genuine value—if it's paying cash distributions, for example—you can find a buyer for it. The nature of illiquidity is that you may have to take a steep discount if you want to cash out. But the vast majority of limited partnership investors, well over 90 percent, hold onto their interests until the partnerships terminate. They are truly long-term commitments.

Every limited partnership is a custom deal. It needs new legal opinions, new offering materials, new sales literature. Virtually all limited partnerships have sales loads. Thus, only 80 or 90 cents of the dollar you invest in a limited partnership is likely to go into the deal. An open-ended mutual fund, on the other hand, keeps selling its standard deal. Many funds sell directly, eliminating sales commissions. Thus, the initial load on a mutual fund is likely to be lower than the front-load on a limited partnership.

Annual costs, too, are likely to be higher with a limited partnership than they are with a mutual fund. In a partnership, management costs are paid directly. In a mutual fund, management costs (of the businesses in which you're ultimately investing) are paid by the companies that issue the stocks or bonds. Funds charge only relatively small administrative fees. Similarly, nothing in a mutual fund is comparable to a limited partnership's "back-end" fees to the general partner. Thus, limited partnerships appear to be more expensive than mutual funds. (The costs are not really comparable because other levels of management—corporate executives—are paid when you invest in a mutual fund.)

## HOW HAVE LIMITED PARTNERSHIPS PERFORMED?

It has become fashionable in some circles for investment advisers to scorn limited partnerships. The mainstream press has largely echoed their complaints. *Forbes* (April 21, 1986), for example, asks "But where are the customers' mansions?" Money magazine (December 1987) runs an article on "Limited partnerships' drastically limited performance" one month; the next month, *Money* (January 1988) quotes a so-called real estate expert that limited partnerships "generally stink." At the root of this disdain is the contention that heavily-loaded limited partnerships rip investors off and there's no chance for profitability.

The debate over limited partnership loads misses the point. It's not how much you pay someone else that matters; it's what he or she does for you.

A short history of limited partnerships provides some perspective. As investment partnerships, they were first used mainly as tax shelters. Fees were high, partly because of the legal work involved and partly because sponsors charged all the traffic would bear. When investors made money on tax savings alone, who begrudged the sponsor his fee?

In the early and mid-1970s, profit-oriented limited partnerships first became widely available, mainly in real estate and oil and gas. Again, fees were high, as a carry-over from the tax shelter business and because of the expenses involved in a broad public offering. At the time, though, inflation pushed up the prices of oil and real estate. Investors made money, and complaints were few.

In the 1980s, the limited partnership business expanded. More sponsors offered more deals in more types of businesses. Because of increased competition and increased scrutiny, loads came down. Instead of 60 to 70 percent of an investor's money going to work for him, 80 to 90 percent became the norm.

However, the 1980s were not favorable years for limited partnership investing, no matter what kinds of loads were used. First, oil prices collapsed just as oil and gas partnerships were raising record amounts of money. With few exceptions, oil and gas partnerships formed in the early 1980s were disasters. Investors bought high and sold low. If they leveraged their investments, borrowing money at peak interest rates, the damage was even worse.

Real estate, too, went into a cyclical downturn. Especially in the oil-producing states, where many partnerships bought properties, values plummeted. The leverage made things worse for many partnerships.

## NOT ALL GLOOM AND DOOM

There have been some bright spots, though. Many real estate partnerships that avoided the Sunbelt and concentrated on the Northeast, Midwest, and Hawaii, did well in the 1980s. Low-risk partnerships, oriented toward producing steady cash flow, generated fair to good performances. Those are the kinds of partnerships we will be discussing in the next chapters.

Some limited partnerships have done extremely well. Cable TV deals, by and large, have amply rewarded investors because the industry has prospered in the last few years. Despite the loads, limited partners made money.

There's really no such thing as a no-load investment. If you decide to invest in real estate directly, you'll spend time and money searching for the right property. If you make an acquisition, there will be legal, evaluation, and closing costs. The mountain cabin you buy for $100,000 actually costs $105,000 or $110,000 or more when you add everything up.

It's not always outrageous to invest $110,000 in a real estate partnership and own $88,000 worth of property if you have a 20 percent front-load. Sure, you're paying someone else more than

144     *Partners-in-Cash*

you would have spent if you did it yourself. Do-it-yourselfers can
achieve a higher return if they have the talent and the inclination.

But not every investor can do it alone, or wants to. For those
investors, a limited partnership may be the only way to include
certain types of assets in their portfolio. The people who today hold
their noses while they point at limited partnerships would have
been in a much different posture in the economic circumstances of
the late 1970s. And who knows what the 1990s will bring?

It's the investment climate, not the load structure, that will
make or break a partnership investment. If you want to be directly
involved in real estate, oil and gas, cable TV, or equipment leasing,
limited partnerships may be the only reasonable way into the
game. Don't be afraid as long as you know the basics and you work
with an adviser you trust. The key question to ask: Has the general partner made real (i.e., cash) profits for his limiteds in previous ventures?

## KEEPING YOUR BALANCE

Most investors should have a balanced portfolio. They should hold
some financial assets, such as stocks and bonds, for times when
inflation and interest rates are low. They should hold some real
or hard assets, such as real estate or oil and gas, for protection
against inflation.

If you want a manager for your financial assets, you are probably
best served in a mutual fund. If you want a manager for passive
business interests, a limited partnership may be appropriate. In the
next few chapters, we'll describe partnerships that are capable of
generating immediate cash flow. Many of these partnerships also
offer the potential for increasing cash flow and for capital appreciation as well.

### Summary

*Pros:*
- Access to certain types of investments. For investors who
  want a direct play in real estate, or in other types of businesses, limited partnerships may provide the only way without a huge investment of time and money.

- Inflation protection. Limited partnerships may do well in inflationary times, while financial assets likely will be in trouble.

- Size. Limited partnerships tend to be smaller and more focused than mutual funds, giving investors a better idea of how their money will be spent.

- Taxation. Limited partnerships avoid the corporate income tax, dramatically reducing the total tax bite. Distributions may be partially or totally tax-deferred.

- Stability. Limited partnerships don't crash in one day.

*Cons:*

- Illiquidity. Limited partnerships generally lock you in for 10 years or more. To sell earlier, you have to accept a discount.

- Economic vulnerability. If the business sector in which your partnership is involved (such as oil drilling) hits the skids, your investment will go down, too.

- Costs. A limited partnership is a costly way to organize and run a business. Operating results have to be very good to make up for the sponsor's compensation.

- Complexity. Often, the offering documents intimidate investors. You may have to rely heavily on your broker, accountant, attorney, or financial planner.

*Recommendation:*

Ten to 30 percent of your portfolio should be in investment real estate. Unless you're prepared to devote the necessary effort to direct property ownership, limited partnerships are the most sensible way to own real estate. Other types of limited partnerships are suitable for investors who are willing to bear above-average risks, and who fear future inflation. Usually, no more than 10 percent of your portfolio should be in nonreal estate partnerships.

Proceed carefully before investing in a partnership because getting out isn't easy. Plan on staying in for the entire holding period. Read the offering materials and question your adviser. You are looking for evidence that the sponsor is financially strong, with a record of making money for investors.

# 15

# Mortgage Partnerships: Low-Risk Real Estate Deals

Real estate is by far the most common limited partnership investment. In recent years, about $13 billion per year has been invested in all types of public limited partnerships. Between 50 and 60 percent of the total went into real estate.

Real estate is the leader even though the past few years have been rough on some real estate partnerships. Over the long term, real estate has more than held its own against stocks, bonds, gems, gold, antiques, bank accounts, and so on. Most investors want real estate in their portfolio. Owning real estate is certainly one aspect of The American Dream.

Not every investor, however, wants to own and manage a building. For those who would rather hold real estate passively, limited partnerships can be ideal. You receive tax advantages, growth potential, and high current cash flow. But with real estate still in the "top dog" position, investors should be extra cautious about how they invest their money.

## THE THREE CATEGORIES OF REAL ESTATE PARTNERSHIPS

If you are in the market for a real estate limited partnership, you should know what type of partnership to look for. All partnerships

146

fall into one of three groups: mortgage partnerships, all-cash ownership partnerships, and leveraged ownership partnerships.

## MORTGAGE PARTNERSHIPS MAY
## OFFER PARTICIPATION

Suppose a business associate wants to buy a local apartment building. When he goes to the bank, the loan officer looks over the property, the associate's financial statement, and so on. Sure, says the loan officer. You qualify for our standard fixed-rate loan, now at 10 percent.

That night, over a drink after work, your associate tells you his story. As it happens, you have as much money as he needs to borrow, on deposit at the same bank. Your CD is about to expire. If you decide to roll it over, you'll probably earn about 6 percent on a new CD.

It doesn't take much for minds to meet. You loan him the money at 8 percent, with a mortgage on the building securing the loan. The bank is squeezed out. You earn 8 rather than 6 percent; his interest is 8 instead of 10 percent. Everybody wins except the bank.

In essence, that's how mortgage partnerships work. Money is raised from thousands of investors, some of whom contribute as little as $1,000. Altogether, $100 million or more may be raised. The money is loaned to someone who wants to develop real estate or who wants to buy an existing property. Partnerships make several loans, a dozen or more loans in larger partnerships.

The borrowers pay interest to the partnership, which passes the interest through to the limited partners. Mortgage partnerships are similar to Ginnie Mae mutual funds. You put up money to be used in real estate loans and collect the interest.

Ginnie Mae mutual funds have some advantages over mortgage partnerships. Initial yields tend to be higher with Ginnie Maes. In addition, Ginnie Maes are backed by the federal government. There's no risk of default. That's not the case when your mortgage partnership loans money to buy an office building or to build a shopping center.

Nevertheless, many investors are better off in a participating mortgage limited partnership than in a Ginnie Mae fund. Most mortgage partnerships get their edge by making *participating* mortgages. That is, they are entitled to share in the growth of the underlying property.

Suppose a mortgage partnership makes a loan to help finance the purchase of a shopping center for $5 million. The loan contract calls for a 10 percent participation. The shopping center is sold for $10 million a few years later. That's a $5 million profit, and the mortgage partnership collects $500,000.

In some cases, a mortgage partnership will share in appreciation right away, not just when the property is sold. Suppose the shopping center's net income from operations is $500,000 in the year the loan is made. The next year, net income goes up to $550,000 for a $50,000 increase. The mortgage partnership may receive an extra $5,000 as its 10 percent participation.

Naturally, the buyer of the shopping center will not be eager to give up 10 percent of his profits. There must be a reason for him to do so. Generally, he borrows from a mortgage partnership and gives up a participation because he can get a better deal than he would from the local S&L.

This better deal may simply be a quicker loan, without all the red tape. It may be a loan at a slightly lower interest rate. Or it may be the ability to make partial payments. Suppose he's borrowing from a mortgage partnership at 10 percent. He may be required to pay only 7 percent currently. The other 3 percent is added to the loan balance for repayment later. Typically, a mortgage partnership makes each loan on a case-by-case basis, negotiating the best deal it can get.

## HOW MORTGAGE PARTNERSHIPS DIFFER

For the investor in a mortgage partnership, the result looks something like this. You get a decent current yield, right from the start, that is likely to be comparable to what you would earn from a 10-year Treasury bond.

However, inflation and rising interest rates will devalue the T-bond; the real estate participation is likely to offset the damage, or even put you ahead. Therefore, mortgage partnerships can give you cash now plus a "kicker" to protect against future inflation.

However, all mortgage partnerships are not the same. They differ greatly, especially in the safety of the loans they make. As

*Purchase*

| | |
|---|---|
| Purchase price | $20 million |
| Down payment | $ 4 million |
| First mortgage | $12 million |
| Second mortgage | $ 4 million |

*Foreclosure*

| | |
|---|---|
| Foreclosure sale price | $14 million |
| Return to first mortgage lender | $12 million |
| Gain or loss | 0 |
| Return to second mortgage lender | $ 2 million |
| Gain or loss | ($ 2 million) |

you might expect, the safer the mortgage partnership the lower the ultimate yield you can expect.

Some mortgage partnerships are ultra-safe. They only invest in mortgages that are backed by Ginnie Mae, the Federal Housing Administration (FHA), or some other federal agency. Other partnerships arrange private guarantees for their loans.

Some mortgage partnerships look for safety by making "first" mortgage loans. That is, in case a borrower can't pay a mortgage debt, the property will be taken and sold. The holder of the first mortgage is first in line to get money out of the sale proceeds.

"Junior" mortgages are riskier. Suppose an investor can borrow $12 million from an S&L to buy a $20 million office building, but he really wants to borrow $16 million. He might take out a $12 million first mortgage and a $4 million second mortgage. As the name suggests, the lender who makes the second mortgage has to wait behind the first mortgage lender.

Suppose the buyer can't find tenants for his office building and can't pay his debts, and the lenders foreclose and re-sell the building, realizing only $14 million. The holder of the $12 million first mortgage gets full recovery. The second-mortgage holder gets what's left—$2 million. He is left with a $2 million loss.

## WHY LOAN-TO-VALUE RATIOS ARE CRUCIAL

Investors in mortgage partnerships should be familiar with the "loan-to-value" concept. Even though it sounds daunting, it's vital for evaluating the safety of any mortgage investment. This ratio simply compares a property's total debt to its worth. The lower the ratio, the safer the loans.

In the example of a $20 million office building, a $12 million first mortgage represents a 60 percent loan-to-value ratio. When the $4 million second mortgage is added, the ratio increases to 80 percent. When the foreclosed property was sold for only $14 million (70 percent of the $20 million original value), the first mortgage holders were made whole while the second mortgage holders lost half their principal.

Most public limited partnerships have a policy about loan-to-value ratios in the prospectus. Be sure to know this policy when you're considering an investment.

Some mortgage partnerships make third mortgages or "wraparound" loans, a more complicated type of financing. All of these loans are junior to first mortgages, and hence are riskier. Similarly, some mortgage partnerships make loans to finance properties under construction. That's riskier than lending money against an existing building that's already occupied. The riskier the loans, the higher the yields you can expect.

Recently, when new Ginnie Maes were yielding around 10 percent, new mortgage partnerships were paying from 6 to 12 percent the first year. Over the life of the partnership, typically 10 to 15 years, the yield to investors is expected to be 10 to 13 percent per year, assuming the sponsors' projections hold up. These are just projections, not guarantees. It's tough to tell what will happen next month, let alone over 10 to 15 years.

Some mortgage partnerships are hybrids: Half of the money goes to make loans while the other half goes to buy property. The loans provide high initial cash flow while property ownership may generate more inflation protection and growth potential than partnerships that only make mortgage loans.

## NOW FOR THE FANCY STUFF

Other mortgage partnerships come with "bells and whistles," but they're easy enough to understand once you grasp the basics. For instance, there are *zero-coupon* mortgage partnerships, where the partnership makes loans and expects no interest payments for the next 10 to 12 years.

What's really happening? It's as if the borrower pays interest every month, but the partnership relends him the interest again. The risk increases as you go along, because the loan balance gets bigger. The property may have to keep appreciating, too. If the loan balance ever gets so large that it exceeds the property's value, the borrower will walk away without repaying.

On the positive side, the unpaid interest earns interest at the mortgage rate. Zero-coupon mortgages are called "Pac-Man" mortgages because the interest buildup eats away the owner's equity.

Some zero-coupon mortgage partnerships are among the highest-yielding entries in this category, provided the mortgages are paid off. A $10,000 investment in 1989 may generate nothing for 13 years, and then a $40,000 lump-sum in 2002. That is a 12 percent compound yield before any bonuses from property appreciation.

Another variation is the tax-exempt mortgage partnership. Here, some juggling is done so that the partnership actually lends money to a local government agency, rather than directly to a real estate buyer or developer. The partnership holds *revenue bonds,* which yield tax-exempt interest, like municipal bonds. There's also a participation feature.

Tax-exempt mortgage partnerships tend to be on the low end of the yield range. However, all of the money is free from federal income taxes. So the after-tax yield may be higher for some investors. In addition, these partnerships may earn a higher total yield than comparable municipal bonds, especially during periods of inflation.

## LOW RISKS, LOW RETURNS

How do participating mortgage partnerships stack up? They are sold mainly to conservative investors for tax-exempt retirement plans. The 1986 tax law makes them more attractive to conventional investors because the income will be taxed at a lower rate.

With the exception of tax-exempt mortgage partnerships, all the income from a mortgage partnership is fully taxable. There are no real estate tax benefits. Buying these funds for a retirement fund enables you to shelter that income. Outside a retirement plan, a 10 to 13 percent return on a mortgage partnership may mean a 7 to 9 percent return after-tax.

Mortgage partnerships provide several advantages. They deliver initial cash flow that's comparable to what you would get with other conservative investments, such as CDs or Ginnie Maes. Their participation feature, however, can give them an edge. Yields can grow, and the investment may appreciate.

It's true that mortgage funds generally don't have the full government guarantee of a bank CD or a Ginnie Mae. But mortgage lending historically has been a safe investment. Loans are secured by real estate, and buildings don't disappear. If you're adverse to taking any risks, there are partnerships that invest in federally-backed mortgages. Otherwise, a cautious approach to loan-to-value ratios should provide ample safety. As usual, the quality of the sponsor is vital. Invest with one experienced in real estate lending.

Apart from default risk, you have interest-rate risk, as with any loan-type investment. If rates rise, the mortgage interest you receive will be less appealing. The offset you get from your real estate participation may or may not be enough to protect you from interest rate losses. Some partnerships offer larger participations while others focus more on initial yields.

## Summary

*Pros:*

- High yields. Cash flow ranges from CD or T-bill equivalents, on low-risk partnerships, to returns that rival junk bonds in the riskier deals.
- Low risks. Most mortgage partnerships offer safety of principal because the mortgages are secured by real estate.
- Upside potential. Unlike bonds, mortgage partnerships may generate growing yields if the real estate prospers. There may be inflation protection, too.
- Liquidity. Among limited partnerships, mortgage deals may be the most liquid. They largely trade like bonds, based on current yield.

*Cons:*

- Limited potential. Mortgage partnerships are like any low-risk investment. You cut your upside when you reduce your risks. You won't achieve spectacular results.
- Complexity. Because there may be two dozen mortgage partnerships on the market, it's difficult to pick the one that's

right. Some may be too conservative while others take risks that you won't accept.

- Interest-rate exposure. If inflation and interest rates shoot up, your real estate participation may not compensate for your lagging yield.
- Taxes. All income from mortgage partnerships is fully taxable (except for partnerships that buy tax-exempt revenue bonds).

*Recommendation:*

Mortgage loan partnerships are part bond, part real estate. That's what makes them flexible and suitable for many investors. During the 1980s, while many real estate ownership partnerships ran into trouble, mortgage programs generally provided consistent returns well in excess of inflation.

If you're an extremely conservative investor, and high current yield is a top priority, you can use mortgage loan partnerships for the real estate sector of your portfolio. If you're a more aggressive investor, primarily concerned with protecting yourself against inflation, mortgage partnerships can replace bonds in your portfolio.

In either case, mortgage partnerships (except for tax-exempt funds) are best suited for tax-exempt pension plans. In or out of a pension plan, you should make an effort to reinvest all distributions in a money market fund, bank account, or mutual fund.

# 16

# Safety First: All-Cash Real Estate

Aside from making participating mortgage loans (see Chapter 15), there's another low-risk way to invest in real estate. You can find a small apartment building, for example, and buy it outright. All cash, no mortgages.

Why is this so safe? Because there's no lender holding a mortgage on your property. There's no monthly debt service to pay. And there's no one to foreclose in case you miss a payment.

As long as you meet the regular expenses (maintenance, taxes, insurance), you can hold on to your property. You may break even if only 30 percent of the building is rented. About the worst that can happen is that when you sell you are forced to take less than you paid for it. You won't get wiped out.

All-cash properties may be high-cash properties. With no debt service to cover, cash goes to you instead of to a bank. Suppose you buy a property with a true "9 cap rate." That is, the property's net income is 9 percent of what you pay for it. With no mortgage interest, you can keep the whole 9 percent.

Even a small office building may cost a couple of million dollars. You probably don't have that kind of ready cash. So you get together a few friends (preferably rich ones) and pool your money to buy the building.

However, since none of the investors wants to manage the building, you form a limited partnership. The investors are limited partners while a general partner manages the property. You pay the g.p. a fee while you split the rest of the cash pro rata.

| Investment | $1 |
|---|---|
| Front load (15%) | 15 cents |
| Amount used to buy real estate | 85 cents |
| Real estate yield | 10% |
| Cash flow | 8.5 cents |
| Cash flow return | 8.5% |

## CHECKING THE MATH

That's how an unleveraged limited partnership takes shape. Fortunately for most investors, these partnerships tend to be public rather than private. As we mentioned above, public limited partnerships are widely available, requiring a minimum investment of only a few thousand dollars. They generally raise many millions of dollars to buy several properties.

What do the numbers look like in an all-cash ownership partnership? Let's assume that the partnership buys existing, fully occupied buildings and that the g.p. is a real estate pro. He should be able to buy properties yielding 9 or 10 percent in today's market. However, only 80 or 90 percent of the invested dollars are actually going to buy properties because of the front-end load.

In simple terms, you invest $1 in an all-cash partnership. Of that $1, 85 cents may actually be used to buy real estate, which yields 10 percent. The cash flow is 8.5 cents (10 percent of 85 cents), or 8.5 percent of the $1 investment. That's how a 10 percent investment in real estate pays 8.5 percent.

Moreover, that only counts the front-end load. There are ongoing management fees, too. In practice, most all-cash partnerships produce an initial cash return of 5 to 8 percent.

## GOING FOR GROWTH

As mentioned before, mortgage partnerships have higher yields, probably 6 to 12 percent. Why should anyone invest in an all-cash ownership deal?

Mainly because the growth potential is greater. Rents on the properties may increase, and cash distributions can go up. Assuming a moderate inflation rate of 4 to 5 percent a year, which most real estate sponsors assume, cash distributions may inch up from an initial 6 to 6.5 percent, 7 percent, 7.5 percent, and so on, over the years. Eventually, the yield catches up to and surpasses the yield from a mortgage partnership.

If the cash distributions go up, the value of the properties is likely to rise as well. Suppose a 6 percent yield becomes a 12 percent yield over a 10- or 12-year partnership life. The sale of the properties is likely to return $2 for every $1 invested.

Doubling your money over 10 or 12 years equals a 6 or 7 percent compound return. Cash distributions that grow from 6 to 12 percent average out to about 9 percent per year. Once you account for the sponsor's cut, you may receive the equivalent of 12 to 15 percent compound return, per year, pre-tax. That is 8 to 11 percent after-tax, a touch higher than the pre-tax 10 to 13 percent mortgage partnerships are expected to generate. Of course there are no guarantees. In fact, the return is more speculative because so much depends on property appreciation.

All-cash ownership partnerships have tax advantages, too. Suppose a $100 million partnership earns enough cash to distribute $7 million to its investors, or 7 percent. The partnership may also deduct $3 million for depreciation, leaving $4 million in taxable income. If you are a $10,000 investor, you may receive $700 in cash but only have $400 in taxable income. If you are in a 30 percent tax bracket, you will pay $120 in taxes (30 percent times $400) and receive $580 for a 5.8 percent after-tax yield. (See page 157.)

## OWNING REAL ESTATE FOR
## INFLATION PROTECTION

If your properties grow slowly, you are better off in a mortgage partnership. Mortgage partnerships generally have the initial advantage, and ownership partnerships need growth to catch up. But if inflation reaccelerates, all-cash ownership partnerships are likely to turn in superior performances.

As an illustration, look at what may be the oldest sponsor of all-cash ownership partnerships, Realty Income Corp., known as R.I.C. In R.I.C. deals, the partnership buys properties and leases them to fast-food restaurants, child-care centers, and so on. The stores pay the partnership a percentage of their sales proceeds as rent.

|                              |                | *$10,000 Investor* |
|------------------------------|----------------|--------------------|
| Money raised by partnership  | $100 million   |                    |
| Cash flow to investors       | $7 million     | $700               |
| Cash-on-cash return          | 7%             | 7%                 |
| Depreciation deductions      | $3 million     | $300               |
| Taxable income               | $4 million     | $400               |
| Taxes @ 30%                  |                | $120               |
| After-tax cash flow          |                | $580               |
| After-tax return             |                | 5.8%               |

The first four R.I.C. partnerships were formed in 1970 and 1971. They began yielding 12 percent to investors, the going rate for what was then a new form of investment. By 1978, the yields had risen modestly, from 13 percent in one partnership to 19 percent in another.

The inflationary surge of the late 1970s and early 1980s began to push up the prices of tacos and hamburgers. By 1987, the same four partnerships were paying 21, 35, 52, and 55 percent per year to the original investors. Any partner who wanted to sell could get $21,000 to $55,000 for an original $10,000 investment.

We are not recommending R.I.C.'s partnerships, although they are well regarded. However, they are an example of how all-cash ownership partnerships can provide growth and protection against a future explosion in inflation. They also demonstrate why real estate investors should take a long-term view. If you go into an all-cash partnership, for example, with a 15 percent front-load (about average) it will take three years of 5 percent growth just to break even.

## BUYING BLIND

Besides the long holding period, what are the disadvantages of all-cash ownership partnerships? Many of them are blind pools. Few sponsors have the financial resources to tie up $50 or $100 million worth of properties before raising the money from the public. The usual procedure is to raise the money, and then buy the properties. Investors may have a general idea of how the money will be spent— for example, the sponsor will say it's going to buy existing office buildings and shopping centers. But they really don't know what they're getting.

There's a way to get around this shortcoming. Real estate public partnerships typically have thousands of investors. Although most invest for the long term, there are always some people who want to cash out soon. If you work with a savvy broker or financial planner, you can buy partnership units from the original investors at a negotiated price.

Buying on the secondary market allows you to wait until the properties are purchased and all of the initial kinks are worked out. You often can get higher cash flow than with a startup partnership.

Another disadvantage of the all-cash ownership partnership is its low reward potential. The partnerships are designed with safety in mind—no mortgage debt. To get safety, you give up some upside. While some all-cash partnerships, such as the early R.I.C. deals, have performed very well, the returns would have been even higher with leverage.

## DEFERRED LEVERAGE DEALS

Some partnerships attempt to deliver the low risks of all-cash plus the reward potential of leverage. These partnerships are unleveraged, going in, but borrow money after operations have stabilized, generally in about five years.

Take as an example an unleveraged partnership that owns a restaurant. It raises $10 million, pays a 15 percent load, and places the other 85 percent into the restaurant. Once the restaurant is

| | |
|---|---|
| Partnership money raised | $10.0 million |
| Front load (15%) | $ 1.5 million |
| Real estate investment | $ 8.5 million |
| Fifth year net operating income | $900,000 |
| Property re-sale value | $12.0 million |
| Mortgage loan | $ 7.5 million |
| Loan-to-value ratio ($7.5 million/$12 million) | 62.5% |
| Mortgage interest (@ 10%) | $750,000 |
| Cash flow (income minus mortgage interest) | $150,000 |
| Fees to sponsor from mortgage financing | $500,000 |
| Available for distribution | $ 7.0 million |
| Distribution to $10,000 investor | $7,000 |
| Cash left "in the deal" | $3,000 |
| Cash flow after interest payment | $150 |
| Cash-on-cash return ($150/$3,000) | 5% |

open for business, investors receive 7 percent cash flow per year.

Five years later, the restaurant business is solid. Net operating income is $900,000 per year, and distributions are up to 9 percent per year. Based on comparable properties, and the operating results, the restaurant's resale value is about $12 million.

Suppose interest rates are relatively low, and 10 percent first-mortgage money is available. The general partner may take out a $7.5 million loan. This is conservative, because the loan-to-value ratio is 62.5 percent (the $7.5 million loan is 62.5 percent of the property's $12 million value). At 10 percent, annual interest on the mortgage is $750,000, which is well-covered by the restaurant's $900,000 in net income.

After various fees are taken out, $7 million of the $7.5 million loan may be distributed to investors. The investors get that money tax-free, as is the case with any loan. They're basically getting some of their money back. At the same time, though, the investors still own the properties.

A $10,000 investor, for example, receives a $7,000 payment, leaving him with only $3,000 "in the deal." At the same time, the partnership has only $150,000 to distribute, after paying mortgage interest. The $10,000 investor receives only $150 per year, down from $900.

Remember, though, that the investor now has only $3,000 in the deal, and his $150 distribution represents a 5 percent yield. If the distribution climbs up to $200, $300, $400, the investor's yield rises to 6.7, 10, 13.3 percent, etc. Now the investor has the benefit of leverage after the property has proven itself to be an income-generator.

## HEDGE YOUR MUNICIPAL BONDS

All-cash real estate partnerships are an alternative to municipal bonds. Like munis, they belong in the low-risk sector of your investment portfolio. They're designed to provide safety plus income rather than speculative profits.

Initial distributions from all-cash real estate today may be around 5 to 6 percent, after-tax. That's close to about what you would receive from a muni with a comparable holding period. The real estate probably is riskier, assuming investment in top-quality munis. But the munis will lose value in times of high interest rates and inflation, while real estate is likely to appreciate. In this situation, you may want to balance the munis in your portfolio with high-quality, all-cash real estate.

Within the category of all-cash real estate partnerships, there are dozens of choices on the market today. You can, for example, receive a higher return with a bit more risk by investing in a developmental partnership, where your money is used to develop new properties rather than purchasing old ones.

Because tenants aren't in place and construction costs lie ahead, investors face risks. In fact, you should look for a partnership with some kind of a guarantee against cost overruns. The sponsor, for example, might guarantee that the construction costs will be no more than 85 percent of the value of the completed real estate, as attested by independent appraisals, or he will refund the difference.

In return for taking risks, investors may receive the kind of profits that accrue when you "get in on the ground floor." One all-cash partnership, for example, recently purchased 40 acres near Lexington, Kentucky, for future development. Two weeks later, Toyota announced the construction plans for a major assembly plant nearby. The partnership already has had an offer that would give it a 135 percent profit on the deal.

## LOW-RISK DOESN'T MEAN NO-RISK

Every all-cash partnership does not bring a huge return. Buying real estate without a mortgage removes the risk of debt service, but there's still the risks of operating real estate. If the properties are in areas where there is widespread overbuilding, or if the local economies turn down, they may suffer from low occupancy rates. Or, they may earn lower rents than anticipated. Some all-cash partnerships projected 6 to 8 percent yields when they were sold, but have been able to distribute only 3 to 5 percent because of difficult real estate conditions during the 1980s.

## EVALUATING ALL-CASH REAL
## ESTATE PARTNERSHIPS

How can you tell when a partnership has the potential to achieve the results the sponsor promises? Unfortunately, you can't in most cases. Few investors know enough about real estate to choose the best partnerships.

That's why you work with a broker or a financial planner. It's his or her responsibility to exercise "due diligence" before selling you any type of investment, but especially a limited partnership interest.

"Due diligence" is a term with different meanings to different people, legally and practically. Essentially, it is the responsibility of the financial professional to investigate an investment before recommending it. In return for his sales commission, the broker or financial planner has a responsibility to help you avoid bad deals and select good ones.

Ask your financial adviser how much due diligence has been exercised in examining a particular venture, and by whom. The credentials of the sponsors should reflect years of experience in the type of real estate in the offering. If not, let them learn with someone else's money.

Who else is selling the deal? If a major brokerage firm with a large legal staff has okayed the offering, you can take some comfort.

Has your adviser—or someone from his organization—made a site visit? Even if it's a blind pool, with properties yet to be specified, your adviser can visit other properties from the sponsor's previous partnerships. Has someone talked to the tenants? To local banks? What makes them feel that this sponsor can deliver real estate profits?

Finally, don't be afraid to ask your adviser if he or she is putting money in the deal, alongside yours. That's the best way your broker or financial planner can demonstrate his confidence in the sponsor and in the partnership.

---

## Summary

*Pros:*

- Cash flow. Without a mortgage to pay off, partnerships generally can pay 5 to 8 percent, if they purchase existing properties.
- Low risks. With no mortgage, there's no lender to foreclose. Your property may break even with only 30 percent occupancy.
- Growth potential. Real estate rents can increase cash flow and property values.

- Inflation protection. Investors are direct real estate owners.
- Tax benefits. Depreciation deductions—non-cash losses— can be passed through.

*Cons:*

- Business risks. As a real estate owner, you are vulnerable to low occupancies, low rents, high costs, and so on.
- Limited potential. A successful all-cash partnership does not have the payoff of a successful leveraged deal.
- Long holding period. Making up for the sponsor's front load may take three years, requiring a long time horizon to realize meaningful results.
- Blind pools. Often, you don't know what properties you're buying.

*Recommendation:*

All-cash real estate partnerships are a step up the risk-reward scale from mortgage partnerships. They are not bond equivalents and don't belong in the bond sector of your portfolio. They're real estate investments, suitable for risk-averse investors. If you hold municipal bonds or bond funds, you may find these partnerships an offset in case of increasing inflation.

Don't buy an all-cash deal solely for the initial promised cash flow. Any sponsor can distribute 8 percent for the first year or two—just spend less on real estate and return the excess to investors. Be sure you choose a partnership for its long-term prospects.

Because depreciation deductions are wasted in a retirement plan, these partnerships work best outside such plans. However, aggressive investors—those who want to minimize bonds and bond-type holdings—may consider them for retirement plans. Before you buy a newly-offered deal, ask your broker or planner to shop the secondary market. You may find proven partnerships there, generating cash flow that is higher than the sponsor's new deal promises.

# 17

# Leveraged Real Estate Partnerships: Shooting for More Cash, Later

Suppose you have saved $30,000 and you want to buy a house. If you look for an all-cash buy, you probably won't find much in the $30,000 price range. However, if you qualify for a $70,000 mortgage from the local S&L, you could look for a $100,000 house, and the chances of finding what you want are greatly increased.

Of course assuming a mortgage is riskier. You may have to pay $600 a month just to keep your house. But it may be worth it to live in a $100,000 house rather than a $30,000 house. Virtually everybody buys real estate for their personal use this way, and leverage generally has paid off.

Suppose you want to sell your house two years later, and you get $110,000 from a buyer. On one level, that's a 10 percent profit—a $10,000 increase on a $100,000 purchase price. But you really have a 33 percent profit—a $10,000 gain on a $30,000 outlay.

## MORE THAN JUST TAX SHELTER

That's how leverage works in real estate investment properties as well as in personal homes. It's tougher to cover the monthly debt service, but leverage provides a higher return when property values go up.

Some people associate leverage in real estate with tax shelters. Now that shelters are less important, why use leverage?

163

It's true that some shelters abused leverage. Let's take an extreme example. You buy an office building for $1 million, but you pay only $10,000 in cash and get a $990,000 mortgage. Depreciation on the office building is $30,000 a year, and interest on the $990,000 mortgage is $99,000. That's $129,000 worth of deductions. If the building's net income is $90,000, there is a $39,000 loss for tax purposes. A $10,000 outlay provides a writeoff nearly four times as great.

The catch is obvious. How can you pay $99,000 in debt service if the building's net income is only $90,000? Most shelters solved this by accruing interest. That is, some of the interest was deducted right away but not really paid. The unpaid interest mounted up while the investors kept taking writeoffs. The only way investors could catch up was for inflation to soar. That didn't happen in the mid-1980s, and many highly-leveraged shelters went under, giving leveraged real estate a bad name.

## A RATIONAL VIEW

Now that tax reform has killed this type of deal, leverage in real estate can be viewed rationally. Leverage means borrowing money to buy properties. The more leverage you use, the more properties you buy. Leveraged partnerships may be either public—usually large, multi-property blind pools—or private—usually small deals to buy one specific property.

Loads in leveraged deals are usually higher than in non-leveraged deals because you're paying people to arrange the mortgages. If most real estate partnerships have 10 to 20 percent front-end loads, the 20 percent loads are likely to be in the leveraged deals.

Let's say a partnership raises $100 million. After the load, $80 million is left to buy real estate. If 50 percent leverage is used, $160 million worth of properties are bought. If 60 percent leverage is used, $200 million worth of real estate are acquired. And so on. It's hard to find a partnership today that would use over 80 percent leverage.

Buying more properties means you collect more rents. If the properties go up in value, you make more profits. On the other hand, you're paying interest for the use of the money used to buy the extra properties.

With these principles in mind, the math of using leverage is simple. First, be sure you can pay the interest. If the properties don't yield enough income to meet the monthly mortgage payments, you're in trouble. The lender will take the properties from you.

Second, calculate whether your leverage is paying off. You earn real estate profits from rents and from price appreciation. The cost of leverage is the interest that must be paid. If the interest cost is lower than the earnings, you win with leverage.

Back in the early 1980s, this was a tough call. Mortgage rates were commonly 15 to 18 percent, and even higher. Suppose you took out a 16 percent mortgage to buy a property that paid 9 percent in current operating income. You would need 7 percent annual growth just to break even. That's been the exception rather than the rule in the past few years.

Now, though, 10 percent mortgages are available. If you buy a property that yields 9 percent from rents alone, you're ahead with anything over 1 percent in annual growth.

## COMPARING LEVERAGED AND ALL-CASH DEALS

For example, suppose a $100 million all-cash partnership buys $90 million worth of properties, after loads. At a 9 percent yield, there are $8.1 million to distribute to investors. Another $100 million partnership has a 20 percent load, but it buys $200 million worth of properties, using a $120 million, 10 percent mortgage. The $200 million in properties generates $18 million in income at 9 percent, but the $12 million in mortgage interest drops the distribution to $6 million. The all-cash partnership is ahead by $2.1 million.

Let's say everything goes up 3 percent in the next year. The all-cash partnership is now distributing $8.343 million, up from $8.1 million the first year. Plus, the original $90 million worth of properties have grown in value to $92.7 million. Total return—cash flow plus appreciation—is about $11 million.

The leveraged properties' operating income also goes up 3 percent, from $18 million to $18.54 million. Because the $12 million debt service is fixed, the cash left for distribution grows from $6 million to $6.54 million. The cash flow gap is narrowing, and the $200 million worth of properties grows to $206 million. Thus, the leveraged properties' return—cash flow plus property appreciation—is over $12.5 million. That's better than the all-cash deal, even though the load is twice as great.

If properties appreciate at an even faster rate, whether 5 or 8 or 10 percent, the advantage becomes even greater. Leveraged properties outperform all-cash properties in a growth environment, as long as interest rates aren't too high.

## THE CONTRARIAN VIEWPOINT

Ironically, all-cash partnerships now are the most popular among investors. Leverage has a bad name, because of the experience with some tax shelters, and most people are avoiding it. Yet leverage makes more sense in the late 1980s, with interest rates comparatively low, than it did in the early 1980s, when rates were higher.

This is another case of "what everyone knows isn't worth knowing." If your general partner can buy real estate cheaply, and has staying power, leveraged real estate will pay off for investors. Look for a g.p. with a record of buying leveraged real estate and selling it at a profit; ask if investors are protected by refinancing old, high-rate mortgages at today's lower rates.

|  | All-Cash (Dollars in millions) | Leverage (Dollars in millions) |
|---|---|---|
| Money raised by partnership | $100 | $100 |
| Front load | $ 10 (10%) | $ 20 (20%) |
| Money for real estate | $ 90 | $ 80 |
| Mortgages | 0 | $120 |
| Real estate acquired | $ 90 | $200 |
| Yield from real estate | 9% | 9% |
| Net operating income | $ 8.1 | $ 18 |
| Mortgage interest (@ 10%) | 0 | $ 12 |
| Cash flow to distribute | $ 8.1 | $ 6 |
| Cash-on-cash return | 8.1% | 6% |
| *Second Year (assumes 3% growth rate)* | | |
| Net operating income | $ 8.343 | $ 18.54 |
| Mortgage interest (@ 10%) | 0 | $ 12 |
| Cash flow to distribute | $ 8.343 | $ 6.54 |
| Cash-on-cash return | 8.343% | 6.54% |
| Property appreciation (@ 3%) | $ 2.7 | $ 6 |
| Total return (Cash flow plus appreciation) | $ 11.043 | $ 12.54 |

## EMPHASIZING AFTER-TAX CASH FLOW

Cash-oriented investors may protest that they'd rather have the higher cash flow upfront, rather than depend on growth that may or may not come. However, the initial cash flow may be as great or greater, after-tax, with a leveraged partnership.

There are two reasons for this. First, buying more properties gives you more depreciation deductions. Second, all of the interest expense is deductible.

Let's go back to our example. Assume that annual depreciation equals 3 percent of the properties bought. Thus, the all-cash deal that distributes 8.1 percent in cash initially provides taxable income of 5.4 percent. The other 2.7 percent is sheltered by depreciating $90 million worth of properties. The after-tax cash flow is about 6.5 percent: you receive 8.1 percent but pay about 1.6 percent in taxes.

The leveraged partnership only yields 6 percent in cash the first year. But $6 million worth of depreciation (on $200 million worth of properties) and $12 million in interest expense completely offsets the $18 million in operating income. There is no tax to pay, and there is virtually no difference in after-tax cash flow to the taxable investor.

## CAN ZEROS BE A PLUS?

Some recent leveraged partnerships have advertised initial yields of 9 or 10 percent. How can this be done?

Often, they use some form of zero-coupon financing or accrued interest. This is the mirror image of the zero-coupon mortgage partnerships discussed earlier.

In our example, the partnership uses $120 million worth of debt to buy $200 million worth of properties. Suppose that the partnership actually uses two mortgages. One, for $80 million, pays 10 percent. The other, for $40 million, is zero-coupon, with no interest due.

Now there is $8 million in interest expense rather than $12 million. The extra $4 million can be distributed, raising the total distribution from $6 million to $10 million. Investors receive 10 percent cash flow rather than 6 percent. The tax picture remains the same—no tax liability—and the 10 percent return is not taxed immediately.

|                                                    | All-Cash       | Leverage       |
| -------------------------------------------------- | -------------- | -------------- |
| Money raised                                       | $100 million   | $100 million   |
| Mortgages                                          | 0              | $120 million   |
| Real estate acquired                               | $ 90 million   | $200 million   |
| Depreciation (@ 3%)                                | $  2.7 million | $  6 million   |
| Net operating income (NOI)                         | $  8.1 million | $ 18 million   |
| Mortgage interest (@ 10%)                          | 0              | $ 12 million   |
| Taxable income (NOI minus interest and depreciation): | $  5.4 million | 0           |
| Cash flow                                          | $  8.1 million | $  6 million   |
| Cash flow to $10,000 investor                      | $810           | $600           |
| Taxable income to $10,000 investor                 | $540           | 0              |
| Taxes @ 30%                                         | $162           | 0              |
| After-tax cash flow                                | $648           | $600           |
| Cash-on-cash return, after-tax                     | 6.48%          | 6%             |

The catch is that the unpaid interest compounds every year at the stated rate. If the rate is 10 percent, and the property is sold after 14 years, investors owe about $160 million on that $40 million mortgage in addition to the $80 million conventional mortgage. All $240 million will have to be paid before investors start dividing up any profit.

Essentially, investors in zero-coupon ownership deals are taking their profits now, and reducing their gains from property appreciation.

## HARD TIMES IN THE OILPATCH

Leveraged partnerships are risky. Even some experienced, reputable sponsors had troubles in recent years. They invested in Texas, Oklahoma, Colorado, Louisiana.

When the oil bust took the bounce out of these economies, many buildings lost tenants and rents sagged. In some cases, revenues couldn't cover the mortgage payments, and the properties were foreclosed. Investors may have thought they were diversifying, placing money into real estate as well as oil and gas, but they didn't have proper geographical diversification. Many public real estate partnerships formed from 1980–83 fell into this trap. Sponsors may have learned a lesson, but it has been a costly lesson for investors.

## BUYING RIGHT IS THE KEY

Whether you invest in real estate through a mortgage or an ownership partnership, leveraged or unleveraged, the key is to work with a first-rate sponsor. Good sponsors negotiate acquisitions rather than pay list price. In investing, money is made when you buy rather than when you sell.

Jerry K., for example, was in the market for an office building. He found a suitable building owned by a publicly-held corporation. After extensive negotiations, he reduced a $2.5 million asking price to $1.5 million.

Then, he heard that another buyer had stepped in with a $1.8 million offer. But Jerry discovered that the other buyer wanted to pay the $1.8 million later rather than sooner. In the meantime, an examination of the corporation's financial statements showed a need for cash right away.

So Jerry increased his offer to $1.6 million and convinced the company that $1.6 million now was better than $1.8 million deferred. He succeeded in buying the property for $1.6 million, 36 percent below the initial asking price. According to current appraisals and cash flow, he already has a handsome profit on the property.

When you're considering a real estate limited partnership, ask the sponsor for acquisition war stories such as this one. If the answers aren't satisfactory, ask the question of another sponsor.

———————— *Summary* ————————

*Pros:*

- Profit potential. You buy more real estate when you use leverage. The more you own, the greater your profits if things go right. Leveraged deals may return 15 percent or more, pre-tax, if you're in the right place at the right time.

- Inflation protection. If inflation heats up, few investments will perform as well as sound real estate purchased with leverage.

- Tax advantages. Owning more real estate gives you more depreciation deductions. When you borrow money to buy investment real estate, most or all of the interest is deductible. Thus, it's possible that cash flow is fully sheltered.

*Cons:*

- Risk of foreclosure. Investing with borrowed money is always risky. No matter how persuasive the sales pitch, put leveraged real estate in the high-risk sector of your portfolio because you can lose your property.
- Low cash flow. Paying debt service reduces the amount that's available for current distribution.
- Gimmicks. Some sponsors try to force up distributions artificially, by using techniques such as zero-coupon financing. Be sure you understand how the gimmicks work before investing.
- Losses are magnified. Just as leverage boosts profits on the way up, it can turn a poor investment into a disaster if the properties lose value.
- Illiquidity. If you want to get out of a leveraged deal early, expect to have to accept a stiff discount.

*Recommendation:*

Approach leveraged real estate with care. Stick with experienced sponsors and be sure you know what they are doing with your money. These investments are appropriate only for investors who already have a solid base of safe, income-producing vehicles. If you are well-covered, leveraged real estate may be your best hedge against future inflation.

Timing is vital. Invest in leveraged real estate when mortgage rates are low—say, under 12 percent. If you invest when rates are high, the debt service can destroy the deal. You will likely receive no cash distributions, or phoney ones, if you saddle your real estate with expensive debt. But if you invest when interest rates are around 10 percent, you are likely to get tax-sheltered cash flow as well as appreciation potential.

Leveraged real estate definitely belongs outside of a retirement plan. Inside, the tax benefits are wasted. Moreover, you may run into UBTI (for unrelated business taxable income, one of the perverse monsters of the "Infernal" Revenue Code). If the IRS thinks you are running an operating business with borrowed money inside a retirement plan profits will be taxed. You'll incur a tax obligation for what you thought was a tax-exempt retirement plan.

# 18

# Comparing Real Estate Deals

Evaluating real estate limited partnerships is like dicing a pickle. First, you make lengthwise cuts, dividing them into mortgage loan, all-cash ownership, or leveraged ownership partnerships. That's what we've done so far.

Second, you make the horizontal cuts to form the tiny bits of specific real estate partnerships. Within the leveraged category, for example, there may be a partnership that buys office buildings and one that buys hotels. By no means are they the same.

Before looking at specifics, there are a few more generalities we should examine. First, there's a great difference between investing in existing real estate and investing in real estate development. The return on an existing building is reasonably predictable. Tenants are in place, their leases can be examined, the building itself has a track record.

Development deals are more risky. There's no way of knowing when the real estate will be open for business, or what the costs will be. There's no assurance tenants will be found, or how soon, or how much they will be willing to pay.

Existing buildings can provide immediate cash flow. You buy a building today, collect rents tomorrow. Developmental real estate has a built-in lag. After formation of the partnership, its funds will probably be parked in T-bills or in a money market fund providing you with some cash flow, fully taxable. Once the money is drawn upon for construction, there's no current return. You'll have to wait until the tenants move in.

The fact that developmental real estate does not generate immediate cash flow does not necessarily mean it is a bad deal. More money may be made in the development stage because investors share in the developer's profits. If you take the risks of real estate development and the property turns out to be a commercial success, your earnings can be substantial.

## CATCHING CASH FLOW WITH NET LEASES

There's one more wrinkle to examine. Some real estate partnerships are promoted as *net lease* or *triple net lease.* These partnerships buy properties and turn them over to a tenant, relinquishing all management responsibilities. The tenant does everything, including paying all related expenses and sending the partnership a rent check.

There are two vastly different types of net lease deals. In one, a building is leased to one or to a few major corporations. The corporations promise to pay their rent, no matter what. These investments are called "bond-type" deals, and they are probably the safest of all real estate vehicles. If your office building is leased for 10 years to AT&T or GE, for example, there's little risk that you won't collect your expected cash flow.

There are a few drawbacks to this type of net lease partnership. Because of their safety, lease payments tend to be low. You should receive a competitive current return and have some sort of *escalation clause* that will enable the lease income to go up in future years.

Also, you should have the opportunity to make some money out of the building's appreciation. Even if the tenant has the option to buy the property at a future date, the tenant should be required to pay fair market value, as determined by an independent appraiser.

At the other end of the scale, some partnerships net lease properties to tenants whose credit quality isn't as good. Fast-food chain franchisees are a common example as are hotels, auto service centers, and the like.

Here, the concerns are the opposite from the kind of net lease deal just described. Rents are usually set at a high level to begin with, and often they are fully adjusted for inflation. Generally, rents are tied to the store or restaurant's sales volume.

The weak spot, though, lies in the credit quality of the tenant. If he goes out of business, you won't collect any cash while the sponsor looks for a new tenant to occupy the storefront. You need a sponsor with experience in dealing with these types of tenants.

Development, existing property, net lease—each type of deal can apply to virtually any type of real estate. Here are the main property categories found in real estate limited partnerships.

## Office Buildings

Of all the flavors of real estate, office buildings are vanilla, before you add the fudge or the cherries or the chocolate chips. Office buildings are the benchmark against which other types of properties are judged. When major institutional investors—insurance companies, pension funds—buy real estate, they usually purchase office buildings.

Generally, the tenants in an office building are corporations with medium- and long-term leases. Even when the leases run out, the tenants tend to stick around. Changing a corporation's address is a big problem and expense—everything from employee downtime on moving day to decorating new offices to reprinting all the stationery.

Therefore, office building investments tend to be predictable. There's some inflation protection, but higher rents may not start immediately. Many real estate investors like to buy buildings in which tenant leases are at lower rents per square foot than rents in nearby offices, and the leases are about to expire. Thus, a sharp increase in cash flow can be expected as new leases are signed at higher rent levels.

Currently, office buildings suffer from their own popularity. During the early and mid-1980s, there was a surge in office construction. Nearly every market is oversaturated, and the phrase "see-through" office buildings has come to stand for unoccupied high-rises. Naturally, you can't expect cash flow from an empty office building. More than that, the presence of the excess space depresses rents in other buildings that have tenants. Lower rents are welcomed by tenant companies but they mean less cash flow for real estate investors.

The office market in Denver, for example, is so glutted that landlords recently held an auction. Some prime office space was rented for as little as 35 cents per square foot. In Houston, there are some beautiful new office buildings without a single car in the parking lot.

That's not really surprising. A few years ago, virtually every real estate syndicator was offering deals with Houston and Denver properties. The Sunbelt was "in," so that's what investors would buy. Some sponsors' idea of diversification was to buy buildings in six Texas cities. Overbuilding led to today's glut.

But there are opportunities in the office market today. Although Houston is overbuilt, Westchester County, New York is not. Many areas of the Northeast, bypassed during the Sunbelt stampede, have low vacancy rates. That's particularly true once you go beyond the "glamorous" urban areas to suburbs and small towns.

Special situations can be appealing, too. In one recent offering, the sponsor—a billion-dollar company—was to be a major tenant in a new California office building. Investors assumed that the sponsor, not wanting to be the only tenant in the building, would make every effort to speed rent-up. So far, the deal is doing as well as the sponsors anticipated.

### Shopping Centers

Compared with office buildings, shopping centers have less stability but more inflation protection. Most centers have a mix of "anchor" stores and "local" tenants. Depending on your mix, you can adjust your risk/reward expectations.

Anchor tenants range from department stores in a major regional mall to a supermarket in a tiny "strip" center. Most investors like their anchor tenants to be nationally known, financially strong retailers on long-term leases. Their presence gives the mall long-term stability, attracting shoppers and pulling in other tenants. In leveraged deals, the lease income from the anchors should be enough to cover the debt service.

Anchor tenants, however, negotiate from strength. Developers want to have Macy's or Wal-Mart in their mall. Therefore, the rents paid by the anchors are generally low per square foot. To compensate, developers require that local tenants pay higher rents. These local tenants generally have "overage" clauses in their rents, too. That is, once sales go over a certain level, part of the increase is added to the monthly rent.

As you can see, the tenant mix is crucial. If there is a high proportion of nationally known retailers, the yield is likely to be lower but the cash flow more certain. With more local tenants in the mix, there's higher yield but also more risk, because local tenants may come and go as often as holiday specials.

Inflation protection is probably the outstanding feature of a shopping center investment. Inflation means rising prices. As prices rise, so will the gross volume of virtually every retail store, even if profits don't keep pace. Shopping center investors usually get a return that goes up directly with increases in retail sale volume.

*Glamour May Not Be Great*

Shopping centers have held up fairly well in the 1980s. Especially among centers with national anchors, overbuilding hasn't occurred, at least not to the same extent as in office buildings. Major shopping centers usually aren't built "on spec." Lenders won't advance funds until anchor tenants are in place, and major retailers generally stay out of areas if they fear overcrowding.

Some shopping center sponsors believe that less glamorous properties are better buys. They contend that investors overpay for the regional "destination" malls, with six anchors and fireworks every Saturday night. On a straight-yield basis, investors may well do better with strip centers anchored by discounters or chain drugstores.

It's hard to believe, though, that investors are consistently irrational. It's more likely that strip centers have higher initial yields than malls because mall investors are willing to pay more for what they perceive to be the long-term strength of investing in Class A real estate.

Nevertheless, even Class B or Class C real estate can pay off in the right circumstances. One offering, for example, involved a strip center in a town where the smell of a local paper mill seemed unbearable. Few investors would want to live there or work there. However, the town was growing, and the shopping center was on the right side of town. After a four-year holding period, investors sold out for an attractive profit.

### Apartments

In terms of the number of offerings, if not dollars raised, apartments are probably the most popular type of property for limited partnerships. Sponsors like to sell apartment deals; they offer high yields and generous tax benefits.

The case for apartments rests on demographics. The size of American households is getting smaller, thanks to divorce, unmarried couples living together, married couples who decide not to have children, people living alone, and all the various social changes that have swept the nation. Smaller households, but more of them.

Of this increasing number of households, a relatively small percentage can afford a single-family home. At a 10 percent interest rate, for example, an $80,000 mortgage costs $8,000 a year, just in interest. Even the most generous bank officer wouldn't give that kind of a mortgage to anyone making under $30,000 a year. Many would-be homeowners are priced out of the market. Thus, they turn to apartments. This creates a demand for apartments, pushing up occupancy rates and rent levels.

Owning an apartment building, though, is much different from owning an office building. There often are many tenants on short-term leases. Apartment tenants come and go much more readily than corporate office tenants or retail stores. And while they're around, they often demand more intensive service. In short, apartment buildings are more difficult to manage, and their income is less predictable.

Because of these defects, many real estate investors don't like to get involved with apartments. This reduced demand leads to lower prices for apartment buildings, and thus to higher yields for investors who are willing to take on apartment investing. A fully-occupied office building, for example, might sell for a price yielding 8 percent while a comparable apartment house yields 9 percent.

Congress has always favored apartment investors with tax breaks of some kind. In the 1986 tax act, for example, depreciation schedules on apartments were set at 27.5 years while all other real estate has 31.5-year depreciation. That is, an apartment investor gets almost 4 percent annual depreciation while all others get just over 3 percent. Therefore, more cash flow can be sheltered from taxes.

Again, it pays to be a contrarian in apartment investing. The Sunbelt was just as popular for apartment construction as for office construction, and it's just as overbuilt today. Areas like Columbus, Ohio, were largely overlooked in the early 1980s. One partnership, however, went into a Columbus deal in early 1983. It was structured as a 2:1 tax shelter—investors received $2 in write-offs for every $1 they invested.

Columbus is a college town (Ohio State) with a strong research and high-tech industrial base. That's where the growth has been in the mid-1980s; therefore the housing market in Columbus has tightened. Not only did investors get their writeoffs, demand for their apartments was so strong that they received 8 percent cash distributions each year, tax-sheltered. After four years, the partnership sold property; investors who contributed the minimum $88,000 received $140,000 from the sale, in addition to their deductions and earlier distributions.

## Low-Income Housing

Apartments for low-income tenants receive a special tax credit under the 1986 tax act. A tax credit is better than a tax deduction, because a credit reduces your tax bill, dollar-for-dollar. If you invest in low-income housing, you can qualify for 10 straight years of tax credits.

However, the 1986 tax act permits full use of the credit only for taxpayers earning less than $200,000. If you make more than that, or think you'll make more within the next 10 years, avoid these deals. The headaches will be more than the tax savings are worth.

What if you do qualify? You might invest $10,000 and get a $1,500 or $1,800 or $2,000 tax credit each year for 10 years. You can come out ahead just on tax savings alone. You can cut your taxes by as much as $8,250 per year, for 10 years, if you're willing to invest $40,000 to $50,000. Your annual tax savings may be considered another form of "cash flow."

The real estate may or may not have resale value when the tax credits expire. That depends on what the tax laws are at that time, and what condition the real estate is in. Be sure to invest with a sponsor who has specialized experience in low-income housing, because the legal and operational technicalities are substantial.

## Hotels

Now, we're getting beyond the realm of pure real estate. With an office building or a shopping center or an apartment house, the property owner's role is chiefly to provide suitable space to tenants, and then get out of the way. Tenants may stay for a month at a time or for 10 years.

In a hotel, your "tenants" are the paying customers who check in and out every day. Running a hotel is really operating a business.

Usually, a limited partnership will hire a professional management company to take care of operations. Often, there will be a tie-in to a national franchise, such as Marriott or Holiday Inns, with its telephone reservations network.

This doesn't take the risks out of hotel investing. The occupancy rate one week may bear no resemblance to the occupancy rate the week before. Room rates may have to be cut to stay competitive. Yields are unpredictable and the risks are especially acute with new properties.

On the other hand, there's no better investment than a hotel in a "hot" market. Room rates can be raised at will, even day by day, as long as the traffic will bear the higher tab. Hotel investments can be the most profitable real estate investments, especially in inflationary periods.

One partnership, for example, bought a Holiday Inn near Kansas City International Airport. That year (1985), the Kansas City Royals won the World Series. Travel into the area boomed, the hotel's occupancy rates shot up, and the partners reaped a windfall. That's not likely to happen with an office building.

### Condo Hotels May Offer Tax Shelter

Under the 1986 tax law, condo hotel deals got a special break. In this kind of a deal, each investor owns a specific room. The rooms are then pooled and run as a standard hotel by a management company.

If a condo hotel investor plays an active role in the business, he may be able to deduct his losses from his other income. Or he may claim that the condo is his "second home" and deduct all the related interest expenses. That's not possible with most other real estate investments.

However, an investor can't win on tax breaks alone—the hotel has to generate cash at some point, if there is to be a profit. Most condo hotel offerings are richly priced. That may have something to do with the fact that they tend to involve resort hotels, and the investors get two weeks' free stay at the hotel every year as part of the deal.

### Restaurants

The remarks about hotels also apply to restaurants. They're operating businesses, rather than pure real estate, so returns are unpredictable. Invest in a new chain, and you take the risk that the idea will never catch on. Invest in a Burger King or a Wendy's, and you're likely to pay top dollar.

On the positive side, successful restaurants can be enormously profitable. Don't you wish you had been a limited partner in almost any McDonald's outlet opened in the 1970s? With rent tied directly to volume at the cash registers?

Moreover, small restaurant chains are excellent takeover candidates. They're cash cows, because they collect revenues daily while paying expenses weekly or monthly. They prosper via the "float," or use of money. Some chains have been acquired just for that reason. The investors in some restaurant deals also get options or warrants for stock in the parent restaurant chain, which they might parlay into stock market profits.

### Mini-Warehouses

This category of real estate investment has been tremendously popular with limited partnership investors. Mini-warehouses are rows of garage-like areas that tenants rent by the month, often for $25 or $50 per month. Individuals store the skis and luggage they can't fit into their homes; businesses use them for excess inventory or old paperwork.

The appeal to investors lies in their low-cost construction and management requirements. They're operating businesses, but overhead is usually low. A hotel, for example, might need a 60 percent occupancy rate to break even while a mini-warehouse can break even at 30 percent. Thus, risks to investors can be relatively low.

In addition, rents can be raised, even in periods of low inflation. Suppose you have a tenant paying $25 a month, and you impose a 6 percent rent increase. That tenant isn't likely to spend a weekend moving his stuff to another mini-warehouse, just to save $1.50 a month.

Mini-warehouse partnerships have performed well during the past 10 years, perhaps as well as any other category. They've mainly been structured with little or no debt, so they have avoided the problems faced by some leveraged partnerships in the mid-1980s. Cash generation has been excellent. A mature mini-warehouse (three or four years old) often distributes 8 percent or more to limited partners.

Some mini-warehouse deals include "land-banking" aspects. When you invest in raw land, you sit and wait for an opportunity to re-sell at a higher price. In the meantime, you receive no cash flow and no tax benefits. So why not put up some inexpensive structures, such as mini-warehouses? That will give you a return while you wait for your land to appreciate. One mini-warehouse partnership sold its property to a Japanese corporation at a huge profit. The Japanese tore down the mini-warehouses and built an office high-rise on the site.

Not all mini-warehouse deals work out as well. The concept is still fairly new, so investors don't know what shape the industry will take when it matures. The minis they invest in today may be outdated tomorrow, if someone else comes up with a better idea, or they may prove to be so successful that they will draw a host of nearby competitors, luring customers away with lower prices.

## Health Care Properties

If there's such a thing as a hot category in today's depressed real estate market, this is it. The aging of the United States is an undisputed fact. Every day, another 5,000 Americans reach age 65. Already, there are more seniors than teenagers.

One way to play this market is via nursing home investments. Currently, there is a shortage of 250,000 nursing home beds nationwide. Occupancy rates average 97 percent.

If you buy an existing, well-maintained nursing home, you're virtually guaranteed near-100 percent occupancy. That's because new nursing homes need state-granted construction permits. Yet most states are reluctant to allow much construction, because that will increase the number of Medicaid patients and strain the state's budget. Already, most homes have waiting lists while the demand for nursing home beds increases faster than supply.

The problem here lies with an over-dependence on Medicaid. Government reimbursements tend to be meager, and there is little hope for improvement as long as budgets are pinched. Some states have even cut back their Medicaid payments. At the same time, labor costs for service workers are increasing rapidly. If you own a nursing home that's entirely populated by Medicaid patients, you may be squeezed by high costs and low reimbursements.

Some nursing homes, though, have amenities that appeal to private patients. These patients pay their own way, generally at rates about 30 percent higher than Medicaid rates. That can mean more money to pass through to investors. Nursing homes may generate enough cash flow to enable you to buy nursing home insurance and protect your own assets.

Nursing homes, though, have a stigma for some investors as a result of scandals involving patient abuse and financial corruption. If you're going to invest, convince yourself that your money will produce positive results. Check into the sponsor and the property operator. Visit one of their nursing homes personally, or find reputable people who'll vouch for their integrity.

Another way to tap the senior citizen market is to go after the 90 percent + who don't need nursing home care. You can invest in a "congregate care facility," more simply known as a retirement center. These really are apartment complexes for people over 65.

Typically, retirement centers offer recreational and social programs. There may be an emergency call button in each room, and those who can't manage on their own can sign up for maid service or for meals in a central dining hall. Medical attendants may be on-premises, or there may be a tie-in to a local hospital or nursing home.

The appeal to investors lies in the potential for high yield. Retirement centers charge higher rents than conventional apartments, and the other services may also turn out to be profit centers. On the downside, you're accepting all the management responsibilities of an apartment building along with the added task of caring for the elderly. Your market is limited to affluent people over 65, and there's no guarantee you'll find enough of them to fill your apartments.

--- *Summary* ---

*How the Different Types of Real Estate Compare:*

- Office buildings. Corporate tenants on long-term leases offer stability. Today, you have to find local markets that aren't overbuilt.

- Shopping centers. Leases tied to store sales provide excellent inflation protection. The more national retailers in a center, the more safety in the deal.

- Apartments. Depreciation is more favorable than for other property types. Management is crucial, and you need to avoid areas where rent control is possible. Low-income housing offers 10 years of "cash flow" through tax credits, if you earn less than $200,000 per year.

- Hotels and restaurants. These are operating businesses rather than real estate. Risks are higher than in more traditional real estate, but so are potential profits.
- Mini-warehouses. A top performer in recent years. Partnerships generally are not leveraged to allow for increased cash flow and to cut risks. Since it is a relatively new category, the long-term potential is still uncertain.
- Health care. As Americans grow older, housing for the elderly becomes a necessity. Nursing homes offer safety to investors while retirement centers may provide high profits.

*Recommendation:*

No matter which type of property you're considering, the sponsor will have a great story to tell. And it's true—investors have made money with every category of real estate.

However, every category has horror stories, too. There's no such thing as a sure thing in real estate. The best advice is to look for a sponsor who has experience in the particular type of deal he's offering to you. The more he knows about his specialty, and the longer his record of making money for investors, the better your chances of finding a happy ending.

# 19

# Leasing Funds: High-Yielding Cash Cows

Real estate investing is fairly easy to understand. Most of us have owned a house or rented an apartment. We're familiar with the ideas behind owning property, paying mortgage interest, collecting rents, and so forth.

Equipment leasing, on the other hand, is a less familiar concept to many investors. It may sound too specialized to be worth learning about, but don't decide this too fast; equipment leasing can provide higher, more predictable income than real estate. In an era where cash flow dominates investors' thinking, equipment leasing provides an income stream that few other vehicles can match. Although some people think of equipment leasing as a tax shelter, leasing income funds can be conservative investments that are appropriate for many purposes—from retirement income to college funding.

## HARDWARE FIRST

Let's try to break down the barriers. "Equipment" generally refers to machinery of any type that's used in business. Investors will find it useful to differentiate between high-tech and low-tech equipment.

High-tech refers to computers and related items. It also includes communications equipment and some medical apparatus. The distinguishing characteristic is rapid technological change. Such equipment may soon be obsolete because newer, better equipment is continually being introduced.

183

Low-tech equipment, on the other hand, is not subject to the same pace of change. An airplane may be used for 20, 30 years or longer. The same is true of truck trailers, tractors, marine containers, and so on. Marine containers, in fact, may never become obsolete. When these boxes no longer carry cargo aboard ships, they're used for various other purposes. With a window or two cut out they serve as offices on construction sites. In some countries, old containers become makeshift houses.

## LOCKING IN LEASE INCOME

In terms of leasing, there's a direct comparison with real estate. Just as you signed a lease on your first apartment, promising to pay so many dollars per month for so many months, the same is true with an equipment lease. Whoever wants to use your equipment signs a contract, promising to pay so many dollars for so many months.

That brings us to equipment leasing income funds. Usually referred to as "funds," they are really *public limited partnerships* rather than mutual funds. These funds raise money to buy equipment, then lease the equipment to users, and collect the monthly rents.

Once an investor has come this far, a natural objection arises. "What if," you may ask, "a leasing fund buys equipment but can't find anyone to use it?"

This isn't a problem with reputable leasing funds, the ones that have been around for several years. They only purchase equipment for which a firm leasing commitment already is in place. What's more, they usually only lease equipment to Fortune 1000 corporations with strong credit ratings. So your income is virtually guaranteed for the term of the first lease, generally two to four years.

Here's an example. Suppose Exxon (or GE or AT&T or 3M) needs a new computer. In many instances, Exxon will decide to lease rather than buy. The company may want to avoid a large purchase, or it may not want to be locked in to one type of system.

Exxon may decide to lease from the computer manufacturer. The manufacturer, though, may prefer an outright sale. Therefore, a third party will be brought in, an equity investor. The equity investor buys the equipment and leases it to Exxon.

That's the role an equipment leasing income fund plays. It comes into a transaction that's already well advanced. It provides the money to buy the equipment, then it collects rents from the user.

Let's say a leasing fund buys equipment and immediately leases it to Exxon for three years. It's virtually assured of three years of predictable income. That's not the case with many real estate ventures—who knows how well your apartment building will be occupied or at what rent levels?

What happens when the three years are up? That's a risk, and it's borne by the leasing fund investors. On the one hand, Exxon may be so pleased with its computer, and its people will be so accustomed to using it, that it will re-lease the equipment for another three years. Or, IBM may have come out with a phenomenal technological advance in the interim. If so, Exxon may not want your computer and it may be hard to find another user.

In real life, the former scenario is more likely than the latter. It's rare that any equipment is totally obsolete after three years. But some equipment, particularly high-tech items, will lose most of its value after seven or eight years.

## GETTING YOUR CASH WHILE THE
## GETTING IS GOOD

As protection against possible obsolescence, leasing investors receive high initial rents. In high-tech funds, lease rates are often 2.5 to 3 percent per month. That's 30 to 36 percent per year. A $10 million computer, therefore, might lease for $3 to $3.6 million per year. (A $10 million airplane, on the other hand, might lease for $1.8 to $2.1 million per year.)

Suppose a leasing fund raises $100 million, of which $85 million actually is spent to buy high-tech equipment after all the upfront expenses. Assume a 30 percent lease rate. That's $25.5 million the partnership collects in rents. After management fees, there might be $23 million to distribute to the limited partners.

After three years, then, the limited partners will have gotten back $69 million on their $100 million investment. Few investments of any kind will throw off that kind of cash flow, with that kind of security (leases from top corporate users). Even if all the equipment is totally worthless, after three years, investors have received nearly 70 percent of their capital back.

| | |
|---|---|
| Money raised | $100 million |
| Front load (15%) | $ 15 million |
| Equipment purchased | $ 85 million |
| Lease rate | 30% |
| Total lease income | $ 25.5 million |
| Management fees | $  2.5 million |
| Cash available for distribution | $ 23 million |
| Actual distribution | $ 13 million (13%) |
| Amount reinvested | $ 10 million |
| Acquisition costs | $500,000 |
| New equipment purchased | $  9.5 million |
| Additional lease income (@ 30%) | $  2.85 million |

If the fund buys low-tech equipment, the lease rates will be lower. Investors might expect about 12 percent a year in cash flow, but their equipment probably will be useful for many years, so there isn't the same capital risk.

Let's go back to the high-tech fund for further illustration. Few funds, if any, pay out a straight 23 percent. It's more common that initial cash distributions are in the 12 to 15 percent range. So what happens to the other 8 to 11 percent?

Typically, it's invested in new equipment. Remember, our fund has $23 million to distribute, but instead it pays out, say, $13 million (13 percent of investors' $100 million outlay). The other $10 million is used to buy new equipment. Assuming acquisition costs run about 5 percent, the fund can acquire $9.5 million worth of equipment, which would yield another $2.85 million in cash flow. After fees, around $2.5 million would be available for distribution to investors.

You can see where this is heading. Each year, the partnership acquires more equipment which increases annual cash flow. The cash distributions to investors can be increased, or the excess can be plowed back into still more reinvestment. By the time the initial three-year leases expire, the fund will have more than $85 million sunk in three-year-old equipment. Perhaps another $30 million will be in newer equipment that is still on lease.

## ADDING LEVERAGE TO LEASING FUNDS

Some leasing funds add another wrinkle: leverage. In real estate, adding leverage generally reduces upfront income. So why should an equipment leasing income fund use leverage?

Because equipment leasing is different: They can borrow at 9 percent and immediately buy equipment that will generate cash flow of 30 to 36 percent. Leverage can boost cash flow in equipment leasing.

Let's look at a $100 million fund that decides to use leverage. Loads on leveraged funds are usually higher, because of costs involved with the loans, so let's say $80 million is used to buy equipment, rather than $85 million in the all-cash fund. This fund will be 50 percent leveraged, so it borrows $80 million and buys $160 million worth of equipment.

At a 30 percent lease rate, the partnership collects $48 million the first year. Debt service on a 9 percent, $80 million loan would probably be around $33 million—that's interest and principal. So $15 million would be left, of which $13 million could be distributed to investors.

Say this fund decides to distribute $13 million (13 percent) to investors, the same as the unleveraged fund. That would leave nothing to reinvest, compared with $10 million reinvested by the unleveraged fund.

So it goes for the first three years. While the unleveraged fund is adding about $30 million in new equipment, the leveraged fund adds no new equipment.

| | |
|---|---|
| Money raised | $100 million |
| Front loads (20%) | $ 20 million |
| Money to be invested | $ 80 million |
| Money borrowed | $ 80 million |
| Equipment purchased | $160 million |
| Lease rate | 30% |
| Total lease income | $ 48 million |
| Debt service (interest & principal) | $ 33 million |
| Management fees | $ 2 million |
| Distribution to investors | $ 13 million (13%) |

*After three years, when borrowed money has been repaid:*

| | Unleveraged Fund | Leveraged Fund |
|---|---|---|
| Original acquisitions | $ 85 million | $160 million |
| After first year | $ 9.5 million | |
| After second year | $ 10 million | |
| After third year | $ 10.5 million | |
| Total acquisitions, Now debt-free | $115 million | $160 million |

However, paying $99 million in debt service over three years would completely pay off the $80 million loan. Now, the leveraged fund would own $160 million in three-year-old equipment while the unleveraged fund would own $85 million in three-year-old equipment plus $30 million in newer equipment. If the three-year-old equipment can be re-leased at a reasonable rate, the leveraged fund is in better shape.

## CASH FLOW DOESN'T ALWAYS MEAN YIELD

Up to now, we've been pretty free with terms such as "13 percent distributions" and "23 percent cash flow." Don't make the mistake of thinking that these are true yields, comparable to what you receive from a Treasury bond or a CD.

Let's say that your fund buys a computer and holds it for eight years. Then it sells the computer for 12 percent of its original price. (It could be higher or lower; no one knows for sure what a computer will be worth in eight years.) If this is the case, your computer is losing 11 percent of its value every year.

Suppose you were in that partnership that had 23 percent available for distribution, and it made the full payout. You'd receive 23 percent of your original investment the first year. However, 11 percent would be an (estimated) return of your original capital while the other 12 percent would be the investment yield.

What about our hypothetical fund that pays out 13 percent and reinvests 10 percent? Here, the fund is paying 11 percent return of capital plus a 2 percent cash yield. The other 10 percent is being reinvested in new equipment.

## PARTIAL SHELTER

Don't forget the tax aspects, either. Equipment leasing income funds own their equipment, so they're entitled to depreciation deductions. Leveraged funds get interest deductions, too. Thus, the partnerships will have less taxable income to be passed on to investors.

The investor with the 13 percent distribution, for example, might get $1,300 in cash flow on a $10,000 investment. His share of the partnership's taxable income might be only $600. He might owe

$180 in taxes, in a 30 percent bracket, and wind up with $1,120, for an 11.2 percent after-tax distribution.

## THE REAL PAYOFF

The ultimate yield from an equipment leasing income fund is subject to many variables. You have no way of knowing if your equipment will be re-leased or how much the equipment eventually will be worth upon re-sale. If you're in a reinvestment fund or a leveraged fund, more equipment will be bought and leased, adding to the uncertainty. Nevertheless, these unknowns are in the margin. Especially in high-tech funds, where so much income can be counted on in the early years, the range of returns is fairly predictable.

Sponsors like to compare equipment leasing income funds with Ginnie Maes. In both cases, your capital is returned over the life of the investment. There's no bondlike redemption at the end of the deal. Leasing funds are more risky than Ginnie Maes, because there's no federal guarantee. So yields are expected to be a bit higher. If Ginnie Maes generally yield about 9 to 10 percent, over the long term, leasing funds might wind up with a true return of 11 to 12 percent, not counting tax consequences.

Is it worth it? Why get involved with a leasing fund just to get a few extra points of yield? There's no real hope for growth here, as there is with real estate.

Leasing funds do have several virtues, though. For one, the high current yield gives you liquidity. Most funds pay 12 to 15 percent initially, with the prospect of increasing distributions as more equipment is added. Within seven years or so, you'll probably receive your entire investment back, to reinvest as you please. It's hard to find other investment vehicles today that can match this payout rate.

Leasing funds can give you a win-win regarding inflation. If inflation stays in check, and interest rates stay down, your 11 to 12 percent anticipated yield looks very attractive.

On the other hand, suppose inflation and interest rates heat up. You have some protection because of the early return of your capital. You can reinvest and earn higher yields.

In addition, lease rates are directly related to interest rates. If inflation increases and rates rise, lease rates are likely to be higher than anticipated. In turn, this might increase the resale value of your equipment. "Hard assets"—including low-tech equipment—may actually appreciate in inflationary times. In general, during an inflationary period, investors are better off owning assets—equipment—than acting as lenders by holding bonds.

## LOW-TECH'S HIGH SALES APPEAL

So far, we've been using high-tech partnerships as an example. Most equipment leasing funds emphasize computer equipment and peripherals or other high-tech apparatus. A few leasing funds, though, buy planes or trucks or trailers. In recent years, these low-tech funds have been the best sellers in equipment leasing. Investors seem to prefer low-tech, because the equipment is more likely to retain its value. Some models of jet airplanes sell for as much today as they did 10 years ago, or even a bit more.

In these low-tech funds, the math is a bit different. As we indicated previously, lease rates on such equipment might be 20 percent per year, lower than on a high-tech fund. After expenses, there might be 15 percent available to distribute to investors.

If you buy an airplane in 1987 and sell it in 1997 for 50 percent of its cost, you're losing only 5 percent of its value each year. If the plane sells for 100 percent of its 1987 value, you're not losing anything to depreciation. So a 15 percent distribution can be a true 10 percent or even a 15 percent yield.

Comparing a high-tech with a low-tech fund, high-tech is likely to give you more cash flow in the initial years. Results in a high-tech fund are less dependent upon residual value. If equipment is expected to retain only 6 percent of its original value, then a complete wipeout (zero residual value) would not have that much impact on the overall return.

On the other hand, low-tech funds have less risk of a sudden collapse and a total loss of value, from a technological breakthrough. There's more inflation protection, too. If prices should soar again, any equipment that's not technologically outdated will see its value increase.

## COLLEGE BUILDUP

Some parents use equipment leasing income funds in their college savings plans. Often, these funds generate mostly tax-sheltered cash in the early years. After a few years, though, loans are paid off and depreciation deductions decrease, so there is less shelter. There may be more cash flow, because of reinvestment in new equipment and a drop in debt service. Some funds project 10 percent or 11 percent distributions in the first four years, jumping to 20 percent thereafter.

Therefore, some people buy and hold equipment leasing funds in their own name, during the period of heaviest tax shelter. When the fund begins to throw off large amounts of taxable income, they give the partnership units to their teenage children. (As we've mentioned, a married couple may give away $20,000 per year, per recipient, without owing gift taxes.) Under the 1986 tax law, children age 14 and over pay taxes at their own rate, which usually is much lower than their parents' tax rate. (See Appendix 2 for more on college funding.)

## HOW LEASING FUNDS HAVE PERFORMED

Equipment leasing income funds have a short track record. They were introduced in the mid-1970s by a California company, Phoenix Leasing. Until the mid-1980s, though, most leasing partnerships were tax-oriented, rather than income funds. From the evidence so far, leasing funds have avoided severe setbacks. They've generally delivered double-digit cash flow, and their true yields have compared favorably with money market instruments.

A few years ago, some leasing funds were troubled. Storage Technology, which supplied equipment to several income funds, ran into serious financial difficulties. Re-lease revenues fell—who wants to lease equipment made by a company that may not be around tomorrow? But Storage turned around, lease rates have rebounded, and the leasing funds survived, generally with lower distribution levels.

In selecting a leasing fund, look for general partners with a record of leasing equipment to high-quality users. If high-tech equipment is to be purchased, find out if it can be easily upgraded, to guard against obsolescence. For safety's sake, try to find partnerships where the initial leases (the ones virtually guaranteed by the users) will return at least 70 percent of the equipment's cost, reducing the capital risk to no more than 30 percent.

Some investors object to being locked in for 10 years or more. If they want to sell their units earlier, they generally have to take a steep discount. But there are advantages to investing for the long-term. There's generally a higher yield than you would get from a money market fund, for example. And you won't be tempted to pull out your money and invest in the next "hot deal" that comes along. In terms of financial planning, you're better off with some of your money put aside for the long haul.

If you're still not certain about how leasing can pay off, go to your local video rental store. The store buys each tape once, for perhaps $30, and rents it (leases it) over and over, at $1, $2, or $3 a day. After a few weeks, the store may have recouped its entire investment, and it still owns the cassette, for further rentals.

---

## Summary

*Pros:*

- High cash flow. Most leasing funds pay 12 to 15 percent per year. Although this is partially a return of your own capital, there may be an advantage to getting your money back sooner, to reinvest.
- Safety. The equipment usually is leased to top corporations, so income from the initial leases, covering the first few years, is fairly predictable.
- Low downside. In a well-structured fund—experienced sponsors and creditworthy users—losing money is unlikely. About the worst you'll wind up with will be a money-market rate.
- Tax advantages. Depreciation, and perhaps interest, deductions will shelter some of your cash flow.
- Passive income. Income that's not sheltered likely will be "passive," so old tax shelter losses can be used as an offset.

*Cons:*

- Disappearing principal. Because the ultimate value of equipment can't be known, investors have to assume there won't be a bondlike return of principal. Thus, the early cash flow should be reinvested.
- Business risks. Investors are subject to numerous uncertainties concerning the equipment they buy and lease: technological obsolescence, supplier's failure, falling interest rates (which lead to low lease rates), etc.

- Low upside. Even the best leasing fund won't generate the returns of a good stock or real estate investment.
- No way out. Interests in leasing funds are hard to value. If you decide to sell early, you'll have to accept a discount from what the buyer estimates as net present value. Holding periods may be 10 years or longer.

*Recommendation:*

Leasing funds fit into the bond section, or the fixed-income section, of an investor's portfolio. They're bondlike because they provide a stream of fairly predictable income, without much prospect of long-term appreciation.

Leasing funds probably work best for investors who like the high yields of bonds, but who fear exposure to inflation. When inflation increases, all bonds lose value. Leasing funds, on the other hand, may hold their own during inflation. Lease rates may increase, as interest rates rise, and some types of equipment will hold their resale value.

Therefore, the more concerned you are with inflation, the more suitable you are for a leasing fund. Don't put your entire fixed-income allocation into leasing funds, though. Instead, balance them with Ginnie Maes or Treasuries or municipal bonds. This combination can give you high current income, with protection against inflation or disinflation.

Reinvestment of leasing fund distributions is crucial. For this reason, leasing funds may be suited for retirement plans, where reinvestment is mandatory. If you invest in a leasing fund outside of a retirement plan, make sure all distributions are swept into a mutual fund or a money market fund.

# 20

# Oil and Gas: Where the Cash Really Flows

Investors have two common misconceptions about oil and gas. One, they tend to believe that it's a wildcat, boom-or-bust business. Two, they think that investing in oil has to be unprofitable at today's price per barrel of oil.

There are ways to deal with both concerns. Some oil and gas exploration definitely is highly risky. Most investments, though, offer low-risk opportunities. These low-risk ventures won't give you the "big score" (the kind of a find that has movie cowboys dancing around with oil splattering their ten-gallon hats), but they can give you a competitive return. Any oil investment is a play on future oil price increases.

There are essentially two ways to invest for cash in oil and gas: income funds and developmental drilling. Let's start with the one that has "income" in its name.

## ELIMINATING DRILLING RISK

Few investments are as simple to understand as an oil and gas income fund. Here again, the word fund is used, but investments usually are made through limited partnerships. These partnerships buy "proven properties." That is, they invest in fields where oil or gas already has been discovered.

Income funds sell the oil and gas, collect the revenues, and pay the related expenses. Whatever is left over is shared among the partners. That's all there is to it.

The ingredients necessary for financial success are evident. The fund has to buy well, distribute its products efficiently, and sell its oil and gas at the highest possible price.

Oil and gas income funds were tremendously popular in the late 1970s and early 1980s. Two sponsors, Petro-Lewis and Damson Oil, raised more money than anyone else in the limited partnership industry—more than any real estate sponsors. They had a lot of success stories—people who invested in their funds in the early 1970s prospered as the price of oil soared throughout the decade.

These two sponsors pushed too hard. Petro-Lewis, especially, leveraged extensively. If it raised $100 million from investors, 15 percent would go to upfront costs and the other $85 million might be matched by an $85 million loan to buy $170 million worth of properties.

Petro-Lewis and Damson were whipsawed in the early 1980s. They bought properties at the top of the market and borrowed money at sky-high interest rates. Then the price of oil tumbled. Debt remained while revenues sunk far below projections. The partnerships fell into extreme financial distress that has yet to be fully resolved. Investors have been seriously hurt.

Some financial professionals invested hundreds of thousands of their own dollars with Petro-Lewis and Damson; they recommended those partnerships to clients. In many cases, these advisers spent hours investigating the sponsors; they had entree to the companies' top executives. Yet they were badly burned.

The moral? If a deal so thoroughly scrutinized—and so widely recommended—by so many investment professionals can go sour, no deal is failure-proof. Don't fall in love with any one investment. If the outlook turns bleak, get out.

Be a *contrarian*. Buy oil when the price is down, not when it's reaching record highs.

Most of all, diversify. All investments have some risk. Don't invest so much in any one deal that its collapse would be devastating.

## THE INCOME FUND STRIKES BACK

After Petro-Lewis and Damson ran into trouble, oil and gas income funds fell out of favor. Lately, though, they've been coming back, sometimes called "production partnerships" to avoid the "income fund" stigma. Sales were up sharply in 1986 and 1987.

Why the resurgence? The income funds on the market now either have survived the rough times, or they're backed by major financial companies (i.e., Prudential-Bache, Paine Webber, New York Life). They're avoiding leverage, so they won't get whipsawed.

More than that, investors see a chance to buy low and sell high. Sponsors say that they can buy reserves (unrecovered oil) today at $4 to 5 a barrel. That may be a little bit of hype, because nobody really knows how many barrels of oil are actually in a field, even after the field has been proven. All they have are engineers' estimates. But it definitely is true that oil properties can be purchased for much less than they cost 5 or 10 years ago because the industry has so many distressed sellers.

"Lifting costs" may be another $5 a barrel. That means it costs about $10 per barrel to buy oil and bring it to market. So selling oil at $15 to 18 a barrel, where the price of oil has ranged recently, can be profitable. Most funds today expect to distribute 15 to 18 percent, cash-on-cash, right from the beginning.

## EMPTYING THE BARREL

Just as is the case with equipment leasing income funds, that 15 to 18 percent is not a true yield. Your investment is being depleted every time a barrel of oil is recovered and sold. Ultimately, no oil will be left that can be lifted economically.

Thus, part of that 15 to 18 percent is a return of your own capital. That capital must be reinvested, or you'll wind up with a dry hole.

Taxation also affects your return. Income fund investors don't get to use percentage depletion, the industry's juiciest tax break. They can use cost depletion, which is less generous. Other deductions also may apply. The result is to shelter part of your distribution. A 15 percent distribution may wind up equivalent to 12 or 13 percent after tax.

True yields are projected at around 10 to 12 percent, after tax. Typically, that projection is based upon oil staying in the $15 to 18 range. If oil goes back up to $25 or 30 a barrel, your return can be much higher. Conversely, your return will drop if prices fall.

No one really knows what's going to happen to oil prices. However, an income fund can give you a reasonable expectation of earning approximately 10 percent now, and a chance for higher returns in the future.

## DRILLING FOR TAX BREAKS

Oil and gas income funds are the least risky way to invest in this area, especially if you invest with a substantial sponsor who won't use leverage. If you're willing to take a little more risk, for a slightly higher return, you might try developmental drilling.

Yes, we said drilling. But the drilling programs suitable for cash-oriented investors aren't crapshoots. They go by the name of *developmental drilling funds*. In this type of venture, wells are drilled near already proven fields.

A few sponsors have developed specific fail-safe zones. One might drill only in the Appalachian region of Ohio while another specializes in the Anadarko Basin of Oklahoma while still another stays in Texas' Spraberry Trend. These sponsors have their particular regions well-mapped. They have a history of bringing in commercial wells with 90 percent or more of the holes they drill.

With these programs, investors probably will receive cash flow, and they can expect to receive it fairly soon. Usually, distributions begin within six months of an investor making a capital contribution.

There is a phenomenon in oil and gas drilling known as "flush" production. When the hole in the ground first meets the oil or gas, underground pressure is released. This pressure speeds the early flow of oil and gas. It's possible to get cash-on-cash returns of 25 percent a year from developmental drilling in the early stages. Most successful partnerships initially distribute 12 to 18 percent.

Flush production doesn't last forever. After the initial release, underground pressure eases up. Production—and revenues—generally follows a declining curve after the first year or two.

One investor, for example, went into a Pennsylvania drilling program a few years ago and received a 55 percent payback the first year! Eureka! He poured more money into the sponsors' deals and spread the word among his friends.

Unfortunately, that 55 percent was about all there was. The next four years produced a total of 5 percent in distributions, and then nothing. The sponsor's other programs didn't even do as well.

## DRILLING FUNDS WITH EXTENDED
## PAYOFF PERIODS

Some sponsors of developmental drilling programs, though, have records of paying out over long time periods. They tell investors to expect total returns to be 1.7:1 to 2.5:1. That is, a $10,000 investor might receive $17,000 to 25,000 in cash flow.

This cash flow, it's true, may take 15 years to receive. Some drilling programs started in the early 1960s still throw off some cash. When the true return is calculated—a time-weighted, annual, after-tax yield—it may wind up around 15 percent.

The tax laws help to boost the yield on oil and gas drilling programs. When you invest in real estate, for example, it takes you from 27.5 to 31.5 years to write off your cash outlay through depreciation.

In oil and gas, though, most of your cash outlay goes toward "intangible drilling costs," which include workmen's salaries, supplies, etc. Those costs are immediately deductible. Your first-year writeoff might be 50 to 90 percent of your cash investment, dependent upon how soon revenues start to flow in, compared to 3 to 4 percent from real estate depreciation. (You can get a greater loss if you use leverage, but borrowing money to invest in oil and gas is extremely high-risk, not suitable for most individuals.)

## BANKING LOSSES TO SHELTER
## FUTURE INCOME

The new tax law complicates matters. If you invest through a limited partnership—the standard method—drilling fund losses aren't immediately deductible. So you would "bank" your losses. Then, when income starts to flow, the losses in your bank can be withdrawn to offset that income. You might wind up with years of income on which no taxes need be paid.

Investors in drilling programs also are entitled to a percentage depletion, the juicy tax break mentioned earlier. Without going into the technicalities, the depletion allowance effectively shelters about 20 percent of all the taxable income from a drilling fund.

Let's say you've reached the point where your intangible drilling costs no longer shelter your distributions. You're receiving taxable income from your partnership. But of every $1 worth of income, only 80 cents will be taxed, thanks to percentage depletion. In a 30 percent bracket, you'll owe 24 cents in taxes—effectively dropping your tax bracket to 24 percent.

## DEDUCT NOW RATHER THAN LATER

Some sponsors are offering investors the option of by-passing limited partnership status. Investors can acquire a working interest— a direct piece of the action. They won't have the limited liability enjoyed by limited partners.

Why should investors want to take this option? If they do, they'll be entitled to deduct their losses right away. Say you invest $10,000 in a working interest and get a 60 percent writeoff the first year. That's a $6,000 deduction, worth $1,800 in a 30 percent bracket. Considering your $1,800 tax savings, your net investment would be $8,200 rather than $10,000.

Sponsors tend to downplay the loss of limited liability. "Real" oil people don't hide behind limited partnership status, they say; commercial insurance is available and is more than adequate. Nevertheless, investors should look hard before investing outside of the partnership format.

## HOW DRILLING PARTNERSHIPS
## ARE STRUCTURED

Another major consideration is the structure of the deal. You shouldn't pay more than 15 percent in upfront costs. That is, at least 85 cents out of your invested dollar should be used for operations. But also be wary of deals in which loads are touted as being under 10 percent. Chances are the sponsor is making money somewhere else—he may be doing the drilling himself and charging the partnership more than the going rate.

The arrangement for sharing revenues should be fair, too. Some deals have a *promoted interest*. The sponsor may put up 10 percent of the money used for drilling operations, yet take 25 percent of the revenues. The extra 15 percent is his compensation for running the partnership. Proponents say this is an attractive structure because the sponsor's 10 percent contribution is likely to run into six or seven figures. It's comforting to see the sponsor putting up money alongside yours.

Other analysts prefer the *reversionary interest* format. Here, the limited partners put up almost all of the money—95 to 99 percent. In return, they get 95 to 99 percent of the revenues until they reach "payout," a return of their original investment. After that, the sponsor might get 15 percent of ongoing revenues. This gives sponsors an incentive to see that investors get their money back, so that they can then begin to receive a meaningful amount.

Investors should look hard at the sponsor, too. Be sure there is enough financial strength to ride out any rough times. And look at the record to see if real cash-on-cash returns have been consistently provided to investors. Those records will be in the prospectus that comes with any oil and gas deal. If they're not available, don't invest.

## SPLITTING THE DIFFERENCE

Some sponsors are offering variations that are neither income funds nor pure drilling funds. In a completion fund, for example, a partnership waits until the drilling fund has discovered reserves. Then it puts up the money for the equipment (pipes, pumps, etc.) to complete the well. In return, it gets a piece of the revenues. Because it has no dry-hole risk, returns are expected to be a bit lower than a drilling fund provides.

Other offerings may be part drilling fund and part income fund. The excess writeoffs from the drilling could shelter most or all of the taxes owed by the income fund.

A new wrinkle is the natural gas liquid (NGL) partnership. Here, the partnership owns a processing plant that converts natural gas to liquid form. When the liquid gas is sold, the partnership gets a cut of the revenues.

There's no dry-hole risk, and sponsors project cash-on-cash returns of 20 percent+. However, the returns are dependent upon the price of liquid gas, which are directly related to oil prices. If oil and gas prices fall to extremely low levels, production may cease and there won't be any gas to liquefy.

## FORTUNES RISE AND FALL WITH OIL PRICES

All oil and gas investments are somewhat dependent upon oil prices. (Although the correlation is not perfect, higher oil prices spur people to switch to natural gas, increasing the demand for and the price of gas.) As of this writing, oil has been selling for $15 to $18 a barrel. If it dips back to $10, as was the case in mid-1986, all oil and gas investments will wind up disappointing. But if it rebounds to $25 to $30, where it was throughout 1985, those investments may deliver windfalls.

Which way are oil prices likely to go? Some economists point to the present glut and see no significant price increases for the next five years at least. Others say that the world—the United States in particular—is consuming oil faster than it's being discovered. At some point, the supply-demand balance will tip again, sending prices up.

One analyst, for example, recently estimated that worldwide production capacity is about 70 million barrels a day while demand is around 60 million. Hence the glut. But new discoveries are approximately 40 million barrels a day, far below consumption. Relatively low prices will hold down exploration, and there are no new Mexicos or Alaskas or North Seas on the horizon. Concurrently, the low prices will encourage demand. So it's just a matter of time until demand catches up to and exceeds supply, boosting the price.

## TAX HIKES MAY HELP

Uncle Sam may do his bit to hike prices. It's no secret that federal budget deficits remain incredibly high. Many politicians would like to help close that deficit with a tax on imported oil. An extra $5 or $10 per barrel, for example, could deliver billions to the Treasury.

Such a tax, if passed, would benefit investors. Imported oil would sell for $20 to $23 a barrel, not $15 to $18, to cover the tax. Domestic producers—including investors in income or drilling funds—could raise their prices without being undercut. The extra revenues would boost returns to investors.

Some sponsors use an "escalated" scenario in trying to project future oil prices. They project prices holding around $15 until 1989, then going up 5 percent a year. Such price increases could make a 2:1 deal (cash-on-cash) into a 3:1 deal.

In the meantime, low oil prices are not a total disaster for investors. Costs are down, too. A 10,000-foot well that would have cost $400,000 to $500,000 in the days of the 1981 boom now comes in at around $200,000. Only the best workers and the most efficient rigs are still in use, available at bargain rates. Proven properties also may be purchased at low prices from distressed sellers.

You have to be a real contrarian to invest in oil and gas today. The same people who bought stocks in the mid-1970s, when the Dow was under 600 and the "conventional wisdom" held that the stock market was Death Valley, are buying oil now. They're risk-takers, but the risks seem low. They look at oil as "black gold"— an excellent inflation hedge that also can provide current double-digit cash flow.

───────────── *Summary* ─────────────

*Pros:*

- High cash flow. Initial distributions may be as high as 18 percent in an income fund.

- Inflation protection. Oil prices are almost certain to rise, if the general price indices go up sharply. If those prices rise, so will returns to oil and gas investors.

- Timing. Investing in oil and gas looks better now than in the early 1980s, when such ventures boomed. Costs are lower throughout the oilpatch, and oil prices may well rebound from current levels.

- Tax benefits. Drilling partnerships offer some of the best tax breaks still available, including immediate deduction of most of your investment. Income funds offer partial shelter for current cash flow.

- Passive income. Taxable income generally may be offset by losses from other shelters.

*Cons:*

- Price risk. Oil prices may go down as well as up.

- Business risk. Drilling funds may strike dry holes. Even in an income fund, the oil or gas may run out prematurely, or distribution difficulties may arise.

- Unfamiliarity. Because most investors don't know as much about oil and gas as they do about, say, real estate, they have to rely heavily on a sponsor's honesty and ability.

- High costs. Because investors rely so heavily on the sponsors, fees and expenses tend to be hefty.

- Illiquidity. Cashing out early means swallowing a steep discount in oil and gas.
- Disappearing principal. Without prudent reinvestment, you'll wind up with nothing, when your oil and gas run out.

*Recommendation:*

Oil and gas investments don't fit neatly into our stock-bond-real estate portfolio breakdown. They belong in a separate natural resources category, that also includes precious metals. This category's characteristics include high risks, large profit (and loss) potential, and excellent inflation protection.

Most investors should hold 5 to 15 percent of their portfolio in such assets. (Only those who are extremely risk-averse should avoid natural resources altogether, but only those who are genuinely knowledgeable about these investments should have higher exposure.) In this category, oil and gas income funds are the best bet for those seeking cash flow. They're the least risky, and they're the closest thing to a "pure play" on oil prices/inflation. Drilling funds should be considered only by risk takers who want generous tax benefits.

Finding an experienced sponsor with a reputation for integrity is vital. Make sure that distributions are reinvested as they're received. As long as oil prices remain below $20 per barrel, the benefits of possible price increases outweigh the risks of price drops.

────────────────────── 21 ──────────────────────

# Focusing on Cable TV

Limited partnerships, as a widely available form of investment, have been around for about 10 years. During that time, some real estate deals have worked out well, but many have struggled. Some oil and gas partnerships have made money, but most have been disasters. In other types of partnerships—record masters, coal mining—few investors have recovered any cash at all.

In one category of investment, though, success has been the rule rather than the exception. That's cable television. Values of cable TV systems have risen tremendously across the United States, and almost any investor who went into a straightforward transaction has prospered.

But haven't there been some cable TV horror stories? Yes, mainly concerning big-city systems. Often, in urban areas, costs have been too high while revenues have been too low. But most cable TV limited partnerships operate in suburbs and small towns.

To be sure, there were some cable TV partnerships in which the purchase price was marked up outrageously, to provide more tax benefits to investors. These partnerships have fallen apart, but they weren't serious business ventures to begin with.

More typical are the results reported by Integrated Resources, a major sponsor of limited partnerships in real estate, oil and gas, and equipment leasing. According to its executives, cable TV has been the best area. Six cable TV systems were bought in the late 1970s and sold by the mid-1980s (others have been bought but not yet sold). Among those six completed transactions, average cash returns have been $3.50 per $1 invested, Integrated's executives assert. Another major sponsor of public partnerships, Jones Inter-cable, reports similar results.

204

## SUBSCRIBING TO CABLE TV'S
## GROWTH PROSPECTS

How do you make money in cable TV? First, a limited partnership acquires a local cable TV franchise. The partnership can acquire an existing system or build a new one. Then it collects revenues from cable TV subscribers. Excess cash, after expenses, is passed through to investors.

Over the past 10 years, more and more viewers have signed up for cable TV. Monthly charges have increased. As a result, cash flow to investors has gone up. Greater cash flow, in turn, has pushed up the value of cable TV systems.

To illustrate the economics of cable TV, we'll use an existing system. Most partnerships buy rather than build. Indeed, the United States is so thoroughly wired that it's hard to find worthwhile opportunities to start new systems.

Suppose a cable TV partnership raises $10 million, of which $8.5 million (after all the costs) is available to purchase a cable TV system. The partnership might buy a system with 5,000 existing subscribers.

Those subscribers might pay an average of $25 per month, or $300 per year. So the system's gross revenues would be $1.5 million per year. You can expect 60 percent of the gross revenues to go for operating costs while 40 percent is operating cash flow, as the cable industry calls it. In our example, cash flow would be $600,000. If that's distributed, investors would get a 6 percent return on their $10 million.

Most cable TV partnerships hold onto their systems for at least five years, so they can get tax benefits by depreciating the equipment they've purchased. In our example, first-year depreciation

| | |
|---|---|
| Money raised | $10 million |
| Front load (15%) | $ 1.5 million |
| Money available to buy cable TV system | $ 8.5 million |
| Number of subscribers | 5,000 |
| Average monthly payment | $ 25 |
| Average annual payment | $300 |
| Gross cable TV revenues (5,000 × $300) | $ 1.5 million |
| Operating cash flow (40% of gross revenue) | $600,000 |
| Distribution to investors | $600,000 |
| Cash-on-cash return | 6% |

might be enough to completely offset the partnership's operating income. So investors would keep the entire 6 percent, after-tax.

The general partner will attempt to attract new subscribers and increase monthly income per subscriber. This may be accomplished by raising rates or by persuading subscribers to sign up for extra services (i.e., Home Box Office, Disney Channel).

Let's say that the subscriber base goes up from 5,000 to 6,000 (20 percent) over five years. In addition, the average monthly tab goes up $2 per year, from $25 to $35. After five years, subscribers will be paying $420 per year, and the 6,000 subscribers will provide a total of $2.52 million in gross revenues. If 40 percent of the gross is available for cash flow, then distributions to investors would be over $1 million. Returns would grow from 6 to 10 percent.

In five years, the partnership decides to sell the system. Based on those results, such a system would sell for well over $14 million. Even after the general partner takes a cut, the limiteds could expect to receive at least a $12 million return on their $10 million. That's a 20 percent return, in four years, in addition to cash flow that grows from 6 percent per year to 10 percent per year.

Altogether, compound returns from such a partnership would be about 12 percent, pre-tax, and about 8 to 9 percent, after-tax. That seems pretty solid, in today's environment. But it's still a long way from the $3.50 for every $1 return reported on Integrated Resources' cable TV deals.

For an answer, let's go back to our discussion of leveraged versus unleveraged real estate deals. In this example, we've been assuming the purchase of a cable TV system for cash. Buying an existing system without debt service is an extremely safe investment. It's hard to imagine a circumstance in which you'd lose your money. Even if an economic depression struck the local community, most people would keep up their cable TV subscriptions. How else can you entertain your family for $20 or $30 a month? Indeed, in recent years, cable TV has shown the ability to buck hard times.

When you make a safe investment, you can expect a lower return. To get a higher yield, you need to take some risks. In the case of cable TV, that usually means using leverage. The same partnership just described might borrow $8 million or $10 million and buy a larger cable TV system, or several small systems. That would give it a chance to make more money and to pay higher returns—15 percent or more—to investors. But there's also a greater chance of running into trouble, if the revenues aren't large enough to cover the interest on the debt.

## PICKING THE WINNERS

So cable TV investors have to choose between a safe all-cash deal or a leveraged deal with more risks and more chance for profit. That's a decision common to many types of investments. What other factors should you look for, in a cable TV offering?

It's essential that someone with cable TV experience be in the deal. If the general partner isn't going to operate the franchise, he should have an operator under contract. In either case, the operator should have a record of taking over a cable TV system and producing revenue growth. Cable TV is an operating business, so you need someone who knows the industry.

Next, look at the system or systems to be acquired. If the partnership is a blind pool, read the business plan. If your money is going to construct a new system, be careful. It's not that you can't make money with a "new build"—you can make a lot of money, if things go well—but if a system has no operating history, all the numbers about cash flow amount to little more than guesses.

The same holds true with an urban system. It may be possible to make money there, but the risks are considerable.

## THE CASE FOR CLASSIC CABLE

Most investors are best served by existing *classic* systems. This type of system is in a small town or suburb. People are dependent upon TV for entertainment, having few other options. And they're dependent upon cable TV in particular, for good reception and for variety in programming.

Even if your partnership is buying the right kind of system, it's crucial that it pays the right price. Cable TV professionals talk in terms of cash-flow multiples. Cash flow in cable TV is another way of saying net income from operations. A system with $1 million in cash flow might sell for $10 million—a multiple of 10 times cash flow. It might sell for 12 times cash flow, or $12 million. In recent years, multiples have edged up, to 14 or 15.

The problem is coming up with a common measurement of cash flow, for this purpose. Is it cash flow from the last calendar year? The last 12 months? The latest month, multiplied by 12? Or the projected cash flow for the coming year?

## THE SIMPLE WAY: PRICE-PER-SUB

To avoid such questions, and to simplify comparisons, cable TV deals are sometimes expressed in terms of cost per subscriber. In our example above, where a system with 5,000 active subscribers sells for $8.5 million, the "cost per sub" is $1,700. Partnership sponsors now pay from $1,100 per subscriber up to $2,000 per subscriber, and sometimes more. Industry averages are in the area of $1,500.

This really is just another way of stating the same thing as a cash-flow multiple. If a subscriber will pay you $20 a month, and 40 percent of all your revenues wind up in operating cash flow, then that subscriber contributes $8 per month to cash flow, or $96 per year. If you can acquire that subscriber for $1,200, that's an 8 percent return. If you pay $1,800 to acquire that subscriber, the return is only 5.33 percent.

Obviously, investors would rather pay $1,200 than $1,800. So why would any partnership pay so much?

Some sponsors pay more for systems where they think the growth potential is high. Suppose you have a system where 80 percent of the potential users already subscribe to cable TV. More than half of them already subscribe to a pay channel such as HBO. The average monthly bill is above the national average. This is a mature system, with future growth likely to be modest. Its price is likely to be low, as a multiple of cash flow.

On the other hand, suppose you have a system where penetration is only 50 percent. The average monthly bill is $15, but all the surrounding cable TV systems get $20. You have an opportunity to attract new customers, raise rates, and sell new services. Sponsors may pay more for this type of system, because of the growth potential.

## NEW TECHNOLOGIES AREN'T
## AS THREATENING

Just because cable TV has been a good investment doesn't mean it will continue to be worthwhile. Critics say that growth has slowed down, in recent years. Videocassettes and VCRs have hurt the pay-movie stations. With prices for cable TV systems going higher and higher, it will be difficult for investors to notch those 3.5:1 returns.

It's true that the great growth days of cable TV may be behind it. Future appreciation is likely to be less spectacular. But as the industry matures into a mainstream investment, the outlook is for a slow but sure rise in revenues.

Competitive technology no longer seems like a threat. Just a few years ago, some experts predicted that satellites and dishes and lasers and other high-tech hardware would blur cable TV's future. That hasn't happened, and it isn't likely to. Cable TV even makes money now by selling decoders to backyard dish owners, so they can unscramble satellite signals and watch TV.

Videocassettes seem to be a threat now, but their future is questionable. Cable TV is probably only a few years away from a full-scale, pay-per-view system. With pay-per-view, consumers will be able to order virtually any movie they want, via cable TV, when they want it. The bill will come at the end of the month. They'll have all the benefits of watching a videocassette without the back-and-forth to the video store. In some trial markets now, cable TV operators get 40 to 50 percent of the pay-per-view revenues while others (studios, packagers) get the rest.

For many cable TV systems, the major expenses of wiring a community are in the past. Even including maintenance and system upgrading, the costs of adding new subscribers are relatively low. There may be fewer new subscribers, because the industry is nearing saturation, but most of the money from those new subscribers will go straight into extra cash flow for investors.

In 1984, Congress passed a law that took full effect in 1987. Now, cable TV rates can't be regulated by local governments. So cable TV has become an "unregulated monopoly." The local cable station can raise rates as high as the traffic will bear, but it's improbable that a competitor will go to the trouble and expense of stringing its own cables in a community that already has been wired once.

Deregulation is likely to generate higher cable TV revenues. Another boost may well come from in-home shopping shows. You've probably seen them—you select merchandise on TV and order by phone. Customers are sorted out by zip code, and the local cable TV station gets a cut (usually 5 percent) out of every dollar its viewers spend.

Other "ancillary" revenues are possible: national advertising, home security systems, "two-way" communications. It's hard to know what will evaporate and what will come to pass. Cable TV is an integral part of life for many Americans, and the uses to be made of that cable running into your house may turn out to be greater than imagined. You still can get cash from cable TV, if you invest with the right people and don't overpay.

## Summary

*Pros:*

- Growth potential. The track record has been excellent. As an "unregulated monopoly," the industry's future looks bright.
- Cash flow. Buying an existing system, at 12 or even 15 times cash flow, can give you a bondlike current return, along with all the growth prospects.
- Leverage. You can increase the potential reward by using leverage to buy systems. This increases the risk, but that risk decreases as cable TV becomes a quasi-utility, almost like a telephone or electric power.
- Tax benefits. Cash flow can be largely sheltered by depreciation.
- Liquidity. Interests in cash-generating cable TV partnerships are easier to sell than interests in many other types of partnerships. Nevertheless, cable TV partnerships should not be considered trading vehicles.

*Cons:*

- High prices. Cable TV has been so successful that prices of existing systems have shot up rapidly. It may be harder to go from $2,000 to $4,000 per subscriber than it was from $1,000 to $2,000.
- Business risk. Cable TV really is an operating business. A partnership needs skilled marketing and management.
- Competing technology. Although there's nothing on the horizon now, some new type of telecasting may supersede cable TV.

*Recommendation:*

A cable TV partnership investment may be considered as a substitute for stock ownership. Investors is an unleveraged partnership can get a current return higher than most stock dividends, plus appreciation. Investors in leveraged deals won't get a current return, but there's a chance for large profits after a medium-term holding period.

Compared with a stock fund, there's less diversification—only one industry—but no corporate income tax to contend with. Also, your fortunes are more directly tied to operating results, without worry about how the "market" values your assets.

Unless day-to-day liquidity is important to you, a cable TV partnership can fit in your portfolio, as a stocklike investment. Cable TV's future is as appealing as any in the U.S. economy, and limited partnerships are a proven way to invest.

# Mastering Master Limited Partnerships

Limited partnerships have one great virtue: They avoid the corporate income tax. But they have one great vice: They're not easily sold, after you've invested. Many investors don't like the idea of being locked in for 10 years or more.

Is it possible to shuck the bad and keep the good? Sponsors have been trying. During the past few years, they've introduced the master limited partnership (MLP). Despite some Congressional tampering, which we'll talk about later, MLPs can deliver the best of both worlds. They pay a high yield, with little or no tax due. And they're liquid: You can sell your investment whenever you want to, just like trading on the stock market.

## THE MAKEUP OF AN MLP

Master limited partnerships, like the limited partnerships we've been discussing, are available in all industries: oil and gas, hotels, restaurants, cable TV stations, and pro basketball teams. They share a few crucial characteristics including:

- They're big. Most master limited partnerships control assets valued at $50 million or more. They usually own several properties—many properties—rather than one office building or apartment house. That's what puts the "master" into MLPs.

- They're income-oriented. Most MLPs own existing businesses where cash flow is expected from the opening gun. Leverage is held down. Neither tax losses nor long-term growth are the main goal. For MLPs, the chief purpose is to distribute as much cash as possible, as soon as possible.

This cash flow usually is tax-favored. Deductions incurred by the MLP cut the tax liability for each partner. So the investor generally gets to keep most of his distribution. Recently, about 75 percent of all MLP distributions were sheltered.

The major distinguishing point, though, is liquidity. When an MLP is first issued, investors acquire units, typically priced from $10 to $20 apiece. If a unit is $20, for example, a $5,000 investor will receive 250 units.

Those units, in turn, will be listed on a stock exchange or they'll trade over-the-counter. You can find the value of your units each day, in the stock tables of your daily newspaper. If you decide to sell, a stockbroker can handle your trade, just as if you owned IBM stock.

## THE MLP ROLL CALL

That's the MLP structure. What's behind it? MLPs usually fall into one of three categories—roll-up, roll-out, or rollover.

Roll-ups were the original form of MLPs, involving oil and gas in the early 1980s. Some oil and gas companies had sponsored many partnerships over the years. Most of these partnerships were producing at least some oil at this point.

These sponsors *rolled up* their smaller producing partnerships into MLPs. Investors exchanged their holdings in the small partnership for a pro rata share of the large MLP. Now, they had a share in many more wells, so they had diversification. Plus, of course, the ability to cash out, if necessary. In small oil and gas partnerships, it's usually hard to cash out unless you're willing to sell at a steep discount. In an MLP, expenses such as accounting fees often were reduced, because the costs were spread over one large partnership rather than dozens of small ones.

Roll-outs came next, also in oil and gas. Some major oil companies felt that their stock was undervalued in relation to their oil and gas reserves. So they *rolled out* some of their oil and gas. That is, they took some reserves and split them off from the parent corporation. The reserves were sold to a newly formed MLP. Typically, some of the funding for the MLP came from individual investors while the rest came from the company itself. This allowed the company to retain control over the oil and gas.

The roll-out MLP then owned the oil and gas. Investors received the revenues directly, without having to cope with a corporate income tax.

In both types of oil and gas MLPs—roll-ups and roll-outs—provision was made for reinvestment. That is, the oil and gas might throw off enough cash to distribute 20 percent to investors. But the general partner would hold down distributions to, say, 10 percent. The other 10 percent would be reinvested in new drilling. This would provide ongoing tax deductions, to shelter the distributions. And it might prolong the life of the MLP, if the drilling proved to be successful.

In 1986, MLPs in real estate became popular. There are a few roll-ups and roll-outs. Burger King, for example, rolled out several of its restaurants to an MLP. That MLP now owns those restaurants and collects rents based on their retail volume.

Other deals may be described as "naked" real estate MLPs. These MLPs own one or two or a handful of properties, just like a standard real estate limited partnership. However, the deals are structured for yield and the units are publicly traded. Similarly, some mortgage partnerships are considered MLPs because their units are publicly traded.

Rollover MLPs were popular before the tax law was changed. In these deals, a corporate entity converts or *rolls over* to an MLP and continues doing business in this manner. It's not a roll-out, because there's nothing left behind after the MLP is formed. Recent rollovers include Motel 6, Perkins Pancake Houses, and the Boston Celtics. By functioning as an MLP rather than as a corporation, the corporate income tax is avoided.

## TIGHTENING UP THE TAX LAW

Congress and the IRS feared that rollovers would spread. Corporate America would become MLP America, reducing revenues from the corporate income tax. So, at the end of 1987, the tax law was changed. MLPs now have to pay a corporate income tax.

However—nothing is straightforward when Congress amends the tax law—real estate and oil and gas MLPs are exempted from corporate taxation. In addition, all other MLPs get a 10-year reprieve, providing they were in existence before the end of 1987. For the next 10 years, MLPs already in existence will retain their ability to pass through high cash flow, free of corporate income taxes.

## LOOKING BEYOND HIGH CASH FLOW

Are MLPs really Marvelous Limited Partnerships? Let's look at the two prime selling points—high distributions and liquidity.

MLPs have high payouts because they're designed that way. When a deal is being put together, the investment banking firm looks over the operating history and projects how much cash flow there will be in the next year, if the corporate income tax can be avoided. Then it multiplies that number by 10 or 12 or 14, to get the MLP's asking price.

Let's say Better Burgers wants to convert to an MLP. Its investment bankers calculate cash distributions in the coming year can be $5 million. They multiply by 12 and the Better Burgers MLP is priced at $60 million.

Better Burgers wants to keep 60 percent for itself. So the other 40 percent will be sold to the public. If Better Burgers MLP is valued at $60 million, then the public's 40 percent share will be priced at $24 million. If units are priced at $20 apiece, then 1.2 million units will be sold to the public.

The next year, Better Burgers MLP distributes $5 million, as promised. Better Burgers has retained 60 percent of the MLP units, so it receives $3 million of the distributions. The other $2 million is distributed among the 1.2 million units held by the public. Each unit will be entitled to a $1.67 distribution.

If an investor bought at the original $20 offering price, $1.67 is an 8.33 percent yield. That's probably better than what would have been received as distribution, if he had bought stock in McDonald's. Plus, depreciation on the Better Burgers restaurants can be passed through, lowering the tax bite. Our investor may wind up with a 6 or 7 percent after-tax return.

## CASH FLOW MAY DRY UP

There are a couple of problems with MLPs. The yield is not guaranteed for any length of time. Here, our investor owns a piece of a going business, not an office building with tenants on long-term leases. So results can vary widely from year-to-year.

Better Burgers may launch a smash ad campaign, boosting sales dramatically. Or someone might die from a poisoned pickle in one of their restaurants, choking off their sales. That $1.67 distribution may be $3 next year, or 3 cents.

That's what happened to all the oil and gas MLPs formed in the early 1980s. In 1986, oil prices plunged. MLPs received a lot less for their oil and gas, so they had less to distribute. Investors saw their cash flow cut or eliminated.

What's more, the trading prices of the MLP units dropped as the distributions were slashed. Therefore, any investor who needed to cash out had to accept a lower price.

In addition, this approach is not a very scientific way to put a value on a business. As you might expect, investors generally wind up overpaying rather than underpaying.

The Boston Celtics went public at the end of 1986. The MLP units were priced to yield over 7 percent. Based on that price, the team was valued at about $120 million. Yet several press articles at the time put the value of a comparable sports franchise, if purchased directly, at no more than $75 million. The former owners bought the team for $19 million in 1983. No matter how great the initial yield, it's never a good deal to buy a $75 million asset for $120 million.

## TRADING PRICES GO BOTH WAYS

Liquidity also can have its drawbacks. MLP units are traded like common stocks. Thus, they're subject to the whims of the stock market. If there are more sellers than buyers, the price will go down. This can happen even if the MLP is performing well, or if the underlying assets are going up in value. When you need to sell, the market may be depressed. If that's the case, you'll receive less when you sell.

Thus, you're losing one of the advantages of a limited partnership—direct participation in a business. Your investment results may vary from the results of that business.

Indeed, MLPs have fared poorly in price, once they've begun trading. It's a rare MLP that trades at a higher price than the initial offering level. Much more common are $20 shares now selling for $15 or $12 or $10. Of course, as the trading price drops, the yield may be extremely high, if the payout may be retained.

## SHELTER NOW, PAY LATER

MLP taxation may complicate matters. Suppose you buy an MLP for $20 a unit. In the first year, you receive a $1.60 distribution (8 percent) of which $1.20 (6 percent) is sheltered. You pay taxes only on 40 cents (2 percent), so the after-tax cash flow is over 7 percent.

For tax purposes, the tax-sheltered amount is deducted from your basis, dropping it to $18.80. Suppose you sell next year for $19 a unit. You think you've taken a loss (bought at $20, sold at $19), but the IRS says you actually have a 20-cent gain, and you owe taxes.

For most investors, this kind of recordkeeping makes it hard to know what the tax consequences will be when you sell shares. Worse, the uncertainty and the hassle may keep some investors from buying MLP units. If so, that will reduce the demand for MLPs and hold down their prices.

Similarly, tax-exempt investors may not want to get involved with MLPs. MLP income may be considered "unrelated business taxable income." Tax-exempt investors owe taxes on this kind of

| | |
|---|---|
| Purchase price | $20/unit |
| First-year distribution | $1.60/unit (8%) |
| Sheltered portion | $1.20/unit (6%) |
| Taxable portion | $0.40/unit (2%) |
| Taxes (@ 30%) | $0.12/unit |
| After-tax distribution ($1.60-.12) | $1.48/unit |
| After-tax cash flow ($20/$1.48) | 7.4% |

*Assume a sale after one year, at $19/unit:*

| | |
|---|---|
| Original purchase price | $20/unit |
| Subtract: Sheltered cash flow | $1.20/unit |
| "Tax basis" | $18.80/unit |
| Selling price | $19/unit |
| Taxable gain | $0.20/unit |

income. Many tax-exempt investors are large pension funds, major stock market players. A similar situation exists for foreign investors. If they keep away from MLPs, demand could be considerably lower, and prices would be depressed.

## MLP BUYERS NEED PATIENCE

Calling an investment an "MLP" doesn't automatically make it perfect. There are advantages, to be sure. Most MLPs are specified in advance, so investors know what they're buying. And these MLPs certainly are better than some of the contrived deals of old that were solely tax-oriented.

But MLPs still can sell investors overpriced goods. Distributions can go down as well as up, and so can unit prices. Investors should make sure they know exactly what they're buying, and what they're paying for it. Often, it's better to avoid the initial offering of an MLP. If you really want to buy into a deal, it might be better to wait and acquire the units on the secondary market. If the initial price is too high, it may come down when the units begin to trade.

─────────── *Summary* ───────────

*Pros:*

- High cash flow. Double-digit distributions are the rule.
- Tax shelter. In most MLPs, the cash flow is mainly or completely sheltered from current income taxes.
- Liquidity. MLP units trade like common stocks.
- Track record. Unlike most limited partnerships, which are "blind pools," you know what you're buying with an MLP.
- Inflation protection. Many MLPs are in industries that will do well in inflationary times. If hamburger prices or hotel room rates or oil prices go up, MLP investors stand to gain.
- Growth potential. Even without inflation, there may be growth through business expansion.

*Cons:*

- Operating business risk. Many MLPs are in businesses where results can vary, driving share prices up or down.

- Price volatility. MLP shares may move up and down with the stock market, regardless of how the MLP actually is doing. MLP shares have not done well, even during the pre-crash bull market.
- Disrupted distributions. Some MLPs artificially prop up cash flow for the first few years, generally through some kind of loan. Once the guarantee period expires, cash flow may fall, leading to a lower share price.
- Tax changes. Further adverse taxation of MLPs is possible. As things now stand, nonreal estate and nonoil and gas MLPs may lose value, as they near 1998, when a corporate income tax will be imposed.
- Delayed taxation. When you sell MLP shares, you'll owe the taxes you previously avoided, through sheltered cash flow.

*Recommendation:*

MLPs cover a broad range from real estate MLPs to operating business MLPs that act like stocks to mortgage MLPs that are real estate/bond hybrids. Each MLP needs to be judged on its own merits.

When MLP prices are low, as they have been recently, they offer cash flow that's hard to pass up. But they're only for knowledgeable investors, who have taken the time to read the fine print. Don't buy just because your broker promises "14 percent, tax-free." (Some MLP mutual funds have been announced, but none has actually been launched yet.)

MLPs should be considered speculative investments, for investors who are willing to take risks. They should not be held in tax-exempt retirement plans, because of tax and paperwork technicalities.

# Appendix A

# How to Get at the Heart of Financial Reports

Don't buy blind. That's been one of our key messages throughout this book. Know what you're doing, before you invest. That's true if you're investing directly or working with a financial adviser.

How do you know what you're buying? Research, research, research. To make money, you need to work. Any investment, before it's offered to the public, must comply with a mountain of paperwork requirements. If you fight your way through that mountain of paper, you can learn how your money will be used.

Few people have the time or the inclination to read everything, especially when it's written in language designed to conform to regulations, rather than inform. But, if you know your way through the maze, you can quickly grasp the main points. In this appendix, we'll discuss how to read the annual reports and prospectuses of the most common types of investments.

## CORPORATE ANNUAL REPORTS

If you're a stock market investor, you're buying shares—a portion—of a publicly held corporation. All such corporations must publish annual reports at the end of each fiscal year. Don't buy stocks on rumors; ask to see the latest annual report before you invest.

Don't expect to play detective when you read an annual report. These reports are pored over by professional analysts, trying to find where the bodies are buried. You probably won't find anything that these analysts haven't already unearthed. Instead, ask your broker for copies of analysts' reports.

Why bother to read the annual report yourself? Because it's the best way to get a feel for a company and its current prospects. Start by reading the letter from the chairman or chief executive that begins most annual reports. Sure, he or she will put the best face on everything, but this letter will describe the company's business and highlight its main concerns.

For example, let's take Southmark Corp. In 1988, *Forbes* ran an article about Southmark, stating that the company's "corporate structure and accounting are bewilderingly complex . . . even an expert has difficulty" figuring out its financial situation. An individual investor can hardly expect to master this corporation after spending 10 minutes with the annual report.

But, reading the chairman's letter in the 1987 annual report, you'll see repeated references to real estate, and to the 1986 Tax Reform Act. So you know right away that the company is heavily involved in real estate, and that its fortunes are closely tied to how the industry recovers from tax reform. If you think that real estate is in for a long-term period of difficulty, you can file Southmark and go on to something else. If you think that real estate is in the "buy low" stage of its cycle, you might want to consider this particular company, so you can search for further details.

## Digging for Details

Most annual reports will follow the chairman's letter with descriptions of the company's business, and the industries in which it participates. Generally, you can skip over this material. It's usually just an expansion of the themes you've already encountered in the introductory letter.

Then comes the "financial review"—page after page of numbers guaranteed to glaze the eye and numb the brain. A few of these pages tell most of the story.

First, there's the income statement. Here you can see how the company did in the latest year. There's a section in this statement called "revenues" and one called "expenses." The difference—assuming it's positive—will be income. The key here isn't the magnitude of income, but the direction. If a company's net income and its net income per common share has been increasing from year to year the company seems to be doing well.

Along with the income statement, the balance sheet is considered a basic financial statement. Here is where a company's assets are weighed against liabilities. The balance—and there better be a balance—is the shareholders' equity. That's the corporation's net worth, and it's what you're buying when you invest. Most annual reports will show a "consolidated statement of shareholders' equity," showing the trend over the past few years. Again, increasing equity is a sign of health.

Balance sheets, however, rely heavily on the way assets are valued. For example, a company may have total assets of $20 million, including $18 million of oil and gas properties, valued at cost. If you invest, you're betting that the company bought that oil at good prices, and that the long-term oil price trend will be up rather than down.

### Concentrating on Cash Flow

While the income statement and the balance sheet are the basic financial statements, another—the consolidated statement of changes in financial position—is worth a look. In essence, this is a cash-flow statement. Many businesses report increased earnings that are really paper profits. At some point, a business needs to earn real cash.

For example, depreciation reduces a company's reported earnings, but it's a noncash expense, so it's not really pinching the corporate pocketbook. On the other hand, a company may sell an asset and take back paper, rather than cash, from the buyer. This makes the earnings per share look better, but it doesn't help the bank account.

The "change in financial position" statement washes out all the noncash items and shows how much money the business actually is taking in from operations. Again, you want to see a rising trend. If cash flow or net income or shareholders' equity has been decreasing in recent years, find out why before you invest.

### Now for the Bad Stuff

Perhaps the most revealing section of any annual report comes under the rather drab title, "Management's Discussion and Analysis of Financial Condition and Results of Operations." Here, the company spells out differences in performance year-to-year, and explains why those differences occurred in language that's stripped of all the promotional hype.

You'll come across language like "recognize the decrease in the aggregate net value of oil and gas reserves," "increased borrowing," "economic downturn in real estate," and other discouraging words. If you read just one section of an annual report, this is the most telling.

## MUTUAL FUNDS

Whenever you invest in a mutual fund, you have to receive a copy of the fund's prospectus. That's federal securities law. If anyone tries to sell you a fund without giving you a look at a prospectus, something's wrong.

The fund's prospectus will describe its policies and its investment objectives. You can learn if it will invest in stocks or bonds or both. More importantly, you'll learn about which types of stocks or bonds the fund will hold. There's a big difference between a fund that "seeks maximum capital appreciation through investment in small growth companies" and one that "seeks long-term growth of principal and income through investment in dividend-paying, financially strong companies with sound economic background." A prospectus also will tell you if a fund will use risky strategies such as buying or selling options, buying on margin, selling short, and so on.

## A New Fee Comparison

In mid-1988, the SEC passed a new rule that applies to all mutual funds. Each fund now must include a fee table in the front of its prospectus. Such a table will list all fees, both sales loads and operating charges. Then it will show the results of a hypothetical $1,000 investment, assuming 5 percent annual growth over 1, 3, 5, and 10 years. If you get the prospectuses from a few funds, and compare the results of these hypothetical investments, you'll be able to see which funds have the heaviest costs for investors.

## Scanning the Financials

A prospectus also includes a "condensed financial information statement" that traces the performance of the fund, up to 10 years' worth. For example, the table from Nuveen Municipal Bond Fund's prospectus, issued at the end of 1987, is shown on page 224.

All data is per share. In the first line, "Investment income," we can see how much interest the fund collected during the year from the bonds that it holds. A stock fund prospectus would show dividends received.

The next line, "Operating expenses," shows the fund's costs. Subtract expenses from income and you get "net investment income," which is what a fund has available for distribution. Sure enough, on the next line, we see that all of the net investment income has been distributed over the year.

Looking over the 10-year period, we see that this fund has been extremely stable. Per-share payouts have ranged from 53 cents to 63 cents. The highest payouts came in 1981-82, when interest rates peaked.

The next line, "Net realized and unrealized gains (losses) on investments," shows if the fund's holdings have gone up or down in value. In this fund we note that, while investment income has been stable, the underlying shares have been subject to frequent swings. In 1979-81, for example, when interest rates rose, the fund suffered large losses in per-share values. Most of those losses, though, were recouped in 1982-83 and 1985-86, when interest rates fell and share values rebounded.

| Fiscal Year Ended September 30, | 1987 | 1986 | 1985 | 1984 | 1983 | 1982 | 1981 | 1980 | 1979 | 1978 |
|---|---|---|---|---|---|---|---|---|---|---|
| **Income and Expenses** | | | | | | | | | | |
| Investment income | $ .658 | $ .656 | $ .642 | $ .623 | $ .628 | $ .671 | $ .682 | $ .635 | $ .598 | $ .601 |
| Operating expenses | (.060) | (.061) | (.056) | (.054) | (.054)† | (.046)† | (.052)† | (.061)† | (.070)† | (.072)† |
| Net investment income | .598 | .595 | .586 | .569 | .574 | .625 | .630 | .574 | .528 | .529 |
| Dividends from net investment income | (.598) | (.595) | (.586) | (.569) | (.574) | (.625) | (.630) | (.574) | (.528) | (.529) |
| **Capital Changes** | | | | | | | | | | |
| Net realized and unrealized gains (losses) on investments | (.614) | 1.162 | .650 | (.220) | .490 | .900 | (1.450) | (1.800) | (.090) | (.450) |
| Distributions from net realized gains on investment transactions | (.146) | (.212) | — | — | — | — | — | — | — | — |
| Net increase (decrease) in net assets | (.760) | .950 | .650 | (.220) | .490 | .900 | (1.450) | (1.800) | (.090) | (.450) |
| **Net Asset Value** | | | | | | | | | | |
| Beginning of fiscal year | 8.780 | 7.830 | 7.180 | 7.400 | 6.910 | 6.010 | 7.460 | 9.260 | 9.350 | 9.800 |
| End of fiscal year | $8.020 | $8.780 | $7.830 | $7.180 | $7.400 | $6.910 | $6.010 | $7.460 | $9.260 | $9.350 |
| **Ratios to average net assets** | | | | | | | | | | |
| Net expenses | .68% | .71% | .73% | .74% | .75%† | .75%† | .75%† | .75%† | .75%† | .75%† |
| Net investment income | 6.85% | 6.95% | 7.68% | 7.91% | 7.81%† | 9.99%† | 9.12%† | 7.11%† | 5.65%† | 5.54%† |
| Portfolio turnover rate | 16% | 39% | 28% | 44% | 78% | 42% | 32% | 47% | 37% | 37% |
| Number of shares outstanding at end of period (in thousands) | 95,257 | 76,099 | 58,682 | 47,022 | 36,778 | 26,600 | 20,451 | 16,035 | 9,177 | 5,867 |

† *Reflects the reimbursement of certain expenses by the Adviser.*

Reproduced from the Nuveen Municipal Bond Fund's Prospectus, 1987.

The next line of the table shows that Nuveen Municipal Bond Fund distributed some of those gains, in 1986–87, which it hadn't been doing in prior years. The next line, "net increase (decrease) in net assets," combines the previous two lines. That is, if your bond portfolio loses 61.4 cents per share, because of rising interest rates, and your fund distributes 14.6 cents per share, then the total decrease in value will be 76 cents per share.

## How Investors Have Fared

Then the table traces net asset value, over the entire time period. That's the selling price per share, if you wish to buy or sell. The fund in our example has gone from $9.80 to $8.02, an 18 percent decline, over the past 10 years. About 36 cents of the decline was due to cash distributions, but the rest has occurred because interest rates have gone up more than they've gone down, during this period. From 1978 to 1982, for example, share prices fell from $9.80 to $6.01, as interest rates shot up. Then, as rates fell from 1982 to 1986, share prices recovered only partially, to $8.78.

The last section of this table shows some ratios that allow you to compare different funds. "Net expenses" generally average around 1.25 percent, for mutual funds. Bond funds are usually lower than average, and this fund shows a comfortably low ratio. In fact, expenses have dropped in recent years.

The next line, the ratio of net investment income to net assets, shows the cash flow that this fund has produced. Over a 10-year period, this payout has ranged between 5.5 and 10 percent. Generally the payout has been around 7 percent. Of course, this is a tax-exempt yield, from a municipal bond fund.

The "portfolio turnover rate" shows how much selling is done by a fund. Average turnover is around 90 percent, so this fund looks like it tends to buy-and-hold, rather than trade frequently. On the last line, the number of shares outstanding, we see that this fund has grown nearly twenty-fold in 10 years, as municipal bond funds became popular with individual investors.

## Keeping Up to Date

The prospectus is supplemented by quarterly reports, and then by an annual report. Here, the fund's most recent performance is reported. Thus, you can see how the fund has done, since publication of the latest prospectus.

Also, these periodic reports will show exactly which stocks or bonds the fund currently holds, broken down by the amount invested. Bond funds will show ratings, where appropriate. So you see what type of investments you'll wind up holding, if you choose a particular fund.

# LIMITED PARTNERSHIPS

Public limited partnerships, like mutual funds, come with prospectuses, which you should read before you invest. However, the typical limited partnership prospectus is much larger, and much more intimidating.

The best place to begin is the "Summary of the Offering," which quickly explains the deal. Then, take a look at the "Management" section. As we've mentioned before, the key to a good partnership investment is the general partner. Under "Management," you'll see who'll be managing your money.

For example, a recent prospectus published by Public Storage, a well-regarded syndicator, goes on for nine pages listing the company's personnel. Besides "senior management," there's an administration and finance group, a development group, an acquisition group, a property management group, and so on. Most of the people listed have good qualifications, at least on paper, and they've been with Public Storage for several years. Senior management includes several executives who have been with the company since the 1970s, when it was founded.

Take a quick look at the "Investment Objectives and Policies" section. A lot of this will be boilerplate, cover-your-anatomy stuff ("the extent to which the Partnership is affected by competition will depend in significant part on market conditions"), but you should be able to get the gist of what the partnership plans to do. What kinds of properties will be acquired? New or existing? Leveraged or unleveraged?

From there, go to the "Risk Factors" section. Securities law requires sponsors to inform investors of potential risks. However, sponsors load up this section with every conceivable risk they can think of, as a defense against future litigation. So the challenge is to find the real risks. Every limited partnership will have the risk of illiquidity, and some tax risks (although public partnerships have generally not aroused IRS ire). However, when you read about joint ventures ("actions by a co-venturer may have the result of subjecting property . . . to additional risks") you may want to learn more about the sponsor's business plan.

## Peering into the Past

The most crucial part of the prospectus, though, is the "Prior Performance" section. Here, you can check on the sponsor's track record. Although past performance isn't a perfect indicator of future success, it's the best one that you have. Read this section before making any investment decision. It seldom runs more than six pages, so it's well worth taking the time if you're going to invest $5,000 or more.

Here, you'll see how long the company has been in business, how much money it has raised, and what types of properties it manages. You also may see a section headed "Adverse Tenant Developments" that lists problems in prior partnerships. Today, virtually every syndicator has some problem properties. In fact, you should be suspicious if no problems are mentioned.

Keep the problems in perspective. Just as a stock mutual fund will have some losers, so will a diversified real estate portfolio. The question that you need to ask is: Are the losses under control or out of control?

One sponsor, for example, lists all the vacancies in 13 prior partnerships. Overall, the rate is 0.94 percent, with 3.86 percent the highest. So the company seems to be meeting its goals. Another sponsor, though, sprinkles language such as "not meeting their investment objectives" and "will not attain . . . capital growth and may not completely attain . . . capital preservation." Such a sponsor hasn't delivered what it promised in the past, so you need to be convinced that things will be different before investing in future programs.

## Tackling the Tables

Each prospectus has a section chock full of "Prior Performance Tables" towards the back. Usually, Table III contains operating results. Again, you need to be a professional auditor to thoroughly analyze the statistics. But you can get a good idea of how the partnerships are performing with a quick look at the right numbers.

First, choose past programs that are roughly similar in size and scope to the one that you're considering. If you want an idea of how the sponsor will do with a $25 million unleveraged hotel deal, don't compare it with a $5 million, leveraged partnership that bought apartment buildings.

Then, look at comparable partnerships formed in the early 1980s. Partnerships that were formed in the past few years may be too new for meaningful results; partnerships formed in the 1970s may have walked into a windfall when the real estate market took off.

Once you have selected the appropriate partnerships, look down the operating results in Table III for the line, "cash generated (deficiency) from operations." You're looking for a sponsor where this number is consistently positive. Ideally, this number should be increasing over time, but real estate conditions in the past few years have been so difficult that any sponsor who has kept operating cash flow fairly stable has done a good job.

Again, let's look at Public Storage (pp. 228–29). Here's a page from a current prospectus showing two partnerships formed in 1983. In both cases, cash generated from operations has been edging up.

Cash distributions, as shown on the bottom of the page, have gone from 3 to 4 to 5 percent to present levels, around 6 to 7 percent. (Distributing $40 per $1,000 investment is 4 percent.) If you compare the

| | PSP-9 | | |
|---|---|---|---|
| | 1983 | 1984 | 1985 |
| **Summary of Operations —** | | | |
| GAAP Basis(1): | | | |
| Gross Revenues(2)(3)(13) | $1,578,000 | $2,411,000 | $3,600,000 |
| Profit on Sale of Property | — | — | — |
| Less: Operating Expense(4) | (265,000) | (1,091,000) | (1,823,000) |
| Depreciation and Amortization | (52,000) | (617,000) | (929,000) |
| Net Income — GAAP Basis(1) | $1,261,000 | $ 703,000 | $ 848,000 |
| **Tax Basis:** | | | |
| Taxable Income (Loss)(3) | | | |
| — From Operations | $1,381,000 | $ 532,000 | $ 135,000 |
| — From Gain on Sale | — | — | — |
| Taxable Income (Loss) | $1,381,000 | $ 532,000 | $ 135,000 |
| **Cash Generated:** | | | |
| Cash Generated from Operations | $1,430,000 | $1,544,000 | $1,579,000 |
| Cash Generated from Sales | — | — | — |
| Less: Cash Distributions to Investors | | | |
| — From Operations | (802,000) | (1,629,000) | (2,122,000) |
| — From Sales | — | — | — |
| — From Other | — | — | (50,000) |
| Cash Generated (Deficiency) after Cash | | | |
| Distributions | $ 628,000 | $ (85,000) | $ (593,000) |
| **Tax and Distribution Data per $1,000 Investment** | | | |
| Federal Income Tax Data | | | |
| Ordinary Income (Loss) | $ 31.80(8) | $ 12.26 | $ 3.12 |
| Capital Gain | — | — | — |
| Total Taxable Income (Loss) | $ 31.80(8) | $ 12.26 | $ 3.12 |
| **Cash Distributions to Investors (GAAP Basis)(6)** | | | |
| Investment Income | $ 18.47(8) | $ 16.19 | $ 19.51 |
| Return of Capital | — | 21.31 | 30.49 |
| Total Distributions to Investors | $ 18.47(8) | $ 37.50 | $ 50.00 |
| **Cash Distributions to Investors (Cash Basis)** | | | |
| Operations | $ 18.47(8) | $ 37.50 | $ 48.85 |
| Sales | — | — | — |
| Other | — | — | 1.15 |
| Total Distributions to Investors | $ 18.47(8) | $ 37.50 | $ 50.00 |

Reprinted from a 1987 Public Storage Prospectus.

# OF PRIOR PARTNERSHIPS
## Certified Public Accountants)

| | January-June 1987 | | | PSP-10 | | January-June 1987 |
|---|---|---|---|---|---|---|
| 1986 | January-June 1987 | June-December 1983 | 1984 | 1985 | 1986 | January-June 1987 |
| $5,133,000 | $ 2,914,000 | $ 770,000 | $2,236,000 | $2,411,000 | $4,351,000 | $ 2,607,000 |
| (2,305,000) | (1,059,000) | (144,000) | (452,000) | (1,480,000) | (1,977,000) | (1,069,000) |
| (1,057,000) | (525,000) | — | (170,000) | (928,000) | (1,098,000) | (560,000) |
| $1,771,000 | $ 1,330,000 | $ 626,000 | $1,614,000 | $ 3,000 | $1,276,000 | $ 978,000 |
| $1,089,000 | $ 885,000 | $ 675,000 | $1,597,000 | $ (392,000) | $ 718,000 | $ 639,000 |
| $1,089,000 | $ 885,000 | $ 675,000 | $1,597,000 | $ (392,000) | $ 718,000 | $ 639,000 |
| $2,683,000 | $ 1,692,000 | $ 675,000 | $1,905,000 | $ 925,000 | $2,209,000 | $ 1,396,000 |
| (2,280,000) | (1,466,000) | (424,000) | (1,379,000) | (1,697,000) | (1,697,000) | (1,299,000) |
| $ 403,000 | $ 226,000 | $ 251,000 | $ 526,000 | $ (772,000) | $ 512,000 | $ 97,000 |
| $ 25.07 | $ 20.37 | $ 15.91(8) | $ 37.65 | $ (9.24) | $ 16.91 | $ 15.07 |
| $ 25.07 | $ 20.37 | $ 15.91(8) | $ 37.65 | $ (9.24) | $ 16.91 | $ 15.07 |
| $ 40.77 | $ 30.62 | $ 10.00 | $ 32.50 | $ .06 | $ 30.08 | $ 23.05 |
| 11.73 | 3.14 | — | — | 39.94 | 9.92 | 7.57 |
| $ 52.50 | $ 33.76 | $ 10.00(8) | $ 32.50 | $ 40.00 | $ 40.00 | $ 30.62 |
| $ 52.50 | $ 33.76 | $ 10.00(8) | $ 32.50 | $ 40.00 | $ 40.00 | $ 30.62 |
| $ 52.50 | $ 33.76 | $ 10.00(8) | $ 32.50 | $ 40.00 | $ 40.00 | $ 30.62 |

# OPERATING RESULTS OF PRIOR PROGRAMS

| | 1983 | 1984 | 1985 | 1986 |
|---|---|---|---|---|
| GROSS REVENUES | $ 4,446,000 | $23,312,000 | $17,115,000 | $17,399,000 |
| PROFIT ON SALE OF PROPERTIES | — | — | — | — |
| LESS: | | | | |
| Operating Expenses | 1,756,000 | 12,004,000 | 8,802,000 | 8,789,000 |
| Interest Expense | 2,038,000 | 8,572,000 | 7,937,000 | 7,946,000 |
| Depreciation and Amortization | 1,087,000 | 5,570,000 | 5,775,000 | 5,869,000 |
| NET INCOME (LOSS)—GAAP BASIS | $ (435,000) | $(2,834,000) | $(5,399,000) | $(5,205,000) |
| TAXABLE INCOME (LOSS) | | | | |
| —From Operations | $(7,801,000) | $(3,176,000) | $(8,460,000) | $(8,114,000)(2) |
| —From Gain on Sale | — | — | — | — |
| CASH GENERATED FROM OPERATIONS(3) | $ 1,388,000 | $ 3,769,000 | $ 449,000 | $ (118,000) |
| CASH GENERATED FROM SALES | — | — | — | — |
| CASH GENERATED FROM REFINANCING | — | — | — | — |
| CASH GENERATED FROM OPERATIONS, SALES AND REFINANCING | 1,388,000 | 3,769,000 | 449,000 | (118,000) |
| LESS: CASH DISTRIBUTIONS TO INVESTORS | | | | |
| —From Operating Cash Flow | 272,000 | 4,406,000 | 3,193,000 | 458,000 |
| —From Sales and Refinancing | — | — | — | — |
| CASH GENERATED (DEFICIENCY) AFTER CASH DISTRIBUTIONS | 1,116,000 | (637,000) | (2,744,000) | (576,000) |
| LESS: SPECIAL ITEMS (NOT INCLUDING SALES AND REFINANCING) | — | — | — | — |
| CASH GENERATED (DEFICIENCY) AFTER CASH DISTRIBUTIONS AND SPECIAL ITEMS | $ 1,116,000 | $ (637,000) | $(2,744,000) | $ (576,000) |

## TAX AND DISTRIBUTION DATA PER $1,000 INVESTED

| | | | | |
|---|---|---|---|---|
| **FEDERAL INCOME TAX RESULTS:** | | | | |
| ORDINARY INCOME (LOSS) | | | | |
| —From Operations | $ (167.86) | $ (34.94) | $ (93.08) | $ (90.00) |
| —From Recapture | — | — | — | — |
| CAPITAL GAIN (LOSS) | — | — | — | — |
| **CASH DISTRIBUTIONS TO INVESTORS:** | | | | |
| SOURCE (ON GAAP BASIS): | | | | |
| —Investment Income | $ 5.85 | $ 48.47 | $ 35.13 | $ 5.04 |
| —Return of Capital | — | — | — | — |
| SOURCE (ON CASH BASIS): | | | | |
| —Sales | — | — | — | — |
| —Refinancing | — | — | — | — |
| —Operations | $ 5.85 | $ 48.47 | $ 35.13 | $ 5.04 |
| **PERCENT REMAINING INVESTED IN PROGRAM PROPERTIES AT THE END OF THE LAST YEAR REPORTED IN THE TABLE** | | | | 100% |

(1) Results for fiscal year ended 10/31.

(2) During 1986, the Partnership changed its fiscal year end for income tax reporting purposes from 10/31 to 12/31. The amount presented relates to the period from 11/1/85 to 12/31/86.

(3) Before mortgage reduction. Includes interest income of $738,000 in 1983; $2,415,000 in 1984; $1,026,000 in 1985 and $614,000 in 1986.

"cash generated" line with "cash distributions to investors," you can see that distributions have come mainly from operations, adjusting for some timing differences. Thus, it appears that this is a sponsor who has made money from real estate, enough to provide investors with meaningful cash flow.

By contrast, look at the table of another real estate partnership formed in 1983 pp. 230–231. In 1983 and 1984, this partnership generated over $5 million in cash (including over $3 million in interest income while the money was "parked," before being invested in real estate) and distributed less than $4.7 million. So far, so good.

But, in 1985 and 1986, the real estate ran into problems, cash flow went negative, and barely $300,000 was generated in those two years. Yet distributions topped $3.6 million. Thus, the partnership appears to have paid out money it didn't really earn. When you see such a pattern, you should find out why operating cash flow fell, and why distributions to investors were so high, before investing in a new program.

# Appendix B

# Paying College Costs with Cash-Flow Investing

Why bother? That's a natural question to ask, once you've learned how cash-flow investments work. Why take the trouble to understand a leveraged, high-tech equipment leasing public limited partnership, for example?

You can, after all, simply put your money into 90-day Treasury bills or six-month CDs or a money market fund. Keep rolling them over, as they come due. You'll have virtually no risk of losing any money and you'll get a decent return, probably around 6 percent. If inflation accelerates and interest rates shoot up, you'll get an increasing yield from your T-bills, CDs, or money fund. Why not put all your cash into cash equivalents and worry about something else?

## CASH HAS RISKS, TOO

Certainly, there's nothing wrong with investing in cash equivalents. But when you go for safety and flexibility, you have to give up something. Here, you have to sacrifice some return. In fact, a strategy that focuses solely on cash equivalents may wind up losing real buying power.

As we mentioned, 6 percent seems like a reasonable long-term return from cash equivalents. However, inflation has averaged just about 6 percent for the past 20 years. That inflation rate has been fairly constant, too. From the mid-1960s to the mid-1970s, inflation averaged about 6 percent. Again, from the mid-1970s to the mid-1980s, inflation averaged about 6 percent. Since then, there has been nothing to indicate that the governments of industrial nations have become more prudent about monetary or fiscal policy. So it's reasonable to expect that inflation will average around 6 percent for the next 10 or 20 years.

233

If you earn 6 percent in cash and inflation averages 6 percent, you're keeping up, but you're not getting ahead. That's been the historical experience: Cash equivalents pay about the same as the inflation rate.

Moreover, cash equivalents are fully taxable, unless they're held in a retirement plan. (You can't get at retirement plan cash easily, and you'll have to pay taxes when you take your cash out.) Assuming a 30 percent tax bracket, you would have to earn more than 8.5 percent, from a cash equivalent, to end up with 6 percent, after taxes. If you're in a 40 percent bracket, including state income taxes, you would need to earn 10 percent, pre-tax, to have 6 percent, after-tax. It's very doubtful that you'll be able to earn 10 percent, or even 8.5 percent, long-term from T-bills, CDs, or money funds. Thus if you invest solely in cash equivalents, you're likely to suffer a loss of purchasing power after adjusting for taxes and inflation.

## OPPORTUNITY COST

Perhaps more important, settling for low returns, via cash equivalents, deprives you of the chance to build up personal wealth. Seemingly small differences in current cash flow can add up to surprisingly large amounts of money if compounded and held for the long-term.

To illustrate, we'll discuss the problem of building up a fund to pay for a child's college education. It's a familiar problem for anyone who has children, and it's an excellent example of a certain financial obligation that you can plan for over a period of years. When a child is born, you know that you'll have to face a hefty tab for college in 18 years. Similarly, many people can look ahead to a definite date, when they plan to retire, knowing that they'll then have to live without a steady paycheck.

In long-term investment planning, it's useful to think in terms of three different investment categories: certain, safe, and savvy. By *certain*, we're talking about the cash equivalents mentioned earlier. You know you'll preserve your principal plus receive a modest return. Long-term, you can expect around 6 percent per year.

*Safe* investments are those where there are risks, but they are relatively low. Bonds—except for junk bonds—are very likely to be repaid, especially when the issuer is the federal government or a state or a top-rated corporation. The risk is that the value of the bond will fluctuate over the holding period as interest rates go up or down. Mortgage loans also fall into the safe category. Some real estate, especially existing properties purchased for all-cash, may fall into this safe category. The property's value probably won't fluctuate, but the income is not guaranteed, and it may not be easy to sell when you want to.

In general, you can expect compound returns around 9 percent from safe investments. This is a guideline, not a rule, but you expect a premium—9 percent rather than 6 percent—for going beyond riskless cash equivalents. You can go a bit higher, perhaps with corporate bonds, or a bit lower, if you invest in tax-exempt bonds, but 9 percent is a good number to use for long-term expectations in this category.

Historically, safe investments haven't paid 9 percent. If you go back to the 1920s, corporate bonds, for example, have paid 5 to 6 percent while Treasuries have returned 4 to 5 percent. But the world has changed in the past 20 years. Inflation now is built into our financial system. We accept 3 to 4 percent annual inflation, even point to such rates as low, but in 1971 such inflation rates were alarming enough to lead President Nixon to impose wage and price controls.

If we're going to accept 3 percent annual inflation, and if inflation is actually going to run at 6 percent per year, long-term, then 5 or 6 percent isn't going to be an adequate returns on safe-but-not-certain investments such as bonds. That kind of return now is more likely for cash equivalents, while bonds are probably going to pay around 9 percent.

## INCREASING THE STAKES

If we expect to earn 9 percent from bonds, we'll need to earn more from stocks in order to justify the extra risks. According to Ibbotson Associates, a Chicago research firm, the S&P 500 has only returned 9.9 percent per year in the past 60 years (through 1987). That includes dividend reinvestment. But now we'll want more—around 12 percent—from stocks, long-term. In effect, all investment returns have been jacked up a bit to compensate for the increased inflation that's built into our financial system.

Stocks are risky. After October 1987, nobody doubts that. Yet stocks tend to pay off. Over a 10-year period, from 1978 to the end of 1987 (that includes the Crash), stock mutual funds have gained about 15 percent per year, on average. Over the past 15 years, the average is about 10 percent per year. So you can expect to earn 12 percent per year from stocks, if you know what you're doing. That's why we put stocks in the *savvy* category.

What else belongs here? Other investments where you can aim for 12 percent annual returns, if you understand how your money will be used—junk bonds, for example, or leveraged real estate, real estate investment trusts, limited partnerships in oil and gas, cable TV, or equipment leasing. These vehicles are risky, like the stock market. But if you proceed carefully you may earn 12 percent per year, long-term.

There are also investments where possible returns exceed 12 percent per year. Such returns fall into a different category—speculative. Whenever a promoter talks to you about a 15 or 20 percent annual return, you can be sure he's referring to a high-risk deal. You may want to speculate in such vehicles, but only with money that you can afford to lose. Don't depend on them for college funds or for your retirement, or else you'll discover yet another investment category—sorry.

## CRUNCHING THE NUMBERS

If 9 percent per year, or even 12 percent, seems pretty tame to you, that's because you don't appreciate the power of compound interest. Over the years, such returns can truly help you build wealth. And there's a big difference among shooting for a certain 6 percent, a safe 9 percent, or a savvy 12 percent. Remember the "Rule of 72." Compounded, money invested at 6 percent will approximately double in 12 years. At 9 percent, doubling will take eight years, but at 12 percent, your investment will double in six years.

Let's see how that will affect college funding. Suppose your newborn child receives a grandparent gift of $10,000 when he or she is born. You invest that money for the child's education. After 18 years, when it's time to write the first college check, here's how that $10,000 will have grown (in round numbers), assuming compounding:

| Certain (6%) | Safe (9%) | Savvy (12%) |
|---|---|---|
| $28,000 | $48,000 | $77,000 |

That's right. If you can earn 12 percent per year, reinvested and compounded, you'll get a return of nearly 8:1 after 18 years. It's not easy to do, but doing it will pay off. Sure, 15 percent is better, but why be greedy and chase after high-risk ventures?

On the other hand, playing it certain with cash equivalents, will give you less than a 3:1 return. That's pre-tax. Who knows how much of college education that will buy in 18 years? That's why it pays to stretch for those safe 9 percent returns, and to use some of your money trying for a savvy 12 percent.

College saving won't stop when a child is born. But even if you put away money later, when a child is older, compounding can make a big difference. Here, for example, are comparable numbers for $10,000 given to a six-year-old, after 12 years of compounding:

| Certain (6%) | Safe (9%) | Savvy (12%) |
|---|---|---|
| $20,000 | $28,000 | $39,000 |

Or, if you make that $10,000 gift to a 12-year-old, to compound for six years:

| Certain (6%) | Safe (9%) | Savvy (12%) |
|:---:|:---:|:---:|
| $14,000 | $17,000 | $20,000 |

These numbers assume no taxation. Suppose you receive your 6 or 9 or 12 percent each year, and that it's fully taxable. In our assumed 30 percent bracket, you would really be earning 4.2 percent per year, or 6.3 or 8.4 percent. In that case, $10,000 invested at 6 percent would grow to about $21,000 after 18 years, rather than $28,000. At 9 percent, your money would grow to around $30,000 after tax, rather than $48,000. And, at 12 percent, you would wind up with less than $43,000 after tax, rather than nearly $77,000, if you could earn a straight 12 percent, tax-free! A 30 percent annual tax obligation winds up cutting down your college fund by nearly 45 percent!

If you compounded $10,000 for 18 years, at 12 percent, then paid a 30 percent tax on all the earnings, you'd wind up with about $57,000. As you can see, you would be way ahead of the $43,000 you'd have if you paid 30 percent in taxes, as you went along. So that's why it pays, not only to stretch for current yields, but also to learn about the different tax-exempt and tax-deferred vehicles that we've mentioned.

## THE COLLEGE PLAN

Now that we've set the ground rules, here is how to implement your college plan (or your retirement plan, or just a get-richer plan). First, start saving early. Second, reinvest the cash flow to let it compound. Third, try to avoid or defer taxes whenever possible.

When you're building up a college fund, you can save by taking advantage of your kids' low tax brackets. All children can have up to $500 per year in investment income, tax-free, plus another $500 taxed at 15 percent. After that (for children under age 14), income is taxed at the parent's highest tax rate.

Thus, it pays to have your kids earn up to $1,000 per year from taxable investments, because the tax will be only $75. For this money, you might want to be certain. That is, keep money in T-bills or CDs. If each of your kids keeps about $15,000 in cash equivalents, the tax bill will be small. If you go for safe investments here (government bonds, for example, or government-backed zeros), you can expect around a 9 percent yield, so you wouldn't want to give each child more than $10,000.

Once your child turns 14, though, he or she no longer has to worry about his/her parent's tax bracket. He/she still gets to avoid taxes on the first $500 worth of investment income, but now will be able to earn as much as $18,000 per year, in the 15 percent bracket.

Is this important? It can be. Suppose you have $50,000 invested in bonds that pay 12 percent. If you're in a 30 percent bracket, that $50,000 will grow to less than $67,000 in four years (while the child goes from age 14 to age 18). If your child holds the bonds, in a 15 percent tax bracket, the money will grow to nearly $75,000 in four years. Even after some of the money is used, for the first year's college expenses, the remaining money will continue to grow faster in a child's bracket.

It makes sense for your kids to hold assets where the tax bill can be deferred until after they reach age 14. EE Savings Bonds, for example, permit you to defer taxes until the bonds are cashed in. So such bonds could be given to a young child, letting the interest compound until he or she reaches age 18 and needs the money for college.

EE Savings Bonds now have a minimum yield of 6 percent, but their yield can rise, if interest rates go up. Therefore, EE bonds may wind up paying closer to 9 than 6 percent, and they may be considered safe rather than certain.

Another possibility for young children is a growth-stock fund that pays low or no dividends. Without current cash flow, there will be no tax obligation. But if the stock fund grows as planned, the child can withdraw money to pay for college and pay taxes at 15 percent, as long as he or she is over age 14.

Beyond these choices, it makes little sense to transfer assets to young children. Tax-exempt bonds, for example, should be held in your own name. The same is true for real estate or for other limited partnerships, especially if the cash flow is expected to be sheltered. Once your children reach age 14, it may make sense to transfer high-yield assets to them, if the distributions will be taxable, to reduce the tax bite.

## WORKING OUT A PLAN

Today, the average cost of a year at a private college is more than $10,000. For a big-name school, annual costs will top $15,000. A child born now can expect to spend $30,000 to $45,000 per year to go to college. (That sounds incredible, but who would have believed, 20 years ago, that the cost of a first-rate college would go from $5,000 to more than $15,000 per year?) So, parents of newborn children can anticipate having to pay around $150,000 to put a child through college.

Here's one way to do it. When the child is born, try to get your hands on $15,000 and put it into a six-month CD in the child's name. Tell the bank to keep rolling over the CD when it matures. If you can't find $15,000 for a CD, aim for $10,000 to invest in a zero-coupon CAT or STRIP, also in the child's name. Either way, CD or zero-coupon bond, that nest egg will grow to $40,000–$50,000 in 18 years.

For the other $100,000 or so, plan to give the child $5,000 per year through age 14. Invest that money in EE Savings Bonds and growth-stock mutual funds. A 50–50 balance may be appropriate, but you can emphasize one or the other, depending on how you feel about the stock market's long-term growth potential.

Suppose you don't think you have the discipline to invest $5,000 every year for college. If you have $25,000 or $50,000 to invest right now, you might buy a single-premium life insurance policy, naming yourself as the insured individual.

Once your child turns 14, think about transfering assets rather than making new investments. Anything you hold that will generate taxable investment income—junk bonds, oil and gas income funds, leasing funds, real estate partnerships that are likely to sell properties soon—may be given to your teenager, who will have a lower tax bracket for up to $18,000 worth of income per year.

Then, your child may use the assets which you've given him to pay for college. And you can start over, using your retirement plans as well as tax-exempt and tax-deferred vehicles to build up your own fund for retirement.

# Appendix C

# How to Choose Financial Advisers

We opened this book with a paradox, so we'll close with one. The concept of mutual funds originated to simplify things for investors. Rather than try to pick winners among the stocks available, investors could buy a mutual fund and let the fund's manager choose stocks for him.

By now, however, there are about 2,000 mutual funds available. That's more than the number of stocks on the New York Stock Exchange. Various newsletters and services exist solely to help investors pick the right mutual funds. Investment simplification is in order!

## LOOKING FOR PROFESSIONAL HELP

For many investors, the answer is to find a financial professional—a broker, a planner, a money manager. Some investors use more than one financial professional, to help with their portfolios. The decision is not an easy one. How do you find good financial advisers?

### *Financial Planners*

Almost anyone can print business cards with the words "financial planner" on them. Recently, the federal Securities and Exchange Commission (SEC) reported that "many planners, perhaps even a majority, are fairly new to the planning business." Many planners were found to be poorly educated, for dispensing financial advice.

According to the SEC, most planners who belong to professional organizations are well-educated. But when the SEC went beyond these organizations, to the planners who advertise in telephone books, education levels dropped off.

Your first step should be to check into a planner's qualifications. If he or she belongs to a professional group, such as the International Association for Financial Planning, that's an encouraging sign. If he or she has earned the title "Certified Financial Planner," or is a member of the "Registry of Financial Planning Practitioners," you'll know that he or she has a well-rounded background, tested by a national organization.

But don't accept a financial planner merely on the basis of a few letters after his or her name. Ask how long he or she has been practicing. Two or three years is probably the minimum, but the longer the better.

Ask a planner if he can help with all your financial concerns—investments, insurance, estate planning, retirement planning, tax planning. Most individuals are not well-served by planners whose main goal is to sell one product, such as life insurance or mutual funds.

Ask for references. A planner has to work closely with lawyers and accountants, so speak to these professionals and get their opinions. And ask his existing clients whether or not they're pleased. Make sure that a planner is comfortable with clients such as yourself. If you're a corporate executive earning $50,000 or $75,000 a year, you may not be satisfied with a planner who specializes in small-business owners whose net worth runs into the millions.

Some planners today have accumulated large staffs. You may have an introductory interview with the head of the firm, then work mainly with a junior planner. If the planning firm has considerable resources, you may find this arrangement acceptable. Just make sure you meet the people with whom you'll be working directly, before committing yourself.

Find out how the planner operates. In some cases, you'll start your financial planning by filling out forms for several hours. Your answers will be fed into a computer that will produce a large, handsomely bound volume that will look impressive on your library shelf.

Not only is this an expensive process, it may not be practical. You may never read this large report, and it's doubtful that all the recommendations will be implemented.

You may be better off with a smaller form that's more to the point. What are your goals, in terms of current income and retirement income? How much will you need to put your children through college and to provide for your family after your death? What assets do you have now, and how are they diversified?

An experienced planner can help you summarize this information quickly, so you know where you stand now and where you want to go. He'll show you what you need to do, realistically, to meet your goals. And he'll help you choose specific investments.

Of course, your planner will want to get paid for this advice. Most planners work on a commission basis. If you buy an insurance policy or a mutual fund or a limited partnership that they have recommended, part of your money will go to them as a sales commission. Insist, right from the beginning, that all such commissions are fully disclosed. You should feel comfortable that the financial counsel you receive is worth the money you're paying.

Some financial planners are "fee only." They'll go through the entire planning process but they won't put you into deals where you pay them a commission. Instead, they'll charge you an hourly rate. They claim to be less biased, because they're not receiving sales commissions from investment sponsors. If you work with a fee-only planner, be certain that he has a method for putting his recommendations into action.

A final word about choosing financial planners: Ask for evidence that they invest, alongside their clients, in the deals they recommend. That's not a guarantee of success—anyone can make mistakes—but it's a sign that your planner believes in his own advice.

## Brokers

A broker, essentially, is anyone who brings together a buyer and a seller, collecting a commission for his trouble. There are real estate brokers, loan brokers, business brokers, and so on.

In the world of investments, brokers are generically known as "stockbrokers." Today, that's not a fair description. Brokers deal in all types of "securities"—stocks, bonds, mutual funds, limited partnerships, real estate investment trusts, unit investment trusts, even variable life insurance. Some "stockbrokers" hardly trade stocks at all.

Securities brokers must pass examinations and earn licenses, for these various types of securities. Whenever you purchase a security, such as those mentioned in this book, you'll have to deal with a broker. If you buy a no-load mutual fund or deal with a financial planner, a broker will somehow have to figure in all securities transactions. That's another question to ask a prospective financial planner—Who will broker the transaction if you purchase a product he recommends?

Some investors will want to deal directly with a securities broker. The screening process is similar to the one we mentioned for financial planners. Ask about qualifications. Ask how long they have been in the business. Ask for references. Ask for proof that this broker puts his or her own money into the recommended securities.

Just because a broker works for a major firm—one that advertises on television, for example—don't assume the broker is honest. Brokers from even the biggest Wall Street firms have been charged with churning accounts (trading too much to earn more commissions) or with putting their investors into unsuitable vehicles. You cannot leave your investments unattended; there is no replacement for your awareness and interest.

In the October 1987 stock market crash, many individuals were badly hurt. Typically, the ones who suffered were not the ones who invested in stocks or stock funds: they might have lost 20 or 30 percent of their asset value, but those were largely values that had been inflated by the previous run-up.

Instead, the investors who really got burned were those in exotic, high-risk strategies. Many investors, for example, were selling "naked puts." (Options to buy stocks they didn't own.) In many cases, brokers had persuaded unknowing investors into these strategies, claiming they were low risk and high yield. Investors didn't realize they were greatly exposed to sudden, sharp stock market declines.

To check on a stockbroker, call your state securities commission, with whom he or she must register. The commission can tap a 50-state computer data base and report on the background of any broker. If he or she has been the subject of any disciplinary actions, you'll get a detailed report. The North American Securities Administrators Association maintains a toll-free hotline (800/942-9022) that you can call for a directory of state securities commissions.

## Money Managers

Many investors with large portfolios (say, over $250,000) turn to professional money managers. Usually, these money managers specialize in stocks, bonds, and cash equivalents. They'll charge a percentage of assets under management—usually 1 or 2 percent—to handle your investments. They claim to be able to deliver more personalized service than you'd get with a mutual fund. That is, they'll invest according to your individual needs and risk tolerance.

Often, money managers are recommended to investors by brokers or by financial planners. If that's the case, there's some splitting of fees and commissions involved. You should find out how much you're paying, to whom, before you agree to any money management arrangement.

Again, look for experience and check references. Remember, lots of money managers have done well since 1982, when interest rates started falling and the stock market began rising. Find out how well a money manager performed in the more difficult 1970s.

Investment advisers and brokers generally must register with the SEC, and many financial planners also are registered. You can check up on an adviser's background by writing to the Freedom of Information Office, SEC, 450 Fifth St., NW, Mail Stop 2-6, Washington, DC 20549. Ask if an adviser has been the subject of any disciplinary or enforcement actions. Give the adviser's name and his full business address. Within 10 days, you should hear from the SEC.

# Appendix D

## Profiles in Cash

There's no such thing as a standard way to allocate your assets among the different types of investments we've discussed in this book. Each individual and each family has specific needs. In this appendix, we'll describe four hypothetical cases—based on real-life situations—and give some suggestions for portfolio allocation.

### THE SMITHS

John and Jane Smith are DINKs—a couple with Double Income, No Kids. (Some might spell it DINC, for Double Income, No Cares.) They're in their early 30s, and they plan to start a family within a few years.

Both Smiths have careers, and their current income is $75,000. They own a house, and they have $50,000 to invest. They have no pressing need for more current income to live on. Their salaries are adequate to meet all their expenses, including mortgage payments, and they expect their income to grow, as they advance in their professions.

How should the Smiths invest their $50,000? Here's a suggestion:

- $10,000—Money market fund
- $30,000—Variable life insurance
- $10,000—Fixed-income vehicle

#### A Premium on Life Insurance

The $10,000 in the money market fund provides a cash equivalent. In case of an emergency, there's money to tap.

If they put $30,000 into a variable life insurance policy, they can direct their investment into a stock market mutual fund. Within the life insurance policy, all dividends can be reinvested, and any capital gains can

244

be taken, free of current income taxes. Over a long-term, that $30,000 can be expected to grow.

Putting $30,000—60 percent of the Smiths' portfolio—into stocks may seem high; it exceeds the guidelines we established earlier. With this allocation, the Smiths' cash flow from their investments likely will be below $2,000 per year, or 4 percent.

But the Smiths don't need ready cash. They can afford to take a long-term view. Over a long term, with dividends reinvested, their stock fund investment is likely to pay off. If they need cash—perhaps 20 years from now, to help pay for college for a yet unborn Smith—they'll be able to tap the policy's cash value (subject to tax laws in effect at that time).

Variable life also offers life insurance protection. For a $30,000 premium, they should be able to buy a policy with a death benefit near $200,000. So this investment gives them tax-deferred growth plus life insurance.

For the other $10,000, their basic choices are real estate or bonds. They don't really need income-producing real estate, because their house is their major financial asset, and they don't really need Treasury bonds or Ginnie Maes, because they don't need current income, fully taxed.

Therefore, they should look for some type of vehicle that can provide fixed income, with tax shelter. Choices include municipal bonds, real estate equity (ownership) partnerships, leasing funds, and oil and gas income funds.

Here, the selection depends upon their personal preference, and upon timing. If the Smiths believe that interest rates are relatively high, and they have no great fears of long-term inflation, then municipal bonds are a good choice. They shouldn't buy munis directly, with only $10,000 (they'll buy too few issues), so they can choose a muni mutual fund or unit trust.

If they think that interest rates may rise, or if they're concerned about inflation, a leasing fund might be the better choice. Or, if they're particularly bullish about the long-term prospects for real estate or for oil and gas, that's where the money can go. For example, if they believe that OPEC will soon regain its clout, sending oil prices back to $30 per barrel, they could put the $10,000 in an oil and gas income fund.

Whichever vehicle they choose, they should plan on holding on for the long term. Distributions should be swept into the money market fund. When that fund reaches $20,000, they can take $10,000 of that money for another investment choice.

## THE JONESES

Bob and Barbara Jones have just turned 40, with three children—aged 8, 11, and 15. They earn approximately $100,000 per year, and have accumulated a portfolio of $150,000.

246    *Appendix D*

Earning $100,000 per year, they're certainly no charity case, but they are concerned about coming up with enough money to pay for putting three children through college. Therefore, their portfolio is skewed more toward cash flow and liquidity, less toward long-term growth.

Here's a suggested breakdown:

- $10,000—Money market fund
- $40,000—Bonds and fixed income
- $30,000—Stocks
- $25,000—Real estate
- $15,000—Other (natural resources)

## Sometimes It's Better to Give

If you're handy with a calculator, you can see that those numbers add up to only $120,000. What happened to the other $30,000? The Joneses decided to give $10,000 to each of their children. They can do this without incurring gift taxes, and the children may pay lower taxes, on the investment income.

Let's take a look at the $120,000 the Joneses retain. They put $10,000 into a money market fund for liquidity. Then, 33 percent went into bonds and fixed income vehicles. That will increase the cash flow they'll receive during the next 15 years, as they cope with college bills.

To maximize yields, they put about half of their bond money into a government bond fund that concentrates on long-term securities. Funds that write covered options tend to focus on long-term bonds. These funds are likely to be volatile, but they may generate high returns, long-term, as long as the distributions are reinvested.

For the rest of the fixed-income money, a leasing fund may be appropriate. Cash flow is particularly high—generally 12 to 15 percent—and the distributions can be swept into a money market fund.

## Growth and Income

In this example, we assume that $30,000 (25 percent of the total) is invested in stocks. The Joneses, with three young children, don't have the time to pick individual stocks. Thus, they prefer to invest in proven mutual funds. With $30,000, they can choose two or three funds.

Assuming they pick two funds, one should be a growth-and-income fund or "equity income" fund, emphasizing dividends. There are many available, yielding 5 to 7 percent. The other fund can be a straight growth fund, preferably one that pays a small dividend (perhaps 2 percent) while focusing on long-term growth.

Another $25,000 (about 20 percent of the portfolio) is allocated for income-producing real estate. Here, the Joneses invest $25,000 in a leveraged private placement. That should yield them 7 to 8 percent, fully sheltered, for sweeping into their money fund. There's no liquidity in this investment, but most of their portfolio is easily convertible to cash. This partnership anticipates a property sale in 10 to 12 years; if things develop as expected, the Joneses can expect some cash when they need it, while their kids are in college.

The final $15,000 (over 10 percent of the portfolio) is in the "other" category, in this case emphasizing natural resources. The Joneses might put $10,000 into a gold-stock mutual fund and $5,000 into an oil and gas income fund. They'll get current income and excellent protection against inflation.

## Adding It Up

From this type of portfolio, the overall cash flow should be about 8 percent, or about $9,600 per year, on a $120,000 portfolio. The real estate, the oil and gas, and the leasing fund all shelter the cash flow, at least partially, so they should be held in the Joneses' own accounts. The U.S. government bond fund and the growth-and-income stock fund, which produce high taxable income, should be held in a tax-deferred retirement plan, if possible.

## Lower Tax Brackets

Children age 14 or older pay taxes in their own bracket. Thus, the $10,000 given to 15-year-old Abby Jones can be invested in a high-yielding Ginnie Mae fund or corporate bond fund. The tax burden will be light, and she'll accumulate some money to help pay college costs.

The younger children, 11-year-old Danny Jones and 8-year-old Seth Jones, have different tax pictures. Their first $500 of investment income is tax-free, the next $500 is taxed at 15 percent, and everything else is taxed at their parent's rates, until they're 14. So Danny's money is invested in a low-dividend growth-stock fund, which won't generate much taxes until the shares are sold, while Seth's $10,000 goes into EE Savings Bonds, where the taxes can be deferred until the bonds are cashed in. If the fund shares are sold and the bonds are redeemed while the boys are in college, the tax bite likely will be small.

## MR. BROWN

Tom Brown is a 52-year-old lawyer, divorced, whose only child has graduated from college and whose ex-wife is remarried. He earns $150,000 per year, from his law practice, and he has a $200,000 investment portfolio in addition to a rental condo. His total income tax obligation, federal and state, is nearly $50,000. His goals are to reduce that tax burden and build up more assets for retirement, in 10 to 15 years.

Here's how he might allocate his assets:

- $20,000—Money market fund
- $25,000—Bonds
- $65,000—Stocks
- $40,000—Real estate
- $50,000—Other (natural resources)

## *Looking for Shelter*

Tom keeps $20,000 in a money market fund. As a self-employed professional, he's vulnerable to lost earnings, any time he's sick or injured. He also needs to have a comprehensive disability insurance policy in force.

He's relatively light on bonds, with just over 10 percent of his portfolio invested there. He has little need for more current income. His bonds are municipals, issued by his home state, to escape all taxes on the interest income. He buys discount bonds; that is, he buys relatively low-coupon bonds for less than 100 cents on the dollar. When the bonds mature, after he has retired, he'll get a nice "pop" in his income.

His $65,000 stock portfolio (over 30 percent) is divided among blue-chip issues, bought individually, an aggressive growth fund, and an international fund. The blue chips are a basic holding, providing some dividend income; the aggressive growth fund is a speculation, that may pay off down the line; the international fund, which holds foreign stocks, hedges against a falling dollar and gives him entree to overseas stock markets, that have been strong performers. He intends to increase his stock portfolio through "dollar cost averaging," from future earnings. That is, he'll invest a certain amount each month, in his mutual funds. This will enable him to buy more shares, when prices drop, and will likely improve his long-term results.

He doesn't need to have as much investment real estate, because he owns a rental condo. However, he puts $40,000 (20 percent) into a low-income housing partnership, which will provide apartments for rural residents. He won't get cash flow, but he can get $70,000 worth of tax credits (a $70,000 tax savings) over the next 10 years. Eventually, the apartments may be sold at a profit.

## Hard Assets

A large section (25 percent) of his portfolio is devoted to hard assets. Of the $50,000 total, half goes into an oil drilling shelter. It's risky, but the risk is reduced by the upfront writeoffs. Assuming 50 percent leverage—he puts down $25,000 in cash and signs a note for another $25,000—he can receive $40,000 or $45,000 in tax writeoffs this year. He'll still owe $25,000, but part of the note may be covered by income from the oil wells.

In addition, he puts $25,000 into a gold mutual fund, for inflation protection and long-term growth.

All in all, this portfolio will generate only about $5,000 in cash flow, or 2.5 percent on Tom's $200,000. The muni income is tax-free while the dividends from the gold fund and the international stock fund can be sheltered in his Keogh plan. So he'll have little taxable investment income.

On the other hand, his drilling deductions are likely to save him $15,000 to $18,000 in taxes this year, his low-income housing deal can save another $7,000, and there might be a small tax saving from his rental condo. In fact, the tax savings are so large that Tom must work with his advisers to make sure he doesn't run into the alternative minimum tax.

## THE GREENS

Michael Green has just reached age 65 and retired from his company. He and his wife Mary expect about $20,000 a year from their combined Social Security checks and from bank accounts they've maintained. In addition, Michael just received a $400,000 lump-sum distribution from his long-time employer. The Greens rolled this money into an IRA. Now, they must decide how to allocate the $400,000, to give them maximum current income plus growth potential. The Greens have the time and the inclination to pick their own securities.

Here's how they might allocate their $400,000:

- $175,000—Bonds
- $100,000—Stocks
- $ 75,000—Real estate
- $ 50,000—Other (natural resources)

## Emphasizing Current Income

The Greens want current income, so bonds are important to them. They have over 40 percent of their portfolio in bonds and bond substitutes.

They put $80,000 into Treasury bonds, which they selected: $20,000 in two-year maturities, $20,000 in four-year maturities, $20,000 in six-year maturities, and $20,000 in eight-year maturities. As each $20,000 segment comes due, the principal that's returned is rolled over into eight-year maturities. This gives them a nice mix of yield and safety of principal.

Of the other $95,000, more than half ($50,000) is invested in a fund that buys long-term investment-grade corporate bonds, while the other $45,000 is invested in a leasing fund.

The Greens like to pick stocks, too. Of the 25 percent of their portfolio ($100,000) that's devoted to stocks, half ($50,000) are picked by them, with an emphasis on high dividends and prospects for dividend growth. Another $25,000 goes to an "option income" fund that buys dividend-paying stocks and sells covered calls (options to buy those stocks). Finally, $25,000 goes to an all-cash cable TV partnership. This is a stock substitute, rather than a pure stock investment, but the Greens like the outlook for cable TV and they prefer to get cash flow without worrying about the corporate income tax.

## Safety First

Real estate, at $75,000, is nearly 20 percent of their portfolio. However, the conservative Greens want income more than the risks of owning properties, so $50,000 is invested in mortgage deals (one partnership and one REIT) while $25,000 is invested in a nursing home partnership that promises to yield high cash flow.

The final $50,000 is split between a gold-stock fund and an oil and gas income fund, for inflation protection. Here's a rough idea of the current yield from such a portfolio:

| Investment | Vehicle | Cash flow | Income |
|---|---|---|---|
| $80,000 | Bond rollover | 7% | $5,600 |
| 50,000 | Corporation bond fund | 10% | 5,000 |
| 45,000 | Leasing fund | 12% | 5,400 |
| 50,000 | Individual stocks | 5% | 2,500 |
| 25,000 | Option income fund | 6% | 1,500 |
| 25,000 | Cable TV LP | 7% | 1,750 |
| 25,000 | Mortgage REIT | 12% | 3,000 |
| 25,000 | Mortgage LP | 9% | 2,250 |
| 25,000 | Nursing home LP | 8% | 2,000 |
| 25,000 | Gold fund | 5% | 1,250 |
| 25,000 | Oil income fund | 15% | 3,750 |

Altogether, their income from this $400,000 portfolio is expected to be $34,000, or 8.5 percent. All of this money is collected in an IRA, so it's tax sheltered. The Greens pay taxes on whatever they take out of their IRA, for living expenses.

The leasing fund and the oil income fund are paying out a partial return of principal, so they're actually depreciating. However, any loss of principal probably will be outweighed by appreciation in the stocks, stock fund, cable TV systems, nursing home, and the gold fund. If interest rates go up, income from the bond rollover and the corporate bond fund will rise. Thus, the Greens have built a safe, high-yielding portfolio that has room to grow.

# Afterword

# Cashing In

Throughout this book, we've repeatedly referred to the stock market crash of October 19, 1987. That's because the crash finished what the 1986 Tax Reform Act started: It validated cash-flow investing.

Before the crash, many people thought of "investing" as buying stocks. Such people were, in fact, speculating that the assets they bought—shares in corporations—would appreciate. The amount of appreciation was unknown and the range of possible returns was vast.

After a crash, it's easy to recognize the virtues of cash-flow investing. Returns are more predictable, so the ventures are generally less risky. Periodic cash flow can be reinvested and compounded. If your cash flow is tax-favored, so much the better. Even if your cash flow is fully taxable, today's low tax rates will help you accumulate wealth, through cash-flow investing.

Today, cash-flow investing is more than buying bonds. Bonds wilt when inflation flowers. But the many different cash-flow vehicles now available include inflation as well as deflation hedges. Together, they enable investors to structure portfolios that will hold up in various economic climates. If you understand cash-flow investing, and you build a diversified portfolio, you can enjoy shock-free growth.

If you have enough education and talent to build up an investment portfolio worth worrying about, you can understand the cash-flow investments we've covered. Whether you're a do-it-yourself investor or a manager hirer, you need to know where your cash is coming from. If you don't take charge of your finances, others will do it for you—and perhaps not to your liking.

There are two income-producing activities: people at work and money at work. Put your money to work for you and keep it working. All the time. That's the financial plan that's most likely to get you where you want to be.

# Index

S